THE HEART AND THE ABYSS

THE LIFE OF FELICE BENUZZI

Rory Steele

Connor Court Publishing

Published in 2016 by Connor Court Publishing Pty Ltd

Connor Court Publishing Pty Ltd
PO Box 7257
Redland Bay QLD 4165

sales@connorcourt.com
www.connorcourt.com
Phone 0497 900 685

ISBN: 9781925501049

Front Cover Design: Maria Giordano

Front Cover Photo: Benuzzi family archives

Picture Credits: Barnes, Colella, Manzoni & Smith

Printed in Australia

For Stefania

Avvicinarsi alla vita di un uomo dall'alto, sfiorare gli attimi più intimamente suoi, vederlo, che dico, parlargli e farsi parlare da lui: colloqui di anime, oltre il tempo. Come non essere riempiti di pietosa commozione alla lettura di una profonda biografia? Come non ti assale allora una dolorosa lucidità di te stesso: "E chi sei tu – ti chiedi allora – che cosa sei tu?"
In questa vita che si sfoglia sotto i tuoi occhi tu scopri in fondo te stesso. E vedi ciò che ha fatto e non ha fatto ciò che tu puoi e ciò che non vuoi fare. Meditazione sull'ieri, sull'oggi, sul sempre. Sul correre degli uomini. Così come tu li vedi passare frettolosi per strada. Vedi quanto v'è di vano e quanto d'eterno nelle loro giornate e nelle tue.

To approach a man's life from above, zoom in on his most intimate moments, see him, practically exchange words with him, soul to soul, outside of time. How could reading a tale like that not move you to pity? Not force you with painful clarity to ask yourself: "And who are you, and what are you?"
You see yourself in this life stripped bare before you, you see what he did and didn't do and what you could and what you can't bring yourself to do. Thoughts of yesterday, of now and of evermore. On the scurrying of humanity, you see them in the street. You see what is fleeting and what is lasting in those lives: and in your own.

Felice Benuzzi
Heinrich Mann, Il Frontespizio, April 1933

CONTENTS

Foreword

By Tim Fischer AC
Former Deputy Prime of Australia and
Ambassador to the Holy See

There is something special about a motivated Trieste Roman. Felice Benuzzi was an extraordinary mountain climber, a brave soldier in battle and later a gifted public servant. He was greatly helped by his dedication and determination and his good education, along with some very real luck.

There were many Italians who came down from the Trieste area and the Dolomites to make their mark in Rome and contribute to the nation state of Italy. One other of great renown was Israel Zolli, first Rabbi of Trieste and then of Rome throughout the horrible Nazi occupation of the eternal city, saving many hundreds of Roman Jews from being sent to Auschwitz. Like Felice Benuzzi he narrowly survived the war with many near misses and having to dice with death.

Felice Benuzzi was a brilliant leader whose first posting overseas was to Addis Ababa as a colonial civil servant in the short-lived Italian empire in Africa. There, and in the Italian Army, he served at altitudes similar to his home region in the mountains near Trieste. After the incarceration caused by World War Two, as richly recorded in this book, Felice had a succession of diplomatic postings and promotions, serving in France twice and Australia twice, in Pakistan and as Consul General in Berlin and finally as Ambassador to Uruguay.

Felice travelled all over the world initially when access to modern means of transport was limited, often by ship to and from his postings. When aviation became more readily available he flew sometimes in hazardous conditions, in Africa, in the Himalayas and in South and Central America where in 1976 one of the engines of the Dakota DC3 that he was in failed leading to a terrifying landing. This record of his colourful life points to a bright diplomat making the most of every opportunity, for the community and his country as well as his family but always with an element of risk. This was especially true of the postings a long way from the niceties of life along the Tiber in Rome or the Seine in Paris.

Underpinning all of this was Felice's innate desire to physically and metaphorically climb mountains, to conquer another peak or two. As well recorded here, famously if not infamously, Felice as a prisoner of war broke out of a British camp, with Giovanni Balletto and Vincenzo Barsotti, two other Italian POWs. They climbed Mt Kenya, a 5,000 metre giant mountain in Africa that they could see in the distance and then broke back into the camp, nearly three exhausting weeks later. It was an amazing achievement with the actual escape, for the joy of climbing a magnificent mountain, only to return to captivity voluntarily. No picnic, as Felice observed, but an absolute sustaining sense of fulfilment and satisfaction.

There are many subtle lessons laid out in this book portraying the life and work of a man who should clearly have landed big Embassy postings like London, Washington or Madrid before retiring, but instead ended his career in Montevideo, Uruguay. Perhaps the most important lesson from it all is for those who must spend years working abroad in varied locations with a set of linguistic skills to match, constantly disadvantaged by for ever having to farewell good friends every few years: it may be a nomadic life but it is one that equips not just the roving diplomat but also close family members with a certain curiosity, motivation and worldliness.

This joy is well conveyed in this book that details the lucky life of renowned Italian diplomat, natural leader and accomplished mountain climber, Felice Benuzzi.

INTRODUCTION

He did something no one had ever done before, or would ever do again. He escaped from prison, climbed a mountain higher than any he had seen, and then broke back into the prison to serve out the rest of his sentence. The mountain was on the equator, and snow-capped. He was an Italian government official held in a British military camp.[1]

Felice Benuzzi was obsessed by mountains, and this one – Mount Kenya – had fired his imagination when in 1942 the clouds at last lifted and he first glimpsed it through the barbed wire, a rocky peak studded with glaciers, rising to 5000 metres. He knew about mountaineering, how you had to be fit for it, you needed good equipment and the best intelligence; he knew how easy it was to die in wilderness, especially one prone to blizzards. As a prisoner he could expect no help whatever. He had no map. Any preparation for the climb, like making ropes, would have to be done in secret. Apparently there were wild animals in jungles in the foothills and on the slopes. He would need companions. After a long search he found two others willing to come with him. Their fellow prisoners thought they were insane. They did it in seventeen days, up and back against innumerable odds, re-entered the camp and next morning presented themselves to their annoyed captors.

Far from being insane, Felice Benuzzi was the most rational of men, highly educated and multilingual. He began drafting the account of his escapade while still a prisoner and when he got back to Italy at the end of the Second World War had it published, as *Fuga sul Kenya*. Five years later a version he himself wrote in English entitled *No Picnic on Mount Kenya* spread his fame around the world. It was written with modesty and humour and it explained the fascination with mountains as well as anyone could.

Humans have since primitive times been awed by the upthrust of earth towards heaven, heights where gods might dwell but also ones with forbidding precipices and avalanches. A few centuries ago explorers pushed across the map into the remotest and wildest places, and after them were adventurers who wanted to climb, beginning with mountains close to home. Readers of their exploits were intrigued by tales of reaching for fearsome summits, and of the elation that comes with ascending. By the early part of the twentieth century people were climbing because they wanted to, and because they could. In the 1950s the world's highest peaks were conquered, and then lesser ones that were actually even more risky. In the last third of the century international travel became easier and cheaper, tourism boomed and soon the world and its high places were generally accessible.

The full story deserves to be told not just because Felice Benuzzi once accomplished something truly amazing. By chance he was part of some of the most stunning vicissitudes of the twentieth century – the rise and fall of fascism, colonialism, major conflicts and their aftermath, and the east-west divide. After Kenya he was a diplomat, in Europe and in far-flung locations, and he wrote with colour and wit of places from Berlin to Brisbane, from the Himalayas to Antarctica. Tall and handsome, he was attractive to women. Men who remember him say he was a gentleman, elegant, self-confident, good company. He was fit and athletic, until felled by a heart attack in his kitchen in Rome in 1988: six months earlier he had almost reached the highest point in New Zealand's North Island, and in 1984 scaled Mount Whitney in the United States. His extensive writings reveal him as well-read in several languages; as a thinker and a complex personality; sceptical but spiritually inclined; at times cynical but also emotional.

This life is alluring not only for those bits of it that are rare and strange but also because Felice had the normal spread of character strengths and weaknesses, of up and down moods, of likes and dislikes. He took his wife Stefania with him wherever he could and she was a great strength to him, but still there were times and places when he insisted on being alone; usually gregarious and sociable, his enormous self-discipline made him sometimes seem severe. German was his mother tongue, and in that language he read about his first mountain-climbing hero Julius Kugy: they shared the town of Trieste.[2] Stefania said that in his obsession with mountains Felice had a yearning for purity that she found typically Germanic.[3] On the other hand she saw in everything else about him the quintessential Italian.

Felice had huge respect for the achievements and daredevilry of the earliest climbers who, like Kugy, tackled peaks never scaled before, and with the most rudimentary equipment. He knew he would never be a climber of that calibre, and since for him the joy was in the totality of the mountain experience he was not sentimental about old ways and had no qualms about the progress being made in better clothes, better gear and readier access. Nevertheless his writings show how he straddled the world of the pioneers and the world of tourists. Some of his most evocative words were about walking perhaps a dozen kilometres through untrodden snow to arrive at the foot of a mountain whose summit might not be reached before nightfall.

In the First World War, when armies were fighting in the Dolomites, the Italians found a way to move troops to the heights and ridges by metal steps and pegs driven into the rock, and called this the 'iron way.' The *via ferrata* today, greatly developed with anchored cables, carries climbers young and old in their many hundreds all over the Italian Alps. Felice would have had no problem with that; nevertheless in the last months of his life he helped set up Mountain Wilderness, an international body that aims to protect mountains from the excesses of exploitation.[4]

A recurring theme in his story is failure, failure that is to achieve everything, summed up in the word *incompiuta* – incomplete – which he regularly uses for a mountain almost but not quite conquered, like Mount Kenya, or Mount Illimani in Bolivia, or

Ruapehu in New Zealand. He learned the hard way to come to terms with this continually falling short, acknowledging that the true value is in the effort itself and not the outcome. Mountains, perfect symbols of things that humans might struggle to achieve, were not for him just targets, still less objects important because of their numerical height, something for the collector. He would not climb to boast of having got to the top. What he looked for in climbing was not only nature, not only physical satisfaction, but also solace and even transcendence. It was why he called his memoirs – which he never submitted for publication – *Più che sassi*, or More Than Rocks.[5] It was the more, the perhaps too far, that lured him.

NOTES TO INTRODUCTION

[1] Before 1943 Felice may have seen Mont Blanc, 4808 metres, the highest in Europe, and Monte Rosa, 4634 metres. Mt Kenya is 5199m; its subsidiary peak Point Lenana is 4985m.

[2] Julius Kugy (1858-1944) of Slovene origin was an Austrian then Italian mountaineer. Kugy (pronounced Ku-ghi) is known best for opening up the Julian Alps, and for his writings, notably *Aus dem Leben eines Bergsteigers* (From the Life of a Mountaineer) published in 1925.

[3] Stefania told the author on 12.10.2012: 'Somewhere in some book of his he says 'Aspiro alla purezza' – this is not very Italian. This comes more from the German side, his attitude to 'anelare, desiderare la purezza (yearn for, long for purity)' – there's a sort of dualism in him.'

[4] Mountain Wilderness, founded in Biella, Italy in 1987, is an international non-government organisation dedicated to the preservation of mountain areas, in their natural and cultural aspects. Full information is available at http://www.mountainwilderness.org/.

[5] The prime source for Felice's early years is his memoirs *Più che sassi*: a bound copy of them is held in the National Mountain Museum in Turin (Museo Nazionale della Montagna Duca degli Abruzzi). Its reference there is T00266 T0073: it may be consulted at location B25-G/4. The memoirs were first brought prominently to public attention in *In Alto* LXXVII/1995 pp. 83-99: *Più che sassi – Testi inediti sulla montagna dell'Ambasciatore Felice Benuzzi (1910-198*8) by Marcello Manzoni.

1

DRO AND VIENNA

The Cemetery at Dro

From its base in the Po Valley near Verona the long thin triangle of Lake Garda, the largest in Italy, tapers up like a fjord into the mountains. Feeding into the narrow top of the lake is the Sarca River whose winding course down from the Dolomites takes it, near the very end, past the village of Dro. Cliffs rise above the neat walled and arcaded cemetery at the edge of the village where among its cypresses on 22 May 2013 the ashes of Stefania Benuzzi were placed alongside those of her husband Felice who predeceased her by just on a quarter of a century. He had died a few weeks before their fiftieth wedding anniversary.

The little cemetery contains many Benuzzi graves, as it is a common name hereabouts. Stefania and Felice are there with his parents, Giovanni and Berta, and two of his brothers. Facing this multiple tomb, ten paces across the white gravel, is the resting place of other relatives, notably Felice's grandfather Giacomo Emilio and his uncle Valerio, the black sheep of the family. Benuzzis had lived in Dro for ages, at least back to the time of the grandparents of Giacomo Emilio, when all the territory north from Dro to the Alps and beyond belonged to Austria. Whether the locals liked it or not, Austria controlled their destinies. The family prospered back in those days, owning various properties in the neighbourhood: they were growers of fruit, oil and wine, and producers of silk.

Until Felice, Giacomo Emilio was the best known of the Benuzzis.[1] He had achieved renown as an engineer and architect abroad as well as at home and, like Felice, wrote a memoir – eighty dense pages – of important events in his life. In 2007 the village *Comune* honoured him by publishing the memoir, adding to it a commentary and a good number of illustrations. In the slim volume Giacomo Emilio described his early life in the village beginning with the moment of his birth in 1848, which, he later learned, had been celebrated with the patriotic shout of 'Viva Italia!' Italy as a nation state did not exist then, but the unification of its disparate parts was not far off. He recalled how as an 11 year old he heard the thunder of cannon fire from the bloody battle of Solferino between Austria on the one side and armies from France and Piedmont on the other.[2] The battle took place at the southern end of Lake Garda, and after it the boy watched pass by, at the lake's northern end, the Emperor of Austria's two younger brothers, the Archdukes Maximilian and Karl Ludwig. The latter was then governor of all Tyrol and he proceeded on to Dro to receive homage from the local authorities. Giacomo Emilio remembered his father afterwards amusing the family with an account of the Archduke's silly remarks.

Austria dominated the top half of Italy for most of the nineteenth century. In Vienna in 1814, after the defeat of Napoleon, the map of Europe was redesigned. Austria gained the regions of Lombardy and Venetia, and regained the southern Tyrol region that spilled down over the Alps as far as Lake Garda. The Congress in Vienna was chaired by the Austrian statesman Metternich who referred to Italy as a 'geographic expression.' It seems he did not mean that as a criticism, but rather that Italy was like Germany, made up of various sovereign entities united only by language and culture.[3]

Across Europe in 1848, the year of Giacomo Emilio's birth, many countries witnessed stirrings of revolution and nationalism. In Italy a struggle began, notably targeting Austria. It continued on and off for the next eighteen years until the definitive withdrawal of Austrian armies from Lombardy and the Veneto in 1866. Four years later the unification of Italy was complete and Metternich's remark lost all significance. Unification did not bring to an end Austrian influence over Italy, nor lessen its impact on the lives of the Benuzzi family. For one thing, although it had given up areas of Italy, Austria now entered into partnership with Hungary creating an empire in Europe larger than any country except Russia. Moreover the southern half of Tyrol, the Benuzzi homeland, was still in Austrian hands. The authorities in Vienna had reason to be concerned about the loyalty of the disparate elements of their empire and in an atmosphere of increasing tension its police were ever on the alert for any signs of rebellion. Many Italians considered those territories where Italian was mainly spoken – the Trentino of the Benuzzis, the area around Trieste and a stretch of the Adriatic coast – as 'unredeemed' and this strong belief, known as *irredentismo*, became a movement that aspired to their integration within the new kingdom of Italy.

On the whole, however, Italians had no special animosity towards Austria. There was greater prosperity in its empire, and it was a logical place for Italians near its borders to look for work. Moreover Austria had not arrived in Italy as a conqueror, and it had instead acquired territory there quite often by marriage and diplomacy. It had governed efficiently and once it had gone it still retained a broad degree of goodwill among its former citizens.

Giacomo Emilio, brought up as an *irredentista*, went to Italian schools, where he learned German not very well and referred to it as 'the hated language.' After graduating with a science degree from Padova University he returned to Dro and before long was called up for service in the imperial military forces. He got his first proper job in Vienna, on the national railways. His subsequent career was spent almost entirely on engineering activity in the transport sector, on roads, railways and bridges all over the empire, from Prague down to Serbia, in Vienna and Hungary, returning occasionally to the province of Trentino. Along the way he learned German properly, married Johanna Holzgärtner, and by her had three daughters and two sons, who were Felice's father Giovanni, known as Nino, and Valerio.

The memoirs of Giacomo Emilio, written not long before his death in Dro in 1930, are quite strange. Intended it seems mainly for the instruction and benefit of his offspring, they are filled with detail of his work, of which he was evidently proud, as well as the names, goings-on and quirks of people he worked with. By contrast the memoirs say hardly anything about the family itself, and have almost no anecdotes or affectionate remarks. How his wife Johanna eventually died in Trieste in 1913 after severe sickness and much suffering is summed up in a few sentences and the dry comment that 'you all know about the last stages of her illness so I won't describe them.'[4]

Felice's family remembered Nino as a good man, of few words, who always did the right thing. In Giacomo Emilio's memoirs his birth is alluded to, but there are few other references to him: and none to Nino's Austrian wife Berta, their marriage, or the birth of their four sons. On the other hand the name of Valerio, who may well have been his father's favourite and who had a knack of getting into trouble, is often mentioned. Giacomo Emilio, having recorded how their mother died, urged Nino and his sisters not to forget how much help Valerio had provided her in the final stages, and to be grateful to him for that.

Nino graduated in law from Pisa University and returned to Vienna where he married Berta Rauer in February 1910. At the end of the year Felice was born. He looked so frail at birth that a priest was hastily summoned and it was he who, spurred on by faith and hope, gave the child a name that meant 'happy.' Felice did survive of course, although his health remained delicate for many years. Other brothers followed: Piero in 1913, Gianni in 1916 and Guido in 1918.

After the second son was born, the heir to the Austrian throne was assassinated in Sarajevo and the world went to war. Italy at first stayed out of things. For thirty years it had been in a three-way pact with Austria-Hungary and Germany, but it was never really comfortable with the arrangement as it badly wanted to win back more of those lands where Italian was the main language spoken. In secret negotiations in London in 1915 Britain, France and Russia made it an attractive offer – to grant Italy almost all the territories it sought in the Trieste region and along the Adriatic coast once hostilities were over, if it sided with them. Italy as a result joined in the war, against a single enemy: Austria-Hungary.

The hostilities that had been declared between the two former allies on each side of the Alps made things awkward but not impossible for the many Italian citizens of the empire, like the Benuzzis. For example one future prime minister of Italy, Alcide de Gasperi, who in 1915 was a member of parliament in Vienna, opted to stay on there for the duration.[5] Nino was able to continue as an employee of the legal department of the imperial railway system. His father Giacomo Emilio at first found work in Trieste but then a road-building opportunity came up in Hungary which he took.

The longer the war went on, testing the loyalty of everyone in this situation, the more difficult things became. Although Nino's commitment to the empire was never in question, its railway authorities still took the precaution of posting him to a remote station on the border with Poland.[6] In the company where his father was working, three quarters of the personnel were Italian prisoners of war and Giacomo Emilio related how he did what he could to alleviate their trying conditions, something not easy under the watchful eye of those in charge.

In February 1917 Giacomo Emilio learned that his youngest son had been arrested and interrogated for treasonous activities. Upon his release six months later Valerio was ordered to the front: claiming that he was sick, he succeeded instead in being sent to Vienna. At Christmas the family got together in the capital and the police swooped and thoroughly searched their apartment, this time locking away not only Valerio but also his father. The charges against Valerio were serious and it seemed quite likely that he would face the death penalty. Giacomo Emilio pleaded for leniency with his own interrogators on the basis that Valerio, like various other members of the family, suffered from some mental abnormality. They retorted that the family had a long history of irredentismo, and that every one of Giacomo Emilio's brothers would be investigated. When he pointed out that one of them, Giuseppe, had recently died the investigating magistrate snapped at him: 'We'll dig him up!'

For the whole of 1918 father and son remained incarcerated in Vienna, alongside common criminals and in conditions often close to starvation. Nino together with his younger sister Claudia managed once a week to come to the prison with some scraps of bread for him, although Giacomo Emilio commented drily that this was never enough. In his idiosyncratic way he then brought his memoirs to an abrupt close, describing his release after 321 days of confinement: 'I got up slowly, put on the standard issue tunic, and was led down to the guardroom. There I hugged Nino without a word, got dressed in my own clothes and was allowed to go free.' He concluded with the whimsical addition of the cry that had greeted his birth: 'Viva Italia!'

Italy's war with Austria was fought in high mountain passes in freezing wintry conditions, with frequent landslides and avalanches. More fell victim to the elements than were lost in direct military action. At Caporetto in November 1917 the Italian defences were overwhelmed and the enemy armies then flooded through to threaten the whole Po Valley. But they were checked and forced back at the last line of defence. The tide turned dramatically a year later, when Austria's wartime ally and patron Germany suffered setbacks as fresh American troops arrived on the Western front. Exhausted and suffering terrible losses everywhere the enemy armies were ordered to pull back. Austria was on the verge of collapse, and independence movements within its empire took advantage of the situation. Italian forces entered Trieste and, as its troops headed for home, Austria sought and signed an armistice. Under its terms Italy received all it had been promised in the Treaty of London, subject to what might be decided in the post-war settlement at Versailles.[7] There Italy gained all land below the Alps but the territories along the Adriatic remained to be resolved with the new Yugoslav state. For the Benuzzis the really important fact was that their home province of Trentino as well as Alto Adige to its north and Trieste were all now in Italian hands.

The legacy of the empire continued in a variety of ways to impact on the life of Felice Benuzzi. His mother and grandmother were both Austrian and the only language he spoke for his first eight years was German. His knowledge of it enabled him at school and university to acquire a profound understanding of German literature, and it gave him other opportunities in his diplomatic career. At the very start of it, thirty years after the armistice, he struck up a rapport with a senior Foreign Ministry official, Justo Giusti del Giardino; Justo helped him secure his first diplomatic posting, to Paris, and was also his boss there.[8] In a later assignment, Felice's bilingualism made him a natural Foreign Ministry choice to take part in high-level talks over the issue of South Tyrol, known in Italy as Alto Adige, where language and culture were at the core of the dispute. It was highly sensitive for all concerned, and it was never fully resolved. For Felice the special challenge as a participant in the talks was to defend and promote Italian national interests, all the while having abundant sympathies for those of Austria.

For generations of Benuzzis with family ties on both sides of the Alps there was always a potential for conflict of loyalty, after the birth of the Italian state in the second half of the nineteenth century. The early twentieth century saw Italy and Austria at war; thereafter Mussolini rose to power with a program of extreme Italian nationalism; in due course the Duce became the ally of Austrian-born Adolf Hitler. There was never any doubt, however, where the family loyalty actually lay: they were out and out Italians.

In December 1918 the pressing problem for Nino Benuzzi was to find somewhere safe for his family to live, and where he would be able to work. The Austrian empire was falling apart, and for people such as them whose status was uncertain it was best that they get out of Vienna. Before the end of the year Nino moved the family to Trieste, a city with its own history of ambiguity and division. But one thing was assured – from now on the lives of the Benuzzis would be under the Italian flag.

CHAPTER 1 NOTES

[1] Giacomo Emilio Benuzzi (1848-1933). His memoirs were published in *Giacomo Emilio Benuzzi ingegnere nell'impero austro-ungarico* a cura di Umberto Zanin: *Il Sommolago*, Comune di Dro, 2007. The following section draws heavily on this record.

[2] The battle of Solferino was the last engagement of the second War of Italian Independence. Fought near the village of Castiglione on 24 June 1859, it was the last where monarchs personally commanded their armies. Horrors on the battlefield inspired the Swiss Henri Dunant to lead a movement to establish the International Red Cross.

[3] Prince Klemens Metternich's phrase in a letter in 1847 'more often quoted than correctly understood, was a warning against the possible consequences of a secular and national power threatening the perfect independence of the Holy See.' Menczer, B. (1994), *Tensions of Order & Freedom: Catholic Political Thought*, 1789-1848, Transaction Publishers, p. 139.

[4] Zanin op. cit. p. 113.

[5] Alcide De Gasperi (1881-1954) was born at Pieve Tesino, near Trento. From 1905 he directed the journal *Il Nuovo Trentino*, in which he defended Italian culture and the economic interests of his own region. In 1911 he was elected to the Austrian parliament as an Italian representative. In 1921, with the annexation of Trentino, he was elected to the Italian parliament. Hostile to the fascists, in 1927 he was arrested and sentenced to four years imprisonment; he was active in the resistance during World War II and after it was instrumental in establishing the Christian Democratic Party.

[6] Nino was sent as station chief to Radziechow, midway between Dresden and Breslau/Wraclow (Zanin op.cit. p. 114; interview with Stefania 12.10.2012).

[7] The Treaty of Versailles (signed 28 June 1919) resolved matters with Germany and the subsequent Treaty of Saint-Germain-en-Laye (signed 10 September 1919) dealt with Austria. At Saint-Germain Italy obtained all of South Tyrol to the "geographical and natural frontier (the Brenner frontier)" as it had been promised under the 1915 Treaty of London: that is the Italian-speaking province of Trentino and the German-speaking Alto Adige. In elections held in May 1921, De Gasperi triumphed in Trentino but all four seats in Alto Adige were won by the *Deutscher Verband* with almost 90% of the votes. The following month, in his first speech in the new parliament, Benito Mussolini in fierce nationalist terms denounced the outcome in Alto Adige: Scarano, F. (2012), *Tra Mussolini e Hitler: le opzioni dei sudtirolesi nella politica estera*, Franco Angeli, p. 34.

[8] Villa Giusti, in Mandria near Padova, was where on 3 November 1918 the armistice was signed that ended hostilities between Italy and Austria-Hungary. It was owned by the Count Vettor Giusti del Giardino (1855-1926), mayor of Padova and a senator – and uncle of Justo Giusti del Giardino (1908-1991) – see Chapter 14, note 4.

Mt Ortler 1929

2

TRIESTE

The third of November 1918, the day that Giacomo Emilio Benuzzi was released from prison in Vienna, was also the day that Italian armed forces entered Trieste and the day that Austria sued for peace with Italy. The war was over and the Austro-Hungarian Empire had imploded, due to military defeats, shortages of food and much else, as well rebellion among its many ethnic minorities. It was definitely time for Italians to quit the capital, and this the Benuzzi family did, in December, with the exception of Giacomo Emilio's three daughters who had all married Austrians.

It made sense for the family to return to Trieste where they had been for a while prior to the death of Giacomo Emilio's wife. Back then, before the war, it was an attractive, prosperous and cosmopolitan city of about a quarter of a million inhabitants. As the Empire's only port, it grew in importance during the previous century and its population had multiplied sixfold. A census held in 1910, the year Felice was born, showed that half those living in Trieste normally spoke Italian, a quarter Slovenian and the rest mainly German and Croatian.[1] These folk had got on tolerably well with each other under Austrian rule. But all that had changed. Central Europe, which for decades had funnelled its trade and culture down to this one point had suddenly lost all influence in Trieste. Instead this frontier city was set for the next fifty years to boil and eventually spill over with political and racial tensions between Italians and southern Slavs.

For the moment Italy was the undoubted winner, in Trieste. It had suffered huge casualties and setbacks in the mountains nearby in 1917, but it emerged from the war in a good strategic position, having in the post-war treaty arrangements gained extra territory to the east and south of the city. Italy was determined to stamp its presence throughout these 'redeemed' lands, even in towns and villages where Italian speakers were a minority. Emotions of nationalism and patriotism led to demands that within the new borders people be Italian or nothing. It was in this climate of political fervour that fascism was born, and it was very much at home in Trieste. Here, less than two years after the end of the war, according to one historian:

> the Fascist Duce Benito Mussolini first used a metaphor with an unhappy future in the region when he talked of the urgent need to 'cleanse' the place of ethnic difference. It did not take Triestine Fascists long to convert words to action. In July 1920 they assaulted and burned the headquarters of the local Slovene political movement and its newspaper, thus liquidating, they hoped, Slav 'power' and Slav culture since, as their local paper put it 'a Slavia within Italy cannot be allowed to exist.'[2]

The Benuzzis had had to toe the political line when they lived in Austria. Now, back in their homeland, there was every incentive for them to continue to do so, and not play any part in the changes which anyway seemed to reflect all they had once hoped for. Nino and Berta had always only sought a peaceful life, and meant to bring up their sons in the same spirit. Nino, aged 35, was sure to be able to get work on the railways in Trieste which had been the terminus of the Empire's railway system, since he knew that system well, and its legal aspects in particular. For Berta, who spoke no Italian, it looked to be as congenial an environment as any abroad to raise a family, the youngest of whom was less than six months old. The senior member, Giacomo Emilio, now seventy, might have retired in Dro where his youngest brother Edoardo had been mayor during the war, but instead as an experienced engineer he decided to take part in postwar reconstruction in Trieste. Felice's uncle Valerio, who had just spent a year in gaol and should have learned lessons from the experience, only too willingly dived at once into the turbulent new politics. Fatefully, he was taken on by ITO (*Informazioni Truppe Operanti*), the intelligence department of the Italian armed forces.[3] Valerio had the aptitude and languages for undercover work in an area where the ethnic currents were dangerous, even treacherous.

Nino's first task was to establish his family in their new city. He found a place for them to live in Scorcola, one of the suburbs looking down as from a balcony over the city centre and the port. It was a pleasant area with intriguing communications to match its geography: a tramway built in 1902 that operated conventionally at sea level converted itself then into a funicular railway and trundled steeply through Scorcola up to a level of three hundred metres where, at Opicina, it again proceeded like any other tram. It is still in operation.

***

For Felice the next five or so years were an enchanting time of freedom and discovery. Everything seemed challenging, physically demanding, readily accessible and without particular responsibilities; he had companions, energy, high hopes and plenty of rewards. The fact that here in Trieste his was increasingly a programmed world hardly mattered since the activities he was required to sign up for were ones that suited him perfectly, above all the organised excursions. He embraced and was embraced by the new Italian reality, and he and his friends marched and climbed joyfully, they did what they were told to do and they breathed the heady mountain air.

His earliest memories of life in Scorcola were of the view over the roofs and out beyond the harbour installations, to the near inlets and the curving away east and south of the Istrian coastline. He and other boys in the neighbourhood would watch the coming and going of ships, draw pictures of them and make models from the husks of the fruit of two luxuriant paulownias that grew in front of the house, flowering in mauve and smelling of honey. Just after his tenth birthday he fell quite ill with pleurisy and spent a long time laid up in bed. On the floor above lived a Pole by the name of Tadlewski, who played the piano interminably, often going over and over some piece until he had got it right. For the fevered boy this music – it was Chopin, his mother told him – blended in with the wanderings of his mind which more and more dwelled on the Carso, the rugged limestone plateau and terrain that encircled Trieste. He recalled how:

> my longing to get well and get up became bathed in the colours of the Carso as I had recently seen it, those blazing and doleful colours of autumn when the beech and sumac leaves go golden and bloody and the shadows of the pine groves darken in violet; and this same desire became enveloped in the luminous and unravelling melodies of sonatas, or obscure, agonising ballads, preludes, and nocturnes.[4]

The geography of Trieste and the area around it were to have deep meaning for Felice, not only in these glorious few years but for the rest of his life as well. He later described how someone approaching Trieste from the south, from the sea, might have a three-stepped image of what lay dead ahead: the city, the Carso behind it and then the high Alps back towards Austria. Travellers from the north on the other hand, having left the mountains behind them would enter stony and largely treeless uplands before coming abruptly upon vistas of blue water and sun. A local journalist had aptly written that this experience was like going through silence and coming out with a yell.[5]

While for some this landscape was unappealing, for Felice it always had enchantment. He sensed the Carso was somehow in his veins and under his skin, the vastness of white, grey or yellowish rocks, dotted with flowers and pitted and punctured, fissured by channels forming little bowl-shaped valleys like bomb craters. There was precious little topsoil here for the meagre vegetation in amongst the bare but highly permeable stone surfaces: no water anywhere to be seen, for all precipitation was swallowed down into rivers thundering through underground caverns before reappearing somewhere distant. Equally potent and invisible, to anyone on the Carso, was the felt presences of the Adriatic below and the Alps above.

Felice was drawn back up into the Carso almost as soon as he recovered from his illness. His parents were keen for him to get out and about, and enrolled him in a youth group of the *Touring Club Italiano* which in 1921 had begun organising outings for schoolchildren to places of historical or natural interest near Trieste. Every Sunday boys and girls between 10 and 15 would be taken up into the high country or down into Istria, in all weathers except heavy rain, even when the notorious bora wind howled from the north-east or sheets of ice covered the steep narrow laneways. From the end of the tramway at Opicina the groups of kids would continue on foot to reach:

> anywhere worth seeing within a radius of twelve kilometres from Trieste: to Monte San Primo perched above the pretty little port of Santa Croce where broom will blossom sweetly in June, Monte San Leonardo with its traces of human settlement dating back thousands of years, Monte Lanaro with its infinite vistas, Monrupino's old church on a flat terrace of rock overlooking much of the Carso, the pine-clad heights of Concusso and Castellaro Maggiore, Moncalvo di Gropada and finally the great Orlek gulley which fills with narcissi in spring. If I close my eyes now as I write, I can see all of this, all these images, in a clear and limpid morning air. And I can hear skylarks.[6]

Sometimes, frightened but fascinated, they would be taken down to dark caves, of which the Carso seem to have a limitless number. At Gabrovizza they saw where recent excavations had unearthed the relics of a prehistoric bear, and in the Gigante cave slender and transparent stalactites and solid and severe stalagmites. At San Canzio a whole complex of caverns with whirlpools and abysses, rivers, lakes and waterfalls for kilometre after kilometre – not lit in those days by electricity but by hundreds of little candles that danced in continual motion creating fantastic shadows and flashes of light reflected in the cataracts and the still surfaces of rockpools.

At age 12 he was old enough to go on a major annual outing to a nearby mountain where he and hundreds of others took backpacks and blankets, rolling themselves up in them to sleep on the floor of the school and town hall of the village of Lupogliano – or Lupoglav, for it was in Istria. From the top of the mountain they looked down on the city-port of Fiume – now Rijeka – which like the rest of the peninsula was later lost to Italy. On the far horizon Felice could just make out the jagged Julian Alps, their rocky surfaces gleaming with snow. It seemed somehow possible that in their stacked-up grandeur there might be even more to marvel at than in the horizontal Carso.

The opportunity for him to find out came soon when his father agreed to take him to Monte Nero above Caporetto where five years earlier the fighting had been ferocious.[7] They walked for hours and came across trees struck down by artillery and a landscape ruined by trenches but then mists closed in on them and Nino decided to call it a day. Felice was much upset as it did not seem so far to the top, but from this excursion he had one unforgettable memory, of the delicious dried apricots that his father at this point produced from his rucksack. Decades afterwards the memory of that gesture was stirred by an incident in the Himalayas: as he was gazing awestruck from the window of a cargo plane at the slopes of Nanga Parbat, a nervous local Hunza on board, who may never have been on an aeroplane before, held out to him a handful of the same fruit, nectar again.[8]

He never forgot, either, the next trip into the mountains with his father. They had taken the train to Chiusaforte, close to the border with Austria. They left from there on foot at dawn passing through one village after another, up a track transformed by a sudden downpour into a torrent, up to a mountain refuge where they spent the night. It was fine in the morning and the grass gave off a strong smell, shiny black salamanders crisscrossed the path and the mists ahead shredded and parted. For a part of this climb and joyously Felice, for the first time, had had to use his hands. Before long and without difficulty they reached the summit of Mt Mangart, 2678 metres. There was not a cloud in the sky and the two lakes of Fusine far below like blue-green sleepy eyes seemed to look back up at them. The sun made the jagged ranges gleam and his father named one by one the Dolomite peaks they could see: Marmolada, Pelmo, Civetta, Antelao, Cristallo. All the splendour of the universe lay before them. On the way down his father kept stopping to point out any unusual flowers; he saw his first edelweiss; and, another first, he felt that strange mix of sensations brought on by descending into the valley, exultation at having been so high, muscular exhaustion, regret it was nearly over and hope for future climbs.

In the summer of 1925 the family spent several weeks with Berta's parents in the mountains near Salzburg. Here in one of the gorges they came across a field of snow frozen hard: 'eternal snow' his grandfather called it, and it amazed Felice to be in this way face to face with eternity. He learned to ride a bike that was too big for him: he collided with an elderly lady who ran yelling to his grandfather and had to be generously compensated. For his misdemeanour he was cuffed about the ears. It was the last time that ever happened. But, he recalled ruefully, in time moral blows would rain down on him, and they would hurt more.

Back in Trieste there was no shortage of vigorous outdoor activity. One Christmas he was given a pair of skis, rugged wooden things, and put these to good use with others from the *ricreatorio* youth club he had recently joined. Several of such clubs had been set up by the city authorities in those years with the aim of keeping boys from poorer families out of trouble after school and in holidays, involving them in sports and activities like music and drama. To reach the nearest ski-field he and his friends would get up at four in the morning and take the steep and narrow alleys through the ghostly suburbs, often with the harsh north wind in their faces, to Opicina on the plateau above the city. From the station another kilometre further along they would catch the train to Vremsica, these days well within Slovenia. There was snow there at last, not at all deep and crusted with ice. They would ski down for a hundred metres or so and then struggle up the slopes in herring-bone fashion; sweating but exhilarated they would go down again. At the end of the day, tired out, they would get the train back to Trieste, and walk home. Extra satisfaction would sometimes come when a passer-by, seeing these boys with skis over their shoulder, would turn out of curiosity and express wonderment.

Often Felice and his friends would be confronted with stark reminders of the recent bloody battles fought in the nearby mountains. They travelled once on an excursion organised by their local alpine club to the chain of mountains that later became the border between Italy and Yugoslavia, in an army truck together with a number of war veterans. Some of the former soldiers had vivid recall of those events, of artillery bombardment and bayonet charges. The boys were startled by this surge of heavy patriotism, but those days all around them they were hearing the fascist clarion call for courage and self-sacrifice.

Another time they had the unnerving experience of finding in a cave the relics of war – mattresses, blankets, utensils in good condition as well as letters and postcards whose writing was still legible, all apparently abandoned by soldiers in hasty retreat. Elsewhere, picking their way through prickly bushes and on the lookout as always for unexploded shells, they stumbled over a collection of bones including a skull with a bullet hole through it that seemed to gaze up and want to say something to them. They stared back at it, petrified.

His parents took Felice to see relatives in Dro and then on north of the village into the Brenta mountains. This was to be his first climb to an altitude of 3000 metres, the goal being Cima Tosa.

With his father he scrambled up into the mists as far as a crowded mountain refuge where they slept badly. In the morning they set off late and the weather deteriorated. Nino struggled to find the right way in the thickening mist but they managed to join up with a couple from Lombardy, who had a guide. Unfortunately the poor visibility forced them to give up their climb, and the cost of the guide used up all the cash his father had on him – yet another sign to Felice that his family was not wealthy. The upshot was that they went without food for the rest of the day, which ended with a thirty kilometre trek back to Dro. But for Felice, thrilled to have climbed higher than ever before, and with a guide, it was altogether worth it despite the agony to his leg muscles.

One unforgettable day in August 1925 there appeared at the refuge where Felice and his friends were a personality already familiar to him, and of whom he was in awe. Emilio Comici and his companion pulled out of their rucksacks metal equipment that Felice had only ever heard about, before setting off agilely up a nearby rockface.[9] Comici was ten years older than him but already the most noted of all Trieste's climbers, with the exception, that is, of Julius Kugy who a generation earlier had been the pioneer in the Julian Alps with more than fifty first ascents: Kugy's fame had spread internationally.

Ever since coming to Trieste Felice had been equally drawn to the sea as much as to the mountains, and in fact it was the former that had seemed to promise most for the future: he imagined that as soon as he turned fifteen he would join the navy. His parents when he was very young had given him an atlas which stirred his imagination about foreign travel. At school he devoured adventure stories by the German writer Karl May,[10] and moved on to stories of genuine exploration by the likes of Livingstone and Scott of the Antarctic.

In these carefree years of early adolescence Felice and his friends on their outings chatted about the usual things – school and sport and sometimes girls. They certainly were not the least interested in politics, although one teacher did urge them to read the newspapers and so keep up with local and world events. The fascism that since 1922 had been taking hold of the country, integrating the people into the state by such means as membership of youth organisations, meant nothing special to them. Even less did they focus on the fact of a substantial Slav minority within the new expanded borders of Italy or the expulsions of other Slavs from Trieste's hinterland. They learned a few Slovene words, and were always treated well by the Slovenes, without ever having the feeling of friction or of tension between the different ethnic groups. Years later Felice wondered if on social and political issues his group wore blinkers, as did the massive draught horses that they sometimes saw trundling carts laden with beer down to the port. Only vaguely did they notice the evidence of Italianisation where everywhere placenames and even family names were switched over to a new euphony, and where warnings also went up that the single language of Italian must be spoken in public places.[11]

Looking back on this period, Felice felt it would not be fair to say that his group was blithely happy, untroubled and unaware. Happiness was not assured during their adolescence and they had their crises and predicaments and family ructions. At school the classwork and homework pressed upon them. They fought amongst themselves sometimes and they had their first delicate, secretive and fervent romances. They were aware of the aftermath of the war with its consequences in their city and close by. Nationalist fervour and incessant party rhetoric demanded conformity and discipline. Quite simply, fascism was now synonymous with everyday life and they accepted it like the air they breathed.

CHAPTER 2 NOTES

[1] The Encyclopaedia Britannica entry for 'Trieste' states that in the Austrian census of 1910, nearly two-thirds of the city's population of 229,510 was composed of Italians. However, it is hard to be precise about the data as the Austrian census assessed the

language in common use, not the mother tongue: the Hapsburgs had no interest in fostering internal nationalisms. The effect was to emphasise the dominant languages: in Trieste Italian predominated. Cuomo, P. (2012), *Il miraggio danubiano: Austria e Italia, politica ed economia,* 1918-1936, Franco Angeli, p. 29; Cresciani, G. (2011), *Trieste goes to Australia,* Padana Press, p. 8.

[2] R.J.B. Bosworth, Foreword to Cresciani op. cit. p. xviii.

[3] Valerio Benuzzi (1892-1961): See Canali, M. (2004), *Le spie del Regime*, Bologna: Il Mulino, p. 207. Also Borgomaneri, L. (1997), *Hitler a Milano. I crimini di Theodor Saeveche capo della Gestapo*, Rome: Datanews, p. 185 footnote: 'Benuzzi, già confidente dell'OVRA dagli anni Trenta, è ritenuto da Guido Leto, direttore della polizia politica, «un disonesto al servizio di chiunque lo pagasse» (Benuzzi, an OVRA agent during the 1930s, is reckoned by Guido Leto, chief of the political police, to be a "villain at the service of anyone who pays him".

[4] *Più che sassi* p. 5.

[5] Silvio Benco, at one stage editor of Trieste's *Il Piccolo. Più che sassi* p. 6.

[6] *Più che sassi* pp. 8-9.

[7] As noted in *Più che sassi* p. 13, Monte Nero is called Krn in Slovenian. Caporetto is Kobarid. Felice generally gives the toponomy in both languages, but 'Caporetto' for Italians resonates, as perhaps 'Waterloo' does for other Europeans.

[8] *Più che sassi* p. 14; the account there is drawn almost verbatim from a letter he wrote to his parents from Karachi on 5 December 1955: see Chapter 16, note 8.

[9] Emilio Comici (1901-1940) was the outstanding Italian climber of his generation. Comici (pronounced with stress on the first syllable) was not only credited with a great number of first ascents but was famed for his technique and cat-like elegance. Before a frayed rope took his life at age 39 at his rock-climbing school in Val Gardena, he had been appointed mayor there by the fascist authorities. Felice (*Più che sassi* p. 73) thought Comici was to mountain climbing what his contemporaries Greta Garbo and Marlene Dietrich were to cinema.

[10] Karl May (1842-1912) was a popular German writer noted mainly for adventure novels set in the American West.

[11] See Hametz, M.E. (2005) *Making Trieste Italian, 1918-1954,* Boydell & Brewer, p. 90.

Felice 1930

3

Julian Alps

When Felice was three or four years old he said to his mother one day in Vienna, 'Mamma, ich bin so traurig, ich muss eine Reise tun.'[1] He was so sad that he needed to go on a journey. Relating this to her future daughter-in-law, Berta said it showed how, at the earliest age and ever afterwards, the oldest of her four boys had felt a compulsion to travel. She had no idea, though, why he yearned for it so much. This strange restlessness never left Felice, and it shaped his life in the broad directions he would take and in the narrow choices he made as to what to do next. In part it was a positive and hopeful force, and could spur him to action; but it was also vague and unfocused, drawing him in on himself and sometimes making him moody. It got stronger with puberty and separated him a little from his friends, none of whom shared his view that Trieste was a place to leave behind soon.

The sea – he could easily reach it on foot from home – was a powerful attraction for him. Sometimes with a friend or two and at other times alone he liked to wander around the docks area, to the sound of groaning winches and anchor chains, watching the tugboats and dredges and all the clamour here where, as he wrote in his memoirs:

> merchant ships from everywhere loaded and unloaded, where the smell of bales of jute mixed with wafts from bags of coffee, barrels of wine and cases of rum, and the cranes screeched while the wharf labourers swore. The confusion fascinated me,

and before my eyes the world opened up.[2]

One summer he took up rowing, mainly as a way to get fit for rock climbing with a thorough exercising of his arms and shoulders. On those days he would be up at dawn to get the early tram and down at the port would meet up with the three other members of his crew. The sea was almost always calm and flat at that hour, and he would get a real thrill from the harmonious rhythm of their strokes and the sight of their wake vanishing into the distance. Occasionally they would cut across a ferry taking workers to the naval yards at Monfalcone or fishermen coming back from their night's work or another crew like theirs and there would be shouts of 'Op! Look out! Come on!'

To be a sailor: that was what he had always wanted. Accordingly two months before his sixteenth birthday he was summoned to Venice for the much-anticipated medical examination, the crucial first step for admission to the naval academy in Livorno. He boarded the train full of hope, but with some misgivings about whether he would really be up to the rigid disciplines of a life at sea. At the Arsenale hospital the oculist told him, 'You have the best eyesight in the Adriatic!' but then failure awaited him at the dentist's. He was found to have more fillings than the maximum allowed and so was rejected on the grounds of 'extensive tooth decay.' That moment shattered his dream of a naval career.

Felice returned home in deepest gloom. As his thoughts churned and darkened he could see just one dim light, one way to break out, and that was by going back to climbing. But down that track, too, he ran into more disappointment: his father could not get time off work to take him on the trip they had talked about many times, into the Julian Alps. In the dejection that followed he kept asking himself why he was no good at anything, and what the point was anyway of climbing if just not doing it made him miserable. Mountains after all were nothing but rocks. In a fit of frustration he grabbed his ice-axe and whacked it, meaning to snap its handle; when he failed even to do that he tossed it in a wardrobe.

Back at school he threw himself into studying. At least he had no trouble there. At home he stayed up reading until all hours. But he looked forward to Sundays, and would pore over maps and train timetables. After age fifteen there were fewer and fewer organised excursions, and usually those who wanted to went off on their own without adult supervision. His companion on these outings was Bruno Salvi, small and lithe, orphaned but cheerful and a good talker, liked by everyone. He and Felice were perhaps smarter and poorer than many of their schoolmates: for a fee they could help them out after hours in areas where they were struggling, Latin in particular. The money they earned paid for their travel; food they could get from home; for a bed, they could always find a peasant's hayloft. One evening hurrying to catch the last train home they mistook in the dark the gap in the hedge for a short cut and fell head over heels down a steep slope into a ditch full of slime. Shaken and filthy they then had to sprint, making it just in time to the station where railway staff and the other passengers stared at them disdainfully.

The following year he and his father made two trips to the Julians, the first time with five boys from the *ricreatorio* including Bruno. Late in the day they reached the Val Trenta, famous for the feats of Julius Kugy. There thirty years later Yugoslavia would erect a big bronze statue honouring the pioneering mountaineer, seated and seeming to gaze at the peaks all around that he had climbed, most of them as the first person to do so.[3] In the years ahead Felice would be more influenced by Kugy than any other personality from the past. Like him, Kugy also straddled German and Italian cultures but the older man had initially come down on the other side. In the First World War at nearly sixty years of age he had served as a consultant on mountain matters for the Austrian army, but afterwards he returned to Trieste, his city, and it was there that he died in 1944. He was a climber, a musician, a writer and also a botanist with a great love of nature, and a fascination for every aspect of the mountains, including their names and all the people who lived or worked in them, the peasants, hunters, taverners and guides. For Kugy, as for Felice, to go into the mountains was a transcendental experience and both of them hoped to find bliss up there, and consolation.

The second trip, and it would be one of the last outings he made with his father, was to Italy's northeastern corner. They headed into the mountains from the multi-ethnic, multi-lingual town of Tarvisio; their goal was the mountain called Tricorno by Italians and Triglav by Slovenes. After a first unsuccessful attempt on the mighty Mt Jalovec Nino and Felice moved on to Triglav, climbing up over the rocks steadily during the morning of their second day until a sudden storm broke upon them with much thunder and lightning. They managed to find the shelter of an overhang. Some chilly hours passed and then it began to snow. After that they scrambled up to the top. Although wet through and shivering like a leaf in the wind from the intense cold Felice felt a great calm in his heart, with the triumph of it. Peaks stuck up like islands through the sea of cloud around them, and he was able to name each one of them. They decided to take the quickest way home via Bohinjska Bistrica and there get the train back to Trieste, but this was not without some risk as they did not have their passports with them. When they saw two border guards coming up towards them they greeted them with a nervous 'Dober dan': but the men did not react in any negative way and they carried on down to the station. Nino found an Italian railway official who helped them smooth things over with their local counterparts and they were allowed to get on the train. It may have been a coincidence but at the first station inside Italy a policeman got on board and sat glaring suspiciously at them during the journey.

Felice and his friends now wanted to put themselves to tougher tests, going further and climbing higher. Their excursions often took them into Slovene areas. One time their descent from high country at Crni Kal brought them down to the source of the River Risano. After a short stretch this little river disappeared underground before resurfacing some kilometres away and plunging into the sea. The strange phenomenon intrigued Felice; much later it caused him to wonder whether this turbulent river with mysterious origins and a brief intense life was somehow emblematic of his own adolescence.

***

When he was seventeen the family spent their summer holidays in southern Tuscany, since at that time grandfather Giacomo Emilio had a job at the cinnabar mines of Monte Amiata, a lava dome from an extinct volcano.[4] They stayed in the house of peasant farmers whose pure Italian language intimidated Felice: the way he spoke now seemed to his own ears barbaric. It was one reason why he wanted to get out of the house. Most days he would leave in the morning, wander in the eroded countryside of soft tufa stone and come back in the evening, often without having set eyes on another living soul, happy in this scarred and empty landscape to listen to dogs barking and to take in the scent of broom. Once he went with his father and brother Piero up a path through thick woods of beech and chestnut to the iron cross on top of the mountain. For him those were magical days of hot sun, heady aromas and a bitter-sweet solitude he would later recall every time his plane passed over that area and began banking for its final descent into Rome's Fiumicino airport.[5]

He was soon drawn to another wilderness, much closer to home. On the plateau at the very edge of Trieste the Val Rosandra cleaves down through the limestone, making cliffs and screes on either side of the river that runs through the ravine.[6] Today, a mere thirty-minute walk from the city, rock-climbers come to hone their skills on Val Rosandra's steep walls. It was here that Emilio Comici, the greatest rock-climber of them all, chose to practise, just when Felice and his companions began taking an interest in climbing. They would gather around him and his small group while they exercised their muscles with a heavy stone in each hand, and then watch open-mouthed when after that Comici effortlessly shot up the cliff above them.

One of those companions of Felice's was Paolo Migliorini; the two of them planned a climbing excursion to the Dolomites, carefully saving up for it. Once they climbed for some hours up a saddle on the Civetta but thick clouds closed in on them and they were forced to go back down. On their return to Trieste they examined the most detailed maps and sought out any publication that mentioned the Civetta. They convinced themselves that the saddle they had reached in the mist was on the southern crest at 3010 metres, and had only ever been climbed once before. They were horribly wrong; they then went on to commit a second blunder, deciding to submit a brief account to *Alpi Giulie*, a highly respected magazine.[7] They consulted Emilio Comici, who knew the Dolomites well: he was amused by how earnest they were, shrugged his shoulders and said if they were sure, they might be right. And so it was that the magazine's yearbook in December 1928 published a half-page article by Felice Benuzzi and Paolo Migliorini describing 'the first ascent without guides and the first direct ascent by the Val di Sasse rock wall.' Alas, the next edition of the magazine produced a 'correction' signed by a mountaineer of international repute who brutally spelt out how these wretched boys had mistaken for the southern crest, one of the most magnificent features of the Alps, a very modest rock spur, and then chided them for their false and puerile boasting. Humbly they went along to see Comici, who laughed at their great embarassment. Felice folornly asked him what they should do and he said: 'Don't do anything.' For Felice the conclusion to draw was obvious. They had been taught a bitter lesson and in future should document any achievement meticulously; to wipe out this shame they needed to do some worthy and proper climbing.

But something good came out of that humiliating experience. Towards the end of the winter as he was wandering around town he felt a tap on his shoulder and it was Comici. He wanted to know if Felice was interested in joining a group who at Easter were going to climb Zuc del Boor, in the Carnic Alps below the border with Austria. He accepted on the spot, it was an amazing chance for redemption. Because Emilio said he would need them, he at once went and bought a pair of crampons. On the Saturday evening he caught the train to Chiusaforte. There in the inn were not only Comici and his friends but also another group of climbers, including some household names like Vladimiro Dougan.[8] He felt so privileged to find himself among these mountaineers he kept wondering if it was all a dream. An hour later the two groups split up and Felice with Comici and three others headed off up the track and into the night. No one said a word. In the silence all he could hear was the crunch of their footsteps, the tinkle of pickaxes and the dull scraping together of his crampons loose in his rucksack:

> After some woods we passed under a vertical rock wall on our right while on our left a valley appeared, or rather the sky itself studded with stars opened up. We carried on walking in total silence and I had the exhilarating feeling of being alone in this night, frighteningly and sweetly alone, but with stars in my heart. Even now, more than fifty years later, I wonder whether memory dazzles and distorts or whether I knew then that a day was breaking that was more pure and swollen than any in my eighteen years of life so far. Swollen with what? I hesitate to use such an exacting word: swollen with happiness.[9]

Three hours later the party reached a former barracks with a cement floor that now served as a mountain shelter. They lit a fire that soon filled the big room with eye-watering smoke, and did their best to get some sleep on the hard floor. What with the snoring of some, the shifting of embers in the fire and in due course the cold Felice found it impossible to sleep. At three an alarm clock sounded. They all got up and after a coffee were on their way. After crossing a ravine they came to a steep gulley and put on their crampons. Every bootfall made the frozen snow skitter. It was still too dark to go on when they reached the last major outcrop and since an icy wind was blowing they stopped and put on all the clothing they had with them. They then sat side by side on a ledge with their legs dangling over, facing the east like worshippers in some ancient solar ritual.

When it was simply too cold to stay there any longer they went on up a really steep gorge until they reached a frightening ice-covered barrier. Opposite them was a mountain whose snow-covered buttresses were pink in the first rays of the sun and over to their right the glazed secondary summit of Zuc del Boor gleamed like crystal. Comici with the others in his wake began climbing and seemingly without effort disappeared behind an overhang. The summit was clearly visible. Felice was offered a rope but he was determined to do it on his own. Imitating what the others had done, he made it up. The wind at the top was terrific. All around were stupendous snow-covered peaks. Down in the valley there was evidence everywhere of spring and from an invisible church the wind carried up to them the deep booming of bells for the first Easter service.

A few months later came the final school exams, and he passed them without difficulty. The next priority was to get a job that would pay for him to go to university – his father had made it quite plain that, with three other sons to raise, he would not be able to assist him financially. Finding work was arduous and exasperating. After an untold number of staircases, waiting rooms, and frosty rejections in the end he was given a temporary job at the same American car company where Paolo worked. The pittance he was paid at least meant he could do some more climbing.

Next winter he and Paolo set their sights on the highest peaks in Alto Adige on the border with Austria.

In a mountain hut on one of these trips Hans Sepp Pinggera, a wellknown guide, was much impressed by Felice's facility in German, and asked if he would like to come along while he took an elderly German couple who spoke no Italian up the Marmotta glacier. It was there that they came across a cannon left over from the last war still in its original emplacement. It prompted the German gentleman to remark that the Italians knew how to make roads but they were no good as fighters. Felice, who was doing the translating, informed them that in these mountains for the whole of the war the Italians had not let a single Austrian or German through. The awkward moment passed with a joke or two. Felice felt as if a great weight was off his shoulders. It wasn't the first and it wouldn't be the last time something awkward like that happened to him, born and bred as he was astride two worlds, but with his heart wholly on the Italian side.

A fortnight after that incident came news of the Wall Street crash, and for everyone the future looked uncertain. Felice had imagined he would find a job with one of the great Trieste insurance companies but these had been among the first to stop taking on new staff. Also out of the question was that he might this year go to university, a disappointment all the more keenly felt because that was what all his former classmates were doing. It seemed the best thing for him to do now was bring forward the call-up for compulsory military service, and for that his heart was of course set on the *Alpini*, the elite mountain brigade. On the very day he turned nineteen he submitted a formal application to be accepted for the *Alpini* officers' training school in Milan. He was sure he had all the right qualifications: not only could he attach a certificate from the prestigious Julian Alps Society testifying to his climbing and skiing skills to his application but also after a rigorous medical examination at the Trieste Military District he was declared 'in the best possible condition for alpine soldiering.'

In a gloomy mood he turned inwards, doubting his own self-worth. He believed he was capable of great things, he had dreams of a future where everything was possible and yet here and now life seemed empty and dreary. He wrote some secret poems for the girl he was in love with. He read all the time, mainly books on mountain-climbing. He continued to give private lessons and though never formally enrolled sat in on courses at the Commercial

University especially the English ones run by Stanislaus Joyce, whose older brother James had also taught for years in Trieste. And he was lured again to the mountains, more powerfully than ever, and went skiing with Paolo and others and sometimes with Emilio Comici.

Then on 30 January 1930 the fateful telegram arrived not from the *Alpini* but the Military District headquarters, directing him to serve with the infantry in Palermo. It transpired later that he was deemed too tall for the *Alpini*. It was a major turning point in his life which had come about through no desire on his part and in circumstances beyond his control. After a fit of anger at the dashing of one more precious hope he came to terms with the unexpected new chapter that had opened for him. Because there was no alternative, he thought he might as well make the best of it, and once he got to Palermo threw himself into the studies part of the program as well as the military drills. At least he was getting to see parts of the country he knew nothing about. In the graduation process at the end of the training period he did well enough to be granted his first choice of regiment, and his pick was the Grenadiers of Sardinia whose headquarters were in Rome.[10] It was to that city that he headed next, with important consequences for the rest of his life.

CHAPTER 3 NOTES

[1] Detail provided by Stefania in written answers to questions, passed to author 9 May 2013 (together with her translation: "I'm so sad, I want to go on a trip!").

[2] *Più che sassi* p. 39.

[3] The statue by the sculptor Jakob Savinsek is in spectacular wooded scenery in a mountainous area midway between Bovec and Kranjska Gora.

[4] Monte Amiata (1738 metres) is south of Siena and east of Grosseto. Cinnabar is the common ore of mercury.

[5] *Più che sassi* p. 46.

[6] Wedged between Trieste and the Slovene border Val Rosandra is a national park of great natural beauty.

[7] *Alpi Giulie*, the journal of the Trieste branch of the Italian Alpine Club, began publishing in 1896, at the outset every two months and subsequently twice a year.

[8] Vladimiro Dougan (1891-1955) climbed extensively in the Julian Alps, notably with Kugy, and like him shunned technical aids to climbing.

[9] *Più che sassi* p. 55. Felice retold the story almost word for word and had it published in *Alpi Giulie* Vol 74 – 1980 under the title *Cinquant'anni fa con Emilio Comici sul Zucc dal Boor d'inverno.*

[10] *Più che sassi* p. 66. Felice joined the 1° Reggimento Granatieri di Sardegna, one of the oldest Italian regiments whose origins go back to 1659: its name refers to the royal house of Sardinia and Piedmont, not the island. Stefania's written notes of 9.5.2013 (see note 1 above) state 'it was a great disappointment to him when the army sent him to the Granatieri in Sicily. Later in life he was grateful for it because it was an eye-opener to all the many problems in the south. Once he became an officer he was sent for six months army duty in Rome.'

Julius Kugy statue in Val Trenta

4

ROME

He had every reason to be excited when he arrived in Rome, in his twenty-first year. The army had brought him here, promoting him as a junior officer, and would look after him for his first six months in the capital, until he completed his national service.[1] For ten years after that the military would still have a certain hold over him, but that did not worry him. At the end of the draft he had every hope of being admitted to the University of Rome, given the good scores achieved in his school exams. And now the subjects he had studied there, Latin and History in particular, were coming alive for him in this city of the Forum and the Pantheon and the Vatican, where emperors had walked and where the Church had thrived and built sumptuously for twenty centuries.

There was naturally another, more contemporary reason for excitement. In the eight years since his Blackshirts had marched on Rome and the King had handed him the reins of government, Mussolini had made this city the headquarters of his fascist system. The new leader had in 1929 reached a new accord with the Church, and had begun a program of reconstruction and demolitions, opening up areas of the old city. Felice would have seen the building sites and the countless men with pickaxes and trucks laden with spoil creating a boulevard from the Colosseum to Piazza Venezia. In that great space, with Victor Emmanuel's vast white marble monument soaring up on one side, the crowds would from time to time gather and roar 'Du-ce! Du-ce!' when Mussolini came out on the balcony to harangue them. The message and the fervour meant little to Felice, but here he was, transported to the palpable throbbing heart of fascism.

For several years now the regime had required its citizens to conform to ideals of nationalism, patriotism and militarism, and at the core of its program was paramilitary education. In 1926 a new law set up the Balilla youth movement for boys from eight to eighteen years of age, and Felice had accordingly been taught military discipline with the slogan 'The Book and the Gun for the Perfect Fascist.' Under fascist doctrine boys could expect to fight for their country, girls to patriotically become mothers, and all in due course to become members of the Party. For Felice this was absolute everyday normality, including the trips to the mountains and the indoctrination at altitude. Fascism had found particularly fertile ground in Trieste, the epitome of the land that had been redeemed, and its alpine clubs had become little bastions of fascism. Felice, indifferent to the ideology, nevertheless had donned the uniforms, had marched and sung with everyone else. That was the reality in the Italy of the 1920s and 1930s.

It was a natural step for him when he commenced at the university in October 1931 to join the student militia, in which he would be an officer since he had already attained that rank with the army. A few months earlier, wrapping up his period of conscription, he had formally pledged his loyalty to the state. He now enrolled in the national body of soldiers on leave (UNUCI), partly because this also was logical and moreover was likely to bring economic benefits.[2] All of it fitted seamlessly in with the way he was brought up. Neither his family nor his own instincts had any quarrel with an insistence on discipline, sacrifice and patriotism. While he was not an out-and-out conformist and did take risks in climbing, he always respected authority.

In the same way it made sense to belong to the fascist student body, the *Gruppo Universitario Fascista*, or GUF, set up a few years earlier.[3] The benefits in doing so included the prospect that members might be given help in finding a job. But perhaps of even greater interest to Felice, the GUF was also responsible for extracurricular activities, including culture and sport, and it organised events and competitions known as *littoriali*.[4] Under Mussolini, sport had become a national priority, with promotions, incentives, propaganda and the building of new stadiums. As a consequence Italy's medal tally at the 1932 Olympic Games in Los Angeles was second only to that of the United States. Sport was a priority of Felice's, too.

His arrival at university coincided with a new, sterner approach by the authorities towards student behaviour. No longer to be tolerated were the playful attitudes and antics of *gaudeamus igitur* – goliardia, in Italian – that had long been a feature of student life. The regime saw universities as the training ground for future leaders, and they were to be serious and disciplined places, monitored by the Party. Professors were moreover required to sign pledges of loyalty to the regime, and virtually every one of them did: in 1930, out of 1250 throughout the country only fifteen refused.[5]

The crux of the matter for Felice was that he had got here. He had achieved this major personal objective. He was about to embark on a degree course in jurisprudence at the University of Rome, founded by popes in the fifteenth century, and known then and still today as *La Sapienza*. The name derived from the sign above its marble front door: *Initium Sapientae Timor Domini* – a quote from the Psalms meaning Fear of the Lord is the Beginning of Wisdom. In the seventeenth century the brilliant architect Borromini had been commissioned to rebuild it, and it was in his splendid creation close to Piazza Navona in the city centre that Felice in 1934 completed his degree. He was one of the last to do so: Mussolini had ordered that a new and larger campus be built elsewhere and it was opened the following year.[6]

The law degree course that Felice was about to embark on had a substantial arts and literature component. It was this that interested him above all. Already he was someone who had read widely, not only in German and French as well as in Italian but also in classical Latin and Greek. In his teenage years he had roughed out what he fancied might be a novel, and had contributed the one article to an alpine magazine about his botched climbing in the Dolomites. From now on he would be a regular contributor of articles to journals. The opportunity came up, almost certainly proposed by one of his professors, to write for a literary magazine in Florence. This was *Il Frontespizio*, and it published quality material, with catholic leanings.[7]

Felice was no more religious than he was political, which is to say he was knowledgeable but not devout. The church was also part of his world as he matured, and he duly went to Mass and accepted its doctrines without question. He would have been glad that, under what became known as the Lateran Treaty, church and state had established a new working relationship which confirmed Catholicism as the nation's religion: one practical outcome was the return of crucifixes into schools. It was no coincidence that in that same year of 1929 *Il Frontespizio* had made its first appearance. The magazine, like so many other institutions including the church, found a way to reconcile its core beliefs with those of the regime.

In 1931 Giuseppe De Luca, a priest and the driving force behind *Il Frontespizio* as well as its theological adviser, mentioned in a letter to a colleague that he had passed on to a university student 'the famous little volume *German Theology*, the most famous religious work in pre-Lutheran Germany.'[8] The student was undoubtedly Felice: the following September the magazine published an article by him on this esoteric text, remarkable more for its elegant prose than any analysis in it. Felice could evidently write well, and he contributed five more articles to *Il Frontespizio* before he graduated from the university, and three or four more in the years after that. His writings are noteworthy for a number of reasons. They show considerable maturity for a university student. They delve into some of life's deep mysteries. Several of them target Germany, but indirectly, via literary criticism. They mirror contemporary political turmoil in Europe, and even the Duce's growing nervousness towards the Führer. And they shed light on the character and personality of the author.

In April 1933 *Il Frontespizio* published an article by Felice on Heinrich Mann, a novelist who mainly wrote on social themes. Later that year Mann's attacks on the authoritarian and increasingly militaristic nature of German society since Hitler's rise to power made him opt to leave the country. Felice liked the way Mann posed questions about where society was headed and whether there were any remedies to the troubles it faced, but he found Mann unable to offer answers, and his arguments though sometimes strong were often weak. As for Germany, Felice in his article said there was no denying it had contributed enormously in education, economics and the sciences. However, this nation so rich in means and memories and despite having been traumatised by the 1914-18 war had still not found its true soul. Without naming Italy, he stated his own position starkly: 'Perhaps we are the only ones so far who have realised that the future can only blossom in the healthy soil of a people sure of their historical purpose.'

Three months later he again took aim at Germany, in an article entitled *Teutones*. He began with a critique of recent trends in German literature and then went on to address elements of the national character. Beyond Germany's borders, he wrote, the best-known image was that of *Gemütlichkeit*, 'of the good-natured, methodical, perhaps pot-bellied burger, quite fond of a beer.' But Felice was more interested in another national trait, that of *Sehnsucht*, a dark and impatient yearning to travel which had within it the feeling of unattainable happiness, of a lust for mystery, of expansion and fusion with outermost limits. In the German soul with all its contrasts he saw an overdeveloped aesthetic sense of individualism so pronounced that it could lead to disintegration, fragmentation and disruption. In religion, this had borne down on the unity of the Church, producing the Reformation. He reckoned the Germans to be dreamers and asked rhetorically: How could this deep propensity to dream not be exploited for any political, economic and materialistic purpose, such as the *Drang nach Osten*? That urge to look East had its roots in German history, but perhaps Felice was already aware that Hitler both in his *Mein Kampf* and after becoming Führer already had his eyes on neighbouring Slav territory. *Sehnsucht* was potentially tragedy, Felice wrote, especially in the context of the Mediterranean, and he instanced the Goths who had invaded Italy and the German crusaders who reached the Middle East. He concluded his article: '*Sehnsucht*: that yearning of the Germans will give them no peace in this world.'

In January 1934 he wrote a third article partly focusing on Germany with the title *Disfacitori* – as in his previous article he chose an unusual word to convey an idea of wrecking or disintegrating. Again he enclosed the issues that seem to be troubling him inside literary criticism. His targets were realist authors like Louis-Ferdinand Céline and Erich Maria Remarque whose *All Quiet on the Western Front* had been published a few years before. For Felice these authors were too negative, atheistic, nihilistic, and he ended his article with some thoughts that seem strange today but perhaps were not so odd for a young man back then:

> All right, here I am at my desk. I'm writing, thinking, hoping, struggling. For things here at hand and others further away, moral, professional, sporting things. Today I can almost grasp them, tomorrow they seem to slip away. I run forward. I stop, start again: I'm alive.
>
> Then one day the great call comes. I get up out of the trench and am struck by a bullet. What was it all for, that struggling day after day and year after year, all those books and competitions and affections? Nothing whatever, if it was all only for me, only for the sake of it – which is how those realist writers would have it.
>
> But beyond today and tomorrow and the day after that lies the future, and eternity. If you live life to the full day after day then death itself is an act of living. And on this basis, even if you

come in late in the race of days, you are still in time in the race
of eternity. That's all there is to it, the rest is absolutely nothing.

And if my life can have a wind like that boosting my soul, if it
has been one life however brief or insignificant, then that bullet
in my skull will have taken nothing whatever from me, when
some ploughman one day digs up my scattered bones.

Those 'realists' are wrong! Living is not just living. It can be
dying, too.[9]

These articles by Felice reflect the fearsome impact Hitler was
already having on Europe. For Italy the dilemma on how to respond
to this northern phenomenon was exquisite, because Hitler
admired Mussolini and his fascism, including the way he sought
to invigorate the national spirit and ready his people for war. For
the time being Italy did not fear German rearmament as others
did, but it was rightly alarmed by the signs that Hitler wanted to
take fascism much further, to extremes, especially on race. Both
worrying and hurtful, too, was the demeaning portrayal by the
Nazi Party of Italians as a 'mongrel race.' The insult was keenly felt
by Mussolini, who came away from his first meeting with Hitler
in June 1934 with negative and contemptuous impressions of the
man. The following month Austrian Nazis assassinated Chancellor
Dollfuss and a German invasion seemed imminent: Mussolini
promptly sent the army up to the border to guarantee Austrian
independence. For that, he would have had Felice's full support.

Il Frontespizio had no inclination to criticise German politics
directly. In another article of December 1934 under the heading
Sport and Culture it allowed Felice to condemn the 'Kultur of the
German world' for its hotch-potch of clumsy notions, in contrast
with the Duce's programs for cultural unity and vitality, which
he believed were also what was sought by Catholicism. Culture,
he added, should not be 'intellectual gymnastics' but creative
and beautiful. Alongside it should be physical culture, and this
should not be a mere trial of strength but also an expression of a
guiding spirit. These rather waffly sentiments echoed some of the
Duce's own pronouncements. In 1932 Mussolini had contributed

a chapter for the Italian Encyclopedia on the Doctrine of Fascism, asserting that Fascism aspired to 'a life free from the limits of time and space, a life in which the individual, through the denial of himself, through the sacrifice of his own private interests, through death itself, realises that completely spiritual existence in which his value as a man lies.'

The pressures building up at home and abroad can be felt in the articles Felice wrote at this time. At no point, however, despite the credo of the magazine he was contributing to, did he make an effort to seek answers in religion to the vexing questions of life and death. Nor did he look for political answers, although he did sometimes echo the language of fascist Italy. He had no qualms, it seemed, with the prospects of war, nor with the charter of the university militias requiring the student military elite to be ready 'to sacrifice themselves on scaffolds or fall in the trenches.' The Duce had made it quite clear in the Italian Encyclopaedia that his people should be ready to face war and so also death:

> Above all, Fascism, in so far as it considers and observes the future and the development of humanity quite apart from the political considerations of the moment, believes neither in the possibility nor in the utility of perpetual peace. It thus repudiates the doctrine of Pacifism – born of a renunciation of the struggle and an act of cowardice in the face of sacrifice. War alone brings up to their highest tension all human energies and puts the stamp of nobility upon the peoples who have the courage to meet it.

In 1932 an obelisk, hewn from a single great piece of Carrara marble, was erected in Rome outside the main entrance to an impressive new sports complex now known as the Foro Italico. Down the side of the monument in large letters was written MUSSOLINI DUX: it stands in the same place today. Just across the Tiber River, in the Flaminio area of the city, was then located a smaller facility, the National Stadium, which had an open-air swimming pool with changing rooms and decked seats for spectators and another pool indoors.[10] The complex was managed by the Lazio sporting club and one of its training staff, a Japanese national, was impressed by the prowess of the young man who had come there for some exercise. He invited Felice to join a squad training for national and international competitions. In the summer of 1933 Felice entered the national championships and came second in the 200 metres breast stroke, and, swimming for Lazio in the mixed relay, again came second. He had further swimming success in 1934, placing twelfth in a competition on the Tiber and winning an award as the first one home of all the breast stroke swimmers. He was given the task of training students for the university littoriali competitions as well as the breast stroke swimmers of the Lazio club.[11]

Every day at lunchtime the Lazio swimmers would go up and down the pool and in the summer of 1934 two German girls would come most days to the National Stadium to swim and sunbathe for a couple of hours, and to watch the fit young men. Felice could not fail to notice them and when he heard them conversing in German he came over and joined in. It was the seventeen year old Stefania Marx, there with her sister Lily, who attracted him more. They began to go out together. Felice could not know it yet but his life had just taken another decisive turn.

CHAPTER 4 NOTES

[1] Details of Felice's military career are from the archives of the Italian Ministry of Foreign Affairs, Fascicolo C.D./2 Archivio Riservato Benuzzi Felice.

[2] MFA archives show he joined the Unione Nazionale Ufficiali in Congedo d'Italia Sezione Roma, commencing 27 January 1932, membership card no. 133171.

[3] Initially formed in 1920, the GUF was restructured in 1927 with the aim of preparing for the new leadership of the nation. Personalities who later became famous in the history of anti-fascism, including, Italo Calvino, Pietro Ingrao, Aldo Moro and Giorgio Napolitano, had all like Felice joined the GUF. See notably Ben-Ghiat, R. (2005), 'Italian universities Under Fascism', *Universities Under Dictatorships,* Michael Grüttner & John Connelly (eds), Philadelphia: University of Pennsylvania Press, p. 166 and Bongiovanni, B. (2003), *Storia dei Guf: organizzazione, politica e miti della gioventù universitaria fascista 1919-1943,* Bollati Boringhieri, p. 133.

[4] Fascism drew heavily from classical Roman symbolism: lictors were officers and the symbol of their authority were fasces, or bundles of rods. The first lictorial games

were held in 1932. Many of those later to become famous in Italy and abroad, including in art, literature and film production, made their debuts in the littoriali.

[5] Ben-Ghiat *Italian Universities under Fascism* op. cit. p. 56 and Blinkhorn, M. (2006), *Mussolini and Fascist Italy,* Routledge, p. 39.

[6] Simone, G. (2012), *Il guardasigilli del regime: l'itinerario politico e culturale* di Alfredo Rocco, Franco Angeli, p. 209.

[7] *Il Frontespizio*: A literary magazine founded by Piero Bargellini, a militant Catholic, and published in Florence monthly from 1929 to 1940.

[8] Roncalli, M. (1999) (ed), *'Giuseppe De Luca – Fausto Minelli', Carteggio,* vol. 1 Roma: Edizioni di Storia e Letteratura, p. 155.'

[9] *'I Disfacitori* was selected for special reference by Ruth Ben-Ghiat in her *'Fascism, Writing, and Memory: The Realist Aesthetic in Italy, 1930-50', The Journal of Modern History,* Vol. 67, No. 3, The University of Chicago Press (1995) as an example of contemporary literary criticism of realist novels in Italy. See also Ben-Ghiat, R. (2004), *Fascist Modernities: Italy,* 1922-45, Berkeley: University of California Press, p. 232.'

[10] Built in 1911, it was later renamed the National Stadium of the National Fascist Party. It hosted some of the 1934 football world cup matches including the final between Italy and Czechoslovakia. The Lazio and Roma football clubs both used it until 1953, when it closed. It was demolished and replaced with the Stadio Flaminio in 1957.

[11] On 21.2.34 Felice was interviewed in the journal *Il Littoriale* – formerly the *Corriere dello Sport*, taken over in 1927 by Leandro Arpinati, an early collaborator of Mussolini's. See Wu Ming 1 & Santachiara, R. (2013), *Point Lenana*, Einaudi, p. 263. *Il Frontespizio* in December 1934 (in the introduction to his article *I Disfacitori*) described Felice as 'one of Italy's best swimmers.'

5

MINISTRY OF COLONIES

It must have been a little weird for the seventeen year old Stefania, shy and far from home, to be approached by the tanned and strapping Italian boy who addressed her in perfect German – although with a spongy Viennese accent, so unlike hers from Berlin.[1] She felt safe with her older sister Lily beside her, Lily who had already been in Italy for quite some time and who anyway had confidence enough for both of them. But, quite apart from the fact that this stranger was smiling and handsome, she was disarmed and reassured at the same time by his easy flow of the language that in Rome she only shared with Lily.

When Hitler came to power the writing was on the wall for Germany's Jews, even for those like the Marx family that had converted to Lutheranism. Stefania's father Otto left as soon as he could for the safety of London. Lily, too, got out of the country quickly but she had always wanted to go to Italy and so headed for Perugia where the university catered specifically for foreigners. Their mother, Alix, stayed on mainly to look after Stefania while she finished her school year as well as take care of family affairs. But in 1933 anti-semitic laws were introduced to restrict the education of Jews: public schools were where students prepared for university and took the necessary exams, and now Jews were not allowed to attend them.

The Marx family was well-to-do. Otto, who raced cars and was one of the first in Germany to do so, had run a clothing factory and after that a private bank. Everything had gone well until the stock market crash of 1929 which hit them hard, although Otto was able eventually to pay off all his clients, and avoided having to sell the family home. They lived in a substantial seventeen-room apartment with a central staircase, up to the next floor and then to the roof with a garden. Stefania remembered their getting a dog that on the first day leapt off that roof, falling to its death on the pavement below. She also remembered the little observatory up there, reached by a ladder: astronomy was a hobby of her father's. Otto had another hobby – a scale model of the battle of Waterloo set out on a large table. He loved books, had thousands of them, and paid a librarian to come once a week to arrange the shelves properly. A cook and two housemaids lived in, and there was also a gardener.

Lily and Stefania shared a bedroom upstairs and they had a governess who was on that floor as well. Each year the governess would take them to the seaside, in Belgium: it was usually cold and not much fun, but their parents hoped it would anyway be bracing. Lessons with the governess were under a strict regime, with one lesson after another, including on the piano. But when the economic crisis in 1929 came, she was the first member of staff who had to go, to the girls' great regret as she had lavished on them the affection their mother found hard to offer them. After that when Stefania went to school, where the curriculum was even more disciplined than at home, she would be taken there in a carriage by a man in a leather jacket.

Their parents were always entertaining, with eighteen or twenty at dinner. The girls would hide behind the curtains, and whisper to each other about the guests. At those times when visitors came and they were allowed to be present, they could only speak if they first asked permission to do so. At the end of the evening Alix would come up to kiss them goodnight. She was beautiful, always immaculately dressed. Every morning she would ride her own horse in the Tiergarten and was keen for her daughters to learn to ride and swim and play golf, although Stefania at least was too young for it. Alix did however insist they learn languages and that had real long-term benefits since both Lily and Stefania were in due course able to make a living by teaching them.

When the family split up in 1933, Otto went to England where he sold seeds, going from farm to farm. Alix rented out the big apartment to diplomats in Berlin and that provided an income. She was a determined woman with seemingly a greater business sense than her husband. To make ends meet she sold many of Otto's books and also took a cosmetic course and earned a diploma. When subsequently she joined her husband in London she made good use of her new qualification as a beautician and attended to ladies in society.

It was Alix's idea that her daughters be together in Perugia. Stefania reluctantly agreed to travel there alone, but only if it would not be for long and then she could come home. Her mother said of course, but when Stefania arrived in Italy Lily told her there was no question of either of them going home. It was July, the heat was terrific, and she had no summer dresses. Lily, formidable of intellect and with an outgoing character, was coping well in Italy. She continued to do so when the going got tough, with the introduction of anti-Jewish legislation – at that point Lily went underground for many years, and lived with the Haiti ambassador to the Vatican and his wife. But for now those developments were not even on the horizon. The two sisters moved to Rome. Lily decided that, since they could not afford to go to the beach, they should instead go regularly to the swimming pool at the National Stadium. In those days they used to speak in German to each other – and that gave Felice his opening gambit. It was one of the last training sessions before an international event, and a week or two later he went with the swimming team to Budapest for a triangular competition between Italy, Hungary and Yugoslavia. He raced, but did not distinguish himself.

After he got back to Rome he and Stefania began going out

together. He had just graduated in jurisprudence but he was a young man with no job, no money and without any support from his family. They would go to the park and sit together on a bench or once in a while have a pizza together. When it was clear that her young sister was infatuated with this good-looking fellow with poor prospects, Lily wrote to their parents saying she was worried, and that made them worried, too. They wrote to Stefania, warning that she was too young and should be careful. She replied that she had so far been a well-behaved obedient daughter, but on matters of the heart she would look after herself absolutely. In any case Felice was a great moral support for her, particularly when she repeatedly failed secretarial exams. She did get a job but almost at once was told she was no longer needed: Felice was waiting outside and comforted her, saying it was not the end of the world and she would definitely find work somewhere else. One thing she was able to do for him was type the thesis for his degree.

They were both constantly short of money. Felice managed to scrape up enough to live on from lessons he gave in Latin, Greek and History at the Meschini Institute, a private school of languages.[2] But he had one or two things in his favour, financially. First were the perks that derived from his membership of the university militia and of the National Union of Officers on Leave, which entitled him to free transport. Secondly the Lazio sporting club let him have a small apartment which he shared with another team member, in exchange for helping out with the training squad.[3]

One of the things Stefania liked about Felice was his guileless idealism. She saw him as something of a dreamer, who set himself impossibly high standards. She would never describe him as 'shrewd.' An early example came when he sat the exams to join the foreign service. He had always wanted a diplomatic career and a life of travel but the competition for entry was tough and one requirement was fluency in two foreign languages. He had excellent German but only fair French and so was a borderline case. But he let himself down when he was asked a question for which he had no answer: instead of talking his way around it, he simply said he didn't know. He was rejected. This meant going for a second best career option – in the colonial service.

***

The first article that Felice contributed to *Il Frontespizio* after meeting Stefania was one on sport and culture, whose final thought was that winning was not everything, and losing should spur a person along the hard road of life ahead. There was growing evidence that for Italy in particular the road ahead was going to be difficult, and that Europe was facing a major crisis. During the first year that Felice and Stefania knew each other, the leaders in the main countries took decisions that before long would put the world at war.

In March 1935 Hitler publicly announced that the German army would be expanded to 600,000 men, six times the number stipulated in the Treaty of Versailles that had settled matters after the First World War. By then he had completed his mimicry of Mussolini, declaring himself Führer, taking total control of the armed forces and reaching an agreement with the Pope. But Hitler had also alarmed Mussolini when the two leaders met in Italy the previous June by shouting at him that his priority was the integration of Austria into Germany.[4] Mussolini already knew that such a move would pose a real danger to Italy's Alto Adige region, where the vast majority of the German speaking population was all for the Führer. A month later the Chancellor of Austria was assassinated by Nazi agents and this so incensed Mussolini that he ordered Italian troops to the border. This rift between the two fascist leaders delighted Britain and France. Winston Churchill had the previous year expressed outright admiration for Mussolini, describing him as 'the greatest lawgiver among living men.'

In April 14 1935 Mussolini hosted a meeting with British Prime Minister Ramsay Macdonald and French Foreign Minister Pierre

Laval at Stresa on Lake Maggiore, to deal with the threat from Germany. In general terms they agreed to uphold the international post-war agreements reshaping Europe, and resist any further attempt by Germany to harm those agreements. But the real importance of the meeting was its failure to mention Mussolini's known colonial ambitions in Africa.

In the second half of the 19th century Britain and France had seized and colonised vast chunks of Africa, and Germany, Belgium, Portugal and Spain had also done quite well. Italy had achieved less with only a foothold in Libya, Eritrea and Somalia: moreover it had suffered an ignominious military defeat at Adua in Ethiopia in 1896.[5] Mussolini's long-held aim was to revenge the shame of Adua but not only that: he wanted an expansion in Africa so that, as he frequently stated, Italy might also have its 'place in the sun.' From 1932 onwards he had been planning to return in force, and had also quickly taken advantage of a minor skirmish between Ethiopian and Italian forces at Walwal in December 1934 to step up his rhetoric. The following month, in a further meeting with Pierre Laval, France ceded to Italy some territories in Africa and – confirming the French and British silence at Stresa – gave the Duce a free hand in Ethiopia.

Over the following months Italy continued to send troops, arms and ammunition to Eritrea in readiness for the invasion. But it was Great Britain that most undermined the Stresa agreement when in June it entered into a secret naval agreement with Germany. For Mussolini this was an act of hypocrisy made worse when his two former partners at Stresa then imposed sanctions on Italy. At that point all restraints on him were lifted. Without support now from London and Paris and fearing isolation he felt he had no alternative but to turn to Berlin. Hitler welcomed him with open arms. At dawn on 3 October 1935 Italian armed forces invaded Ethiopia.

It seems that Felice was not in the crowd in Piazza Venezia, the largest to gather in the first fourteen years of fascism, to hear the

Duce announce from his balcony the start of the war. Stefania said that she had not been there, and thought that Felice might not even have been in Rome at the time.[6] They never spoke of politics or the things that Mussolini was saying, but instead of literature, the articles he was writing, of his swimming. They would have talked about Felice's passion for climbing. That summer, as Stefania prepared for a holiday in the Dolomites with her mother, he had the idea perhaps of putting her to some test: in any case he wrote to Emilio Comici in Trieste to ask if he could meet her and walk with her in the mountains and see how she fared.[7] Comici came to Misurina where they were staying, and he and Stefania had a morning together on a rockface near the lake, and he taught her how to use a double rope. After the lesson Comici reported to Felice that 'your girl will do all right in the mountains.' Felice at once sent a message to her saying he would come up on Wednesday and they could both climb a nearby peak. Bad weather however prevented their doing that. Because Comici was busy elsewhere during that fortnight, they didn't see him again. Five years later the famous climber fell to his death not far from Misurina.

With the rhetoric and fervour of fascism engulfing the country, Felice was inescapably caught up in it. The war in Ethiopia was tremendously popular, including with the Church and intellectuals and the lower and middle classes. Many students stepped forward as volunteers. The Duce had effectively mobilised his people: in December that year in a 'national day of faith', women in their thousands donated their wedding rings to the cause in exchange for a cheap metal substitute. It seems Felice accepted Mussolini's aims in Africa. With his university course over he was still a lieutenant in the reserves, in his old unit, the first grenadier regiment of Sardinia. He found temporary work in an insurance company while on the lookout for something more substantial, and the prospects seemed good in the colonial service given both the probable expansion of Italy's presence in Africa and the setback he had had regarding a diplomatic career.[8] Like every other Italian,

Felice could not imagine at the end of 1935 that the dream of a 'place in the sun' would lead within ten years to the ruin of the nation.

In 1936 he sat the entrance exam for the Ministry of Colonies which would before long change its name to the Ministry of Italian Africa. No records are available for this period of his life but it is clear that he was indeed accepted a 'colonial volunteer' with a requirement for him to spend six months assigned to an overseas jurisdiction. Stefania recalled only that for this the Ministry sent Felice to Libya. One of the rare references in any of his writings to his time in Libya is in the Italian, but not the English, account of his Mt Kenya experience, when he describes a moment of absolute silence in a cave near Benghazi.[9]

Towards the end of 1936 Felice left Libya and may have returned briefly to Italy. In December he contributed a final article to *Il Frontespizio*, which ceased publishing in 1940. In it he recounted a singular episode that perhaps he had only just witnessed, as he passed through the Suez Canal. He was sitting, he wrote, on the bridge of the troop ship *Piemonte* on its way to Eritrea. He referred to the human cargo as 'legionaries' which may indicate that they were members of the fascist university militia, since these were formed in 'legions.' Suddenly from the darkness of the night came the shout of a small boy on the canal bank: 'Viva l'Italia!' After a stunned pause, those on the ship practically as one responded with 'Evviva!' The boy, whom the author calls 'the unknown balilla' referring to the fascist youth movement, and it is the title of the article, yells in Italian: 'Hail to the Duce!' The roar in return was the standard fascist response of 'A noi!' Felice concluded his short article:

> After that, silence returned. Each of us on board felt in his heart the confirmation hardly needed of what it means to be Italian. We and our ship then represented all Italy for that lad who most likely had never seen it: an Italy which for him as well as for his people was on its way to win a place in the sun. Our ship continued its slow journey between the two banks of the Canal,

its prow headed for the seas of Eritrea.[10]

This is the only time Felice ever left any record of actual sympathy for the regime. It is essentially a brief and factual account. It describes a moment laden with emotion and patriotism: he was prone to both.

CHAPTER 5 NOTES

[1] Stefania provided a detailed account of her early life in an interview filmed and produced by Personal Documentaries Ltd, 1 Umbria Street London SW15 5DP UK. Many of the details in this chapter were provided to the author in interviews in October 2012 and May 2013, and in written answers to questions. She also gave interviews to the authors of *Point Lenana* (op. cit. especially pp. 263-267).

[2] Stefania's written answers: 9.5.2013. The Meschini Institute was founded in Rome by Erminio Meschini (1880-1935): he invented a form of shorthand which became officially recognised. The institute began as a language school and was located in Via del Tritone; subsequently it broadened its scope, and moved more than once: its current address is 17 via Piave.

[3] *Point Lenana*, p. 261.

[4] The two leaders met on 14 June 1934 in the Palladian Villa Pisani, near Padova. An account of their meeting is in Martucci, M. (2005), *Hitler turista: viaggio in Italia*, Greco & Greco, pp. 26-27 and Corvaja, S. (2001), *Hitler and Mussolini: The Secret Meetings*, New York: Enigma Books, pp. 34-36.

[5] Du Bois, W.E.B. (2007), *Africa, Its Geography, People and Products and Africa – Its Place in Modern History*, Oxford University Press, p. 57 succinctly summarises the defeat: 'In 1895 began the Italian attempt of the Italians to take Abyssinia by force. The commander, Baratieri, attacked against his best judgment, and the result was a battle at Adua, March 1, 1896. Five thousand Italians were killed and 2,000 taken prisoners. The Italian hopes of conquering Abyssinia were destroyed.'

[6] *Point Lenana*, p. 296.

[7] *Point Lenana*, pp. 283-4.

[8] MFA Archives: Submission by the Prefecture of Rome to the Foreign Ministry: Risposta a nota 21305/729 del 6.XII.1947: 'per breve tempo è stato occupato nella Società d'Assicurazioni Alleanza Securitas Esperia, sita in Via delle Mercedi (for a brief period he was employed by the insurance company Alleanza Securitas Esperia, in via delle Mercedi).'

[9] *Fuga sul Kenya* p. 140. He also alludes to Libya in a letter to his parents of 5.12.55, after a visit to Peshawar: 'Giro per i bazar... che per colori, volti, costumi, odori non trova riscontro a Karachi, ma – nei miei ricordi – soltanto con Bengasi ed il Cairo (I wander around the bazaar ... whose colours, faces, costumes and smells have no counterpart in Karachi but bring to mind only those of Benghazi and Cairo).'

[10] *Il Frontespizio* December 1936 p. 13. Felice says it was just after El-Qantarah, midway between Port Said and Ismailia. The 'A noi!' or 'To us!' was first a 1918 war cry then a fascist one, answering the implied question 'To whom the victory (or glory)?'

6

DIRE DAWA

'We have been patient with Ethiopia for forty years!' the Duce declared on the evening of 2 October 1935, announcing the commencement of war – but at the time of the humiliation at Adua in 1896 the country was better known as Abyssinia. Difficult to conquer militarily. According to the 1902 edition of the Encyclopaedia Britannica 'the whole country presents the appearance of having been broken up and tossed about in a remarkable manner, the mountains assuming wild and fantastic forms, with sides frequently abrupt and precipitous, and only accessible by very difficult passes.' There were no roads. Moreover between the populated central plateau of Abyssinia and the coast was an expanse of low-lying land that was arid, uncultivated and unhealthy. The Encyclopaedia concluded its survey of the country: 'It is, in a great measure, owing to Abyssinia being thus cut off from intercourse with the civilised world by this inhospitable region, which for three centuries has been in the hands of its enemies, that it is at present so sunk in ignorance and barbarism.' Also problematic for any foreign intruder was the fact that the population was divided into distinct races and subdivided into tribes with chiefs in many cases who were 'fierce and turbulent in character, and addicted to cruelty.'[1]

In these forty years Italy had improved its strategic position, gaining a firm hold on both Eritrea and Somalia that were neighbours of Ethiopia and good launching points for an invasion.

Forces under the command of General Emilio De Bono crossed the border from the north, and although Adua fell on 6 October his further progress seemed to Mussolini altogether too cautious and he replaced him with Marshal Pietro Badoglio. The Duce wanted a speedy end to the war, by every possible means, including the use of chemical weapons. Hundreds of tons of mustard gas were accordingly dropped on the battlefield, and sometimes on the local population. After seven months of fighting Italian troops were able to capture and occupy Addis Ababa.

On 9 May 1936 in front of a festive crowd in Rome Mussolini declared that with this victory Italy finally had its empire. In his speech Mussolini drew for inspiration on the glory of the ancient Romans, as he loved doing – from classical times he had already taken the title of Duce for himself as well as claiming the fasces, the rods and axe of magisterial power, as the symbol for his party. His program for Ethiopia was to be on that same grand ancient model: marching, conquering, bringing civilisation, including via the building of roads and edifices. Road construction had top priority, partly because his imperial predecessors had been spectacularly good at it and partly because this closed country needed to be opened up and made easier to control. Security was also high priority since the locals were offering tough resistance even after the end of military operations. To rule over the country and crack down if necessary Mussolini chose the hard-line general, Rodolfo Graziani, as the Viceroy of Ethiopia.

On 19 February 1937 two students threw hand grenades at the new ruler and other senior Italians who had gathered for an official ceremony, killing seven and wounding fifty including Graziani himself. Savage and indiscriminate reprisals resulted immediately throughout the capital, whereby the worst elements in the Italian community including the fascist Blackshirts went on a wild rampage against the indigenous population, torching their houses and bashing with clubs and iron bars those who tried to flee. Over the following days the reprisals took a systematic military and legal form under the direct control of the authorities. Graziani gave orders to kill nearly three hundred monks in a famous monastery thought to have harboured the assailants. In fact it was Mussolini himself who insisted on the greatest repression in a message to the Viceroy, two days after the assassination attempt: 'Not one of those already arrested and those to be detained should be released except under my order. All civilians and priests suspected under any pretext should be executed without delay. I await confirmation.' Graziani responded at once: 'Since the 19th up to today three hundred and twenty-four summary executions have been carried out …. this figure does not of course include the repressive measures taken on the 19th and 20th of February.' Over the following months more than five thousand executions took place, among them those of a substantial number of young educated Ethiopians and all the officers and cadets of the Holeta Military Academy.[2]

Graziani's repression was not carried out uniformly throughout the country, and in the end his extreme policy failed for all it did was provide life-blood to the Ethiopian resistance. In December he was replaced by a member of the Italian royal family, the urbane Amedeo Duke of Aosta, one of whose first acts to was to remove the gallows set up in different piazzas in Addis Ababa. Aosta, educated in Britain, admired the way the British Empire was administered. In a radically different approach, the new Viceroy respected local traditions and devolved power to local authorities. This policy was certainly paternalistic but it was humanitarian and effective. Over the next few years the country witnessed a notable degree of social and economic progress.

The task Italy had set itself in Ethiopia was impossibly ambitious. Mussolini's goals were to modernise the towns and create a highway system, to build schools and hospitals and set up a judicial system, and massively develop agriculture through irrigation. To assist with these projects hundreds of thousands of immigrants were to be brought in from Italy, and the hope was that most would settle permanently. While there were some notable achievements, overall the project stalled and in due course collapsed. The costs of setting up an empire in this way and at this speed were colossal, even before Italy's entry into the war. As its strategic situation took a turn for the worse, local resistance to Italian rule increased and the countryside became more unsafe. Immigration was a dramatic indicator of failed ambitions: by the end of the five year colonial period Italy's entire community in Ethiopia numbered fewer than 55,000 with only a tenth of those being farmers and their families.[3]

As if the colonial project were not in itself difficult enough, it was greatly and unnecessarily complicated by the question of race. When Mussolini in 1935 announced that Italian forces were about to invade Ethiopia he spoke to the crowd of 'an African country... without a trace of civilisation' being up against a 'people of poets, artists, heroes, saints and navigators.' When military operations were over, the rhetoric about the biological, cultural and moral superiority of the colonisers became central in the new Italian African Empire, and it may have spurred on Graziani and those under his command to greater cruelty. This derived in part from Mussolini's vague fear about the fecundity of non-white races, as well as from his notion that a 'pure Italian race' with roots in the greatness and culture of ancient Rome might foster national identity and unity.[4]

Legal racism was introduced into Ethiopia following a directive from Alessandro Lessona, Minister for the Colonies, that 'whites must lead lives wholly separate from those of the natives.' Mixed marriages were forbidden but the laws went further: under legislation introduced in December 1937 'An Italian citizen at home or in the colonies having sexual relations with a female subject of Italian East Africa or with a foreign female from a people with comparable traditions, customs or social and juridical concepts faces a penalty of one to five years incarceration.'[5] For the authorities it was imperative that they stamp out the problem of cohabitation with native women which too often led to the production of 'half-castes.' Another decree banned whites from residing in indigenous quarters; commercial activities were also required to be conducted in separate markets for whites and colonial subjects. The latter were excluded from whites-only public areas, and taxi drivers and bus operators were not allowed to convey members of the local population. All of this made cooperation between colonisers and colonised difficult in the extreme, and practically ruled out the chance of preparing a local elite who might take on some responsibilities. This was what Britain and France had done in their African colonies, with notable success. They also had a tradition of properly training those they were sending out to administer the colonies, so that many such civil servants felt they were on a mission to bring betterment to far-flung peoples and places. In Italy's case however it was not uncommon for those sent abroad to prove both incompetent and corruptible.[6]

**

Felice arrived in Africa at the end of 1936, on a troop ship, with the militia rank of *capo manipolo* or platoon leader, the same rank he had in the university militia.[7] He was, however, immediately assigned by the Ministry of Italian Africa to political-administrative duties in Ethiopia. In Rome it must have been obvious that this young trainee from northern Italy, intelligent, well-educated and conspicuously tall, was intent on doing as well as he could in the colonial service. His induction period would begin in an outpost in the Harar region.

At such a low rank Felice would have had only scant knowledge of what was happening in the country in general, and in the capital in particular. It is possible that at the time the atrocities were carried out, soon after his arrival, he was unaware of them. Indeed, when referring to them much later, in a 1971 article for the Trieste newspaper *Il Piccolo*, he wrongly asserted that the assassination attempt in Addis Ababa on Viceroy Graziani was in December 1936.[8] In the article he wrote that 'there followed a mindless and shameful reaction meted out on the local population and similar orders were sent out to the governors of the five adjacent regions. All the governors undermined the orders' by finding ways to minimise the repression they had been asked to carry out. The only one who refused to implement them at all was Guglielmo Nasi, the Governor of Harar.

Felice reported for duty on the first of January 1937 in Dire Dawa, 500 kilometres east of Addis Ababa.[9] Founded at the beginning of the century as the main stop on the line between the capital and Djibouti on the Red Sea, the little town had grown up around the railway station and now had some 30,000 inhabitants. Felice's arrival coincided with the opening in the centre of town of the Commissariato, the Italian government's regional headquarters and a fitting example of what Italy had in mind for its new colony. The Commissariato was housed in what was once an imperial building with Arab and Hindu influences and a loggia on three sides. From a small rise, it dominated the town square. To the left of it was the Bank of Italy, and to its right was the office of the Fascist Party, with a theatre complex and an exhibition of Italian products. A few streets away an octagonal Ethiopian church graced a site that under well-advanced plans it would share with a new Catholic church; close by would be a new market, a hospital, an elementary school and playing fields.

From the outset the Italian plan for Dire Dawa was always that it be two towns, one white and one black, divided by a wadi. A fair description of what it was like at this time can be found in the 1938 *Guide to Italian East Africa*, a detailed compendium brought out by the Italian Tourist Union.[10] In many ways this publication is not unlike the old guide books published by Baedeker, providing handy information and advice for travellers. Extraordinarily, nowhere in its more than a hundred pages on Ethiopia does it tell the tourist about the security situation in the country, or hint that moving around it might actually be dangerous. In the pages at the beginning, the contributors are listed and among these is Felice Benuzzi, Dire Dawa: without doubt it was he who contributed the relevant section. The Guide recommended that the visitor wander in the network of small streets in the centre and so gain an insight into the town's distinctly oriental way of life. Heading for the outskirts, the visitor would come to a broad and sandy watercourse, dry all year except for the rainy season. Further along was a sizeable structure within it a mill, a bakery and a power station, and beyond that lay the indigenous part of town known as Megalo.[11] According to the Guide, Dire Dawa was characterised by neat little villas tucked away in perennially flowering gardens but it did not explain that this residential quarter was exclusively European, or that the Indian expatriates once living there had under the new regime been forced to move to Megalo.

It was Felice's good fortune that the region of Harar where he was assigned was governed by a man of great talent. Moreover General Nasi's deputy, the Director General for Political Affairs, was Piero Franca, another worthy individual. He was Felice's boss, and the two of them got on well, helped no doubt by the fact that Franca was also from Trieste, or rather from nearby Istria, which Italy was later to forfeit to Yugoslavia. Some years later Franca wrote a report of Felice's time under his supervision, outlining what this probationary young officer was called upon to do.[12] On a day to day basis Felice for his first thirteen months had responsibility for civil and economic affairs, and once in a while was tasked with political matters. It was his job to deal with the French consulate in Dire Dawa. France had been an ally of Italy's up to the time of the invasion of Ethiopia; afterwards, despite the official freezing of relations between them, it continued secretly to supply Italy with oil and war materials.

Throughout 1937, while Graziani was viceroy, the highest priority for all Italian administrations in Ethiopia was managing the security situation. That summer the resistance to Italian occupation was everywhere, but especially fierce in the Shewa region around Addis Ababa and in the south of the country. Although it was imperative for governors that there be a military response to acts of resistance, they were also required to make efforts to induce local warlords to cooperate with the Italian authorities. The Harar region was among those not yet fully pacified. Franca's report noted that Felice 'took an active part in negotiations that led to the winning over of the Danakil chief Hassan Mathan Farah... and had participated in the leading column that penetrated the Danakil area, driving through to Gauani.' This hot dry area is to the north of Dire Dawa, towards the borders of what is now Djibouti.

Once the Duke of Aosta had replaced Graziani, in November, the situation on the ground began to improve. By early 1938 there was evidence of success with civil and infrastructural projects, especially in the case of road-building. Felice would undoubtedly have been encouraged by the good results that flowed from the new viceroy's peace-building policies. He never actually met Aosta but, as his writings testify, he held him in the highest regard. In any case he would, bolstered by the assessment of his performance as consistently 'outstanding' by Piero Franca, have been confirmed in his intention to make a career in the colonial service. The next step was to apply for formal admission to the service, which meant going back to Italy and sitting for the Colonial Administration Group A exam. Franca granted his request to do this and so in February 1938 Felice set off for Rome. It would be twelve months before he returned to Ethiopia.

***

All this while he had stayed in touch with Stefania. To see her again was an extra reason for him to go home. They had not yet talked about the possibility or desirability of spending their lives together. But Felice must have been worried about how she was coping. The fascist paranoia with race was intensifying: there was talk of the need to send Italian women to the colonies to guarantee complete racial separation and pressure was mounting for unmarried men to find European wives. He may well have heard of an anti-Semitic campaign starting up in Italy: it looked as if life there for Jews was becoming quite difficult.

When he reached Rome the real gravity of the situation was apparent. On 16 February Mussolini had announced that the Italian Jewish problem would be addressed by various measures aimed at drastically reducing the part played by Jews in the life of the nation. In the weeks leading up to a visit to Italy by Hitler at the beginning of May the anti-Semitic campaign waged by the press reached a new level of intensity. On July 14 a leading journal published a manifesto signed by 180 scientists which contained ten principal and ominous pronouncements one of which asserted that 'Jews do not belong to the Italian race.'[13] Mussolini confided to his Foreign Minister (and son-in-law) Galeazzo Ciano that he personally had drafted the greater part of the manifesto. There followed a series of anti-Jewish laws, the first of which, promulgated in early September, prohibited Jews from sending their children to an Italian school or to teach in any Italian school from kindergarten to university.

The race issue, an unambiguous sign that Mussolini was aligning himself more and more with Hitler, now dominated everything. Some senior members of his regime were uncomfortable with explicit anti-semitism, including Ciano, Italo Balbo, governor of Libya, as well as the Duke of Aosta in Ethiopia, but they had no influence on the Duce's policy. With their lives at stake, Jews were having to make critical decisions. Stefania, perhaps recalling how her parents in Berlin had nominally converted to Lutheranism in an attempt to become less conspicuous, now changed her surname from Marx to Marchi.[14] Her sister Lily opted to go into hiding.

For Stefania, the prospects for any sort of continuing relationship with Felice looked bleak even though they did love each other.

She knew from her contacts with them since he went off to Africa that his parents, Nino and Berta, were concerned that their son's career might be harmed, given the way things were going on the race issue, if the two stayed together. It was becoming more and more obvious to her, too, that soon she might have no alternative but to leave Italy for good, and go to England where her parents were. She took the initiative, and told Felice that he should think the situation over carefully, and come to a decision one way or another. She proposed that they should not see each other for a week, and then he should let her know her fate. It was, she said later, the hardest week of her life.

For Felice, the decisive moment had arrived. His instincts had always been to respect authority and the rule of law. The choices he had so far made had been the right ones in a personal and moral sense, and had not conflicted with the demands and policies of the government. But he had seen the nasty underside of those policies as soon as he got to Ethiopia. He would have had some idea of the thuggery of fascist squads in Italy and must have been aware of the hardships that had faced the Slovenes when they were forced to abandon their homes in the 'redeemed lands.' But in colonial Africa fascist policies had gone to extremes, with racial separation between the Italians and the indigenous population, the brutal repression of Ethiopian resistance and the massive use of mustard gas – although with the decent and efficient administration of the Harar region Felice would not have witnessed the worst excesses.

Back home, he discovered extremism and nastiness had now become routine. The regime was intolerant, even of the woman he loved. When the week was up he went back to Stefania and said 'All right, let's get married. As soon as possible.' His natural boldness now came to the fore. He just had to hope that Ethiopia would prove a safe haven for the couple when they were married, that enforcing the new race laws out in the colonies would not become an official priority, and that his superiors might somehow protect him.[15]

They were to be married on 29 September, which happened to be the date of the appeasement in Munich, when Germany succeeded in annexing a sizeable part of Czechoslovakia. Everyone was talking of the risk of war. Stefania dreaded that on the crucial day Felice might actually not turn up. But he did, on time. And despite drenching rain and the absence of any of their parents the wedding went ahead, in a chapel in the church of Santa Maria in Vallicella, a few minutes' walk from the Vatican.

It was done in the nick of time. On 6 October the highest body of government, the Grand Council of Fascism, issued a declaration on race that prohibited marriages between Italians and Jews. On 17 November a decree on 'the Defence of the Race' excluded Jews from a long list of professions and from all public office. Other prohibitions that were introduced barred Jews from serving in the army, vacationing at luxury resorts, placing classified advertisements in newspapers or owning a radio.

Since arriving back in Italy in February, Felice had knuckled down to preparing for the crucial exam to enter the colonial service. When the time came, he sat it and passed. He was now approved for overseas service as an administrative officer of the Government of Italian East Africa.

Over Christmas Felice and Stefania went to Trieste to see Nina and Berta before departing for Ethiopia. They went on from there to Vienna to farewell his grandmother, who was also called Berta. In March German troops had invaded Austria where they had been in fact enthusiastically welcomed by the population. In April a plebiscite there had given ninety-nine per cent support for *Anschluss* – the incorporation of Austria into Germany. Stefania recounted years later how all that side of Felice's family were Nazi supporters. They were invited for tea by an uncle and aunt. The latter, as they came into the house, pointing to a portrait of Hitler on a wall, said '*Das ist unser Führer.*' The aunt of course knew all about Stefania, and was keen to underline how wide the gap was that separated her from them.[16]

CHAPTER 6 NOTES

[1] See http://www.1902encyclopedia.com/A/ABY/abyssinia.html.

[2] 'Henze, P.B. (2000), *Layers of Time: A History of Ethiopia,* C. Hurst & Co, p. 226.'

[3] 'Henze op. cit. p. 224; Sbacchi, A. (1980), *Il Colonialismo italiano in Etiopia 1936-1940,* Milano: Mursia, p. 111.'

[4] Ben-Ghiat Fascist Modernities op.cit. p. 128: 'The duce worried aloud that the "numeric and geographic expansion of the yellow and black races" mean that "the civilisation of the white man is destined to perish."'

[5] Salvante, M. (2010), 'Violated Domesticity in Italian East Africa, 1937-40', *Domestic Violence and the Law in Colonial and Postcolonial Africa,* Ohio University Press, p. 98.'

[6] 'Del Boca, A. (1982), *Gli italiani in Africa orientale: La caduta dell'impero,* Laterza, p. 145; Sbacchi *Ethiopia under Mussolini* op. cit.

[7] *Point Lenana*, p. 361-2.

[8] *Il Piccolo* 13.10.71 article by Arrigo Risano *Il solo modo di governare e' quello di mostrarsi buoni* – it is a tribute to the life of Guglielmo Nasi (1879-1971).

[9] MFA Archives: Felice's handwritten application to sit for the entrance examination, dated 23.1 1948, specifies the precise dates of his government service in Dire Dawa: 'anni 1 mesi 1 giorni 13 di servizio civile al commissariato regionale di Dire Dawa - governo del Harar A.O.I. e precisamente dal 1 gennaio 1937 al 13 febbraio 1938 (one year, one month, 13 days service in the Harar governorate's regional office at Dire Dawa, and to be exact from 1 January 1937 to 13 February 1938).'

[10] Guida all'Africa Orientale Italiana – CTI 1938 *op. cit.; Point Lenana*, pp. 360-362.

[11] The township is called Mägala in Haile, G.M. (2002) *Ya-Ingliz Gize or British Paramountcy in Dire Dawa (Ethiopia), 1914-1946: Notes Towards History* from master's thesis, Addis Ababa University published by Michigan State University — Northeast African Studies, Vol 9, No 2, pp 47-82 (which also contains a sketch map of Dire Dawa on p. 49).'

[12] MFA archives: Note sul servizio prestato dal 1o Segr. di governo BENUZZI Felice dated 20.1.1948 and signed Dott Piero Franca Il Direttore Generale del Personale Ministero dell'Africa Italiana. This ministry ceased functioning under law 430 of 19.4.1953.

[13] See inter alia Michaelis, M. (1978), *Mussolini and the Jews: German-Italian relations and the Jewish question in Italy, 1922-1945,* Oxford: Clarendon Press, p. 163 which contains Ciano's diary extract.

[14] *Point Lenana*, p. 374. MFA archives, however, all dated late 1947/early 1948, refer only to Marx, as in the file SITUAZIONE DI FAMIGLIA in Fascicolo C.D./2 Archivio Riservato Benuzzi Felice where the italics here represent handwritten answers to proforma questions: unitosi in matrimonio il 24 sett. 1938 in Roma
trascritto in Italia nel Comune di Roma
con *Stefania Marx* di nazionalità' *Tedesca* religione *cristiana cattolica*.

[15] There seemed some grounds for hope. According to an entry in Ciano's diary of 29.8.1937 Mussolini had an idea, never realised, to set up a homeland for Jews in northern Somalia. See inter alia Michaelis op. cit. p. 195. On the other had the

Duce had transferred his race mania in Africa to the Jews at home – see Bosworth, R.J.B. (2013), *Italy and the Wider World: 1860-1960,* Routledge, p. 68 and Ben-Ghiat *Fascist Modernities* op. cit. p. 155; if he was consistent, he would enforce anti-Jewish legislation within Italian East Africa.

[16] 'Stefania' – DVD interview produced by Personal Documentaries op.cit. Stefania concluded the telling of that incident: 'But they were kind to me and we left for Addis Ababa, and I never saw them again.'

In army uniform in Addis Ababa with Daniela 1940

7

ADDIS ABABA

On the first day of 1939 Felice began his colonial career. He was appointed 'colonial volunteer,' a title that represented the lowest administrative rank of grade 11. But it meant he was now a fully-fledged officer, and should report for duty in the second week of February at the political affairs head office in the Government of Italian East Africa, the nerve centre of Italian East Africa, in Addis Ababa. He was to spend the intervening weeks in the Ministry preparing for the new assignment. For him and for Stefania this was a stressful period of waiting given the possibility that new racial laws might be brought in and the application of them extended to the colonies. That was logical: for Mussolini racism in Africa had quickly led to anti-Semitism. The previous July an official publication had declared that it was necessary to guard against all forms of racial contamination and accordingly racial laws 'were being drafted and applied with fascist determination throughout the empire.'[1]

It was a relief for both of them finally to set sail on 14 February, and leave Europe and its woes behind. After some days at sea they passed through the Suez Canal and continued on to the port of Massawa in Eritrea. From their ship they could see little islands linked by causeways to each other and to the mainland. In the background the Eritrean uplands rose dramatically to 3000 metres, with the promise of greater heights behind, in Ethiopia.

The quayside they were approaching was lined with ageing stone and concrete buildings, including a mosque with minaret. Here a year or so ago hundreds of thousands of military men and tens of thousands of animals had landed; now it was bustling with the unloading of material for an empire being built in a hurry. Massawa was a small but pleasant town with villas surrounded by trees and flowers, many Italian style coffee bars and restaurants and thriving commercial activity. The heat was humid and oppressive.

They still had several more days of travelling ahead of them. The thousand kilometre Victory Road from the coast to Addis Ababa was not quite completed, and only half of it had so far been sealed. For three years vast numbers of workers from Italy, Ethiopia and Yemen had been carving out a route for it up into the mountains, with sixty-four bridges and many tunnels. Because of the uncertain security situation it was only possible to travel along it in daylight hours.[2]

The capital, when they reached it, was much cooler than the coast they had left behind. Everywhere were signs of industrious activity. Mussolini had long nurtured the idea of making Addis Ababa a grand imperial city with a monumental centre and with the races separated. In 1937 already completed were two new hospitals and the House of Fascism. A start had been made on transferring some 10,000 local inhabitants to a specially-built quarter on the outskirts, but this proved to be an operation beyond the financial resources available and impossible to carry out in a short time. Meanwhile construction was well under way of official buildings in the city and residences for families that had emigrated from Italy, as well as cinemas, dance halls, restaurants, bars and sports fields.[3]

Addis Ababa had been founded less than fifty years earlier by Menelik II who also wanted to establish a modern capital for an empire. The site chosen by the emperor was in a broad bowl on the slopes of Mt Entoto among hills and little valleys criss-crossed by many watercourses. Either to beautify the area and make it more healthy or else to increase the supply of wood for cooking and heating, he had planted a veritable forest of eucalypts, imported from Australia because they grew especially quickly. It was here in pleasant villas set in gardens that the Italian community of some 17,000 of whom a quarter were women resided. The local population was four times that number and they preferred to live in tuculs, round houses made of mud with thatched roofs. For the time being the colonial residences and the traditional tuculs were close to each other.

The master plan for Addis Ababa was officially approved the month before the Benuzzis arrived. It provided for a European quarter in the north of the city in the area of the railway station, linked to the centre by two boulevards, Viale Mussolini and Via Imperiale. The House of Fascism and the cathedral were already in place, and it was here where the main government offices and numerous imposing monuments would also be built. The European quarter was growing up around Hailie Selassies's former palace which was now the residence of the viceroy and where the Government of Italian East Africa currently had its headquarters. This would be Felice's place of work and so with Stefania he began looking for somewhere to live nearby. Quite soon they found a villa near the race course whose great grassy spaces were also used for military parades.

Their house, made of wattle and daub, was comfortable, and had a pleasant garden with trees and flowerbeds around it. It was not far from the expatriate club that was to be the centre of their social activities for the next two years. Most of its members were unmarried, and Stefania only had two or three other wives to keep her company. At home she had an Eritrean cook, who could both speak Italian and cook Italian food. He was assisted by a boy called Ubishet, who said he was 15 but looked much younger: he did all the housework and also served as waiter when they had guests to dinner. He helped Stefania with shopping, was intelligent and alert, and a pleasure to have around.[4]

Life for Europeans in Addis Ababa, as in many other capitals in colonial Africa, was one of ease, privilege and apartness from the indigenous population. But colonising for Italy was something of a novelty, and it had an untried and makeshift quality. Britain and France had two centuries of experience, in America and India and elsewhere, of stamping a presence, settling well in and managing environments that were exotic and sometimes hostile. They had also been the most adept of the Europeans in the nineteenth century scramble for Africa. Their empires were based on domination and racial superiority, but for practical purposes they had worked out a form of governance that devolved a good deal of power to local rulers. Italy however had manifold and conflicting objectives in Africa, including solving unemployment at home through emigration, disseminating Italian and fascist civilisation and turning a subsistence economy into one that could produce surpluses. It would have been difficult to carry out Mussolini's program in Ethiopia under ordinary circumstances. Local armed resistance had from the outset required colonisation by military means, and now Italy was in a period of high international tension with heavy demands on the national defence budget. The intention to have an overtly race-based system multiplied the difficulties of administering the country efficiently.

Felice started work at once, in the political affairs office of the Government of Italian East Africa. He had arrived at a crucial moment. Throughout 1938 while he had been away in Italy the security situation had improved a little. The policy of pacification, adopting a mix of brutality against those rebel leaders who refused to submit and encouragement including financial inducements to those inclined to cooperate with the Italians, had led to a notable degree of accommodation, or at least stalemate. In early 1939 the hard line that former viceroy Graziani had introduced was still being carried out in the Shewa region around the capital by forces under General Cavallero and guided by Governor Emilio Cerulli. But now the situation was deteriorating.[5]

The Duke of Aosta, who had been in Ethiopia for just over a year, was recalled to Rome in March by Mussolini to report on progress being made with the pacification program. The viceroy conceded that the security situation was far from perfect. Groups of armed rebels were able to roam all over the country, and their harassing and skirmishing operations prevented the sort of development activity that the Duce had always intended. Less than ten per cent of the thousands of farmers whom it had been hoped would emigrate from Italy had so far been able to come out and settle. Moreover the ongoing rebellion was an intolerable challenge to Italian authority. Aosta managed to persuade the Duce not to step up the repression. He acknowledged that a firm hand was needed, but argued that the policy of rewarding local leaders who were willing to cooperate was more effective as well as cheaper. Mussolini agreed to this approach, and also to replacing Cerulli with General Nasi, Governor of Harar. This was good news for Felice, all the more so when he learned that Nasi would bring with him to Addis Ababa his own right hand man Piero Franca, with whom Felice had got on well during his time in Dire Dawa when Franca was his boss.

Mussolini told Aosta he needed to deal with Abebe Aregai, the most dangerous and effective as well as the most charismatic of the rebel leaders, who operated in the Shewa region. Aregai was playing infuriating games with the Italians, sometimes seeming on the point of making an assault on the capital and at other times suggesting he was ready to submit and cooperate. The Duce directed that a special effort be made to subdue Aregai during the next six months, before onset of the rainy season.[6]

***

Following the failed assassination attempt on Graziani in February 1937 almost four hundred members of the old Ethiopian aristocracy were arrested and sent into exile in Italy. Some rebel chiefs and many other notables were also deported and imprisoned, mainly on the island of Asinara off Sardinia, and in Tivoli near Rome. After the meeting of Mussolini and the viceroy, those deemed least dangerous and most likely to cooperate were released and sent home.[7] One of Felice's first assignments on commencing work in the political office in Addis Ababa was to assist in the arrangements for receiving them.[8] It was not simply a matter of welcoming the VIPs on their return to their country. Accommodation had to be provided for them, suitable to their status, and in a number of cases this meant the building of new houses. Surveillance had also to be organised, as they were effectively under house arrest. The sheer numbers were problematic, exacerbated by a belated act of clemency of General Graziani who had set free nine hundred held in Libya, without any careful judgement as to which among them deserved their liberty. Moreover many of those now being released were destitute, and the colonial government had no choice but to help them financially.

In June Felice, as part of his training and development, was entrusted by Franca with an assignment of particular sensitivity. Franca, perhaps impressed with Felice's dealings with a tribal leader in the Danakil region two years earlier, sent him to join in the pursuit of Abebe Aregai who now commanded groups of fifty or so men. The rebel leader had stepped up his operations, and may well have hoped that the looming conflict in Europe could help his cause. In recent weeks Germany had invaded part of Czechoslovakia and Italy had invaded and annexed Albania. In April there occurred one of the nastiest episodes in Italy's occupation of Ethiopia. A large group of Aregai's followers that included women and children had taken refuge in a cave at Ankober not far from the capital. To deal with them a unit of the Granatieri di Savoia used first flamethrowers and then artillery with chemical weapons. Confirmed dead amounted to eight hundred. Aregai who was not there remained actively operating in that area.

Felice, a political officer and a civilian, joined a military offensive against the rebels in the highlands east of Addis Ababa. The operations were being carried out by one of the Gruppo Bande, lightly armed irregular forces of battalion size composed of indigenous soldiers under the command of Italian officers and NCOs, as auxiliaries to regular forces.[9] Felice was in the thick of the action. Although he never spoke about it later with his family, he must have been greatly stirred by the experience. As a result of it he was honoured with a medal for heroism in time of war, the Croce di Guerra al Valor Militare. The citation accompanying the award stated that in the month of his involvement with fighting units targeting the rebel leader Abebe Aregai in the Ankober area, he twice took the initiative, together with military messengers, to reach foremost areas and bring back important information that contributed to the success of the operations.[10]

When on the first of July Felice returned to normal civilian activities in the political department in the capital, his probationary *volontario* status was amended to that of *addetto* or attachè.[11] While this change brought no promotion or alteration in salary, it was a further confirmation of his permanency as a colonial official. Life for him, as in the country, became more settled for the rest of the year. His principal responsibility was for cultural policy in Ethiopia, and he was given specific tasks in the field of indigenous arts and crafts. Cultural activities, together with education, fell within the fascist rhetoric of a 'civilising mission' that Mussolini had in mind for his new empire, and led to exhibitions being held in Italy of the work of skilled Ethiopian goldsmiths and weavers of baskets and cloth.

War broke out in Europe in September and Mussolini reluctantly declared Italy's status to be that of 'non-belligerent.' He accepted the advice given by his generals and senior fascist leaders that Italy, despite having a large army, was militarily unprepared and its industries were weak. Moreover its African empire was strung out and in two distinct halves, with British-controlled Egypt in between. Libya was particularly vulnerable but so too was the eastern half of the empire, cut off from the Italian homeland by the Suez Canal. Three months earlier Mussolini had signed a 'Pact of Steel' with Germany and now found himself acutely embarrassed towards his new ally. He reassured German Foreign Minister Ribbentrop who came to see him in Rome in March 1940 that he wanted to join in the conflict but reserved the right to choose the best moment to do so.

That same month negotiations between General Nasi and Abebe Aregai collapsed. For the general they had become something of an obsession because he was convinced that the whole policy of pacification in the country would fail if Ethiopian rebels were able to operate freely in the area around the capital. While Aregai kept intimating that he was prepared to surrender he told other rebel groups that his only intention was to play for time. In April the viceroy went to Rome to ask that Italy's policy of neutrality continue: he was all too aware both that his own forces were no match for the British and that there was a risk of revolt breaking out in the north and centre of Ethiopia once hostilities commenced. Aosta said that if however the decision was for war then he urgently needed additional armoured vehicles, fuel and ammunition. Some of the funds were indeed promptly allocated to him but in the event hardly anything he had asked for reached Africa before war broke out.

During the Duke's absence Felice was promoted to *segretario di governo*, a further advance in his civilian career. Nevertheless in May as a result of general mobilisation he was called up for military duty, and was to serve with the tenth infantry regiment of the Granatieri di Savoia. For nearly six months he wore army uniform, with the rank of lieutenant. On 10 June Mussolini, believing the fate of Europe was now decided in Germany's favour following the success of its armies in France, declared war on Great Britain and France. The military reality for the Italians in Ethiopia was that they were now up against the armed forces of the British Empire soon to be bolstered by the arrival of modernised and fully motorised units from India and South Africa. It was inevitable that from this moment the enemy would have every motive to lend material assistance to rebels in Ethiopia.

On 4 July Italian forces attacked and seized hold of various places in Sudan and in August 35,000 troops under Nasi invaded and captured British Somaliland. In that same period Felice was transferred to active military duty against Ethiopian rebels in the region around the small town of Sendafa east of the capital, and for several weeks participated in the patrolling and skirmishing operations of one of the mobile Gruppo Bande units in the Ankober region. This turn of events must have caused both him and Stefania a deal of stress, for when he left Addis Ababa for the highlands she was in an advanced state of pregnancy. On 9 August their daughter Daniela was born.[12]

***

Felice remained on active military service with the Granatieri di Savoia with the local rank of captain until 1 October, but at least he was in the capital. To the relief of Piero Franca he then returned to work in the political affairs office at the colonial government headquarters where he was required to produce a genealogical chart of all the major Ethiopian chiefs. It was a significant task in a country with a diverse and fragmented population due largely to its rugged geography, a complex of highlands riven by deep valleys. For centuries the word empire had justifiably been used to describe it. To keep it under control, Italy had sought to understand the nature and dynamics of indigenous power and had had a fair degree of success in co-opting those who wielded that power in the different regions. Now it seemed clear to the colonial authorities that their external enemies would want to foment current tensions within Ethiopia and that rebellion there would intensify and spread.

The military success in British Somaliland had been a significant win but Italy's strategic situation elsewhere in the East African theatre soon began to deteriorate. On 13 September, following orders from Mussolini, Italian forces in Libya under Graziani crossed into Egypt but having made modest gains they stopped: they had insufficient armour, reinforcement was problematic and they lacked water. On 9 December the British counter-attack surrounded and destroyed the Italian positions. The following month well-equipped and highly mobile British imperial forces entered Eritrea from Sudan while others attacked Somalia and Ethiopia from the south. To add to the military pressure on the ground the British began an airdrop of propaganda leaflets in Amharic inciting native troops to surrender.

From November to March Felice was given a major role in countering this psychological campaign. He was assigned to a small unit using an aircraft from the air command in Addis Ababa which went out on night sorties dropping its own propaganda material over territory controlled by the enemy. Altogether he completed thirty hours of these wartime flights. In an unpublished article he wrote about this experience:

> Nearly midnight and we were on our way back, coming up to the Blue Nile ravines. The smooth tableland that borders on Gojjam with its soft woven checkerboard fields fell away suddenly into the void. In the moonlight the edge of it sharply separated two worlds, one bright, farmed, inhabited and horizontal with the other black, vile and vertical, disappearing. Here and there the plateau jutted out above bottomless valleys, or broke off into jagged sawtooth peaks with breathtakingly deep and awful glimpses of darkness between one tooth and another...
>
> Alongside the wireless operator I flexed my wrists, those of a desk warrior let loose in the night skies, aching after having heaved out packets of leaflets by the thousands. When areas held by the enemy showed up in the moonlight I threw the packets out with all the strength I could muster, hopefully making sure none got sucked in an updraught and stuck in the undercarriage or the tailplane. Plof-plof-plof they went one by one as the packets were swallowed by the jaws of the night... My thoughts, wandering in high altitude, were interrupted when the wireless

operator rose, turned off his screen, put his headphones down and took the bulletin from the landing field to the pilot. He came back and closed the sliding roof above our heads.

Down there at the foot of Mt. Entoto, practically invisible in its shroud of eucalyptuses, the city lay asleep. The aircraft circled wide over darkened Addis Ababa and slowly lost height. Below on the edge of the main sports fields I could see a little house I knew and in it a mother by a crib would be listening for a three-engine rumble to break the peace of the night. On the airfield a dazzling cone of light at ground level showed where to come in. Then a rectangle of six red lights along the runway started to blaze, expanded giddily before embracing us: we were down. Warm air embraced us, the motors coughed and died and then, almost painfully, all we could hear was silence.[13]

Life for civilians in Addis Ababa had got steadily tougher in the second half of 1940, from the point when Italy entered the war, and all facets of community life were impacted by mobilisation efforts. Petrol rationing was brought in, and the Benuzzis' car was taken from them. To replace it they bought a horse and cart, and their houseboy Ubishet was given the role of driver, something he undertook with immense pride. A lean-to was built in the garden as a stable for the horse.

By early in 1941 the British had achieved air superiority, and were able to use air bases in Egypt, Sudan, Kenya and Aden: moreover their capabilities were augmenting each month as those of Italy dwindled. Assisted by South African aircraft, they began bombing targets in Ethiopia, including the railway from the capital to the coast at Djibouti; after that they turned their attention to Addis Ababa itself. London now was under intensive blitz from Germany, and the British were in no mood to compromise. To the west of Egypt a great threat to them had just formed in the shape of Erwin Rommel and his Afrika Korps. The lesser Italian threat to the east needed to be summarily dealt with.

On 11 February Felice was at the airport during one such raid: caught out on the runway and unable to reach shelter he was slightly wounded.[14]

The war in Ethiopia was soon over. On 26 February General Cunningham's Kenya-based forces which included a motorised South African division captured Mogadishu, the Somali capital, and then advanced towards Harar in Ethiopia. An Indian division under General Platt entered Eritrea and Asmara fell on 1 April. The Duke of Aosta, knowing he would be unable to defend Addis Ababa, decided to offer no resistance to the entry of British troops into the capital. With 7,000 men he retreated to Amba Alagi where, outnumbered and outgunned, he was forced to surrender on 17 May. Nasi managed to hold out until November, in Gondar.

Thirty years later Felice wrote an obituary for Nasi, for whom he had enormous respect not only because he had refused to carry out the harsh orders of reprisal after the failed assassination attempt on Graziani in 1937 but also because of his humane and efficient administration of the Harar and Shewa regions. Clear proof of this, Felice asserted, came following the collapse of Italian forces in Ethiopia in 1941, and with their retreat from the capital.[15] For several days there was a dangerous power vacuum in the city. It was a tribute to the good governance of recent times that no harm at all was done by the local population to the 40,000 strong Italian community of mainly women and children. Others have asserted that the risk of violence against the Italians in Addis Ababa was the reason why General Cunningham deliberately delayed until 5 May the return there of Emperor Haile Selassie.[16]

After the fall of Addis Ababa the Italian community lived in a state of some nervousness and their representatives begged Cunningham for effective protection. To begin with he entrusted the maintenance of public order to the PAI, the auxiliary police force that had been set up during the Italian colonial period. Some ugly incidents ensued. Members of the PAI fired on Ethiopian prisoners who had not yet been released, killing some sixty of them, while others who had been recruited from the community were responsible for the deaths of Ethiopians during a disturbance. At this point the British felt obliged to disarm the uniformed Italians and hand over responsibility for security to the Ethiopian police force that had only just been re-established.[17]

In late April Cunningham advised the Emperor who was travelling in triumph around the country that he might now reclaim his capital. The moment had also arrived to remove the Italian community from Addis Ababa. On 29 April South African soldiers of the King's African Rifles came to the Benuzzi home. Felice, Stefania and their baby daughter were given minimum amount of time to get their things together in one suitcase each. They were then escorted to the nearby racetrack where they joined a mass of Italian civilians now under the control of British military authorities. Those assembled learned they would now all be taken to Dire Dawa. The Benuzzis boarded a bus crowded with others in their situation, for a journey that took five days. In Dire Dawa they were transferred to a hotel. Almost immediately an infantry platoon arrived to separate the men from their families and take them away as prisoners of war.

The Italian empire had been born on 9 May 1936 when the Italian king assumed the title of emperor and it died with the return to Addis Ababa of Hailie Selassie on 5 May 1941. Ethiopia with its capital was the jewel in the crown of this empire with a brief life of barely five years, and it was here that the fascist regime devoted great energy into building roads and infrastructure and to modernising the cities. Mussolini dreamed of a 'demographic colonialism' whereby millions of Italians would emigrate to Africa, from all the productive sectors of national life – farmers, workers, artisans, clerks, traders and those with small businesses. Significant migration did take place but when the Italian empire ended in 1941 the civilian presence was not greater than 150,000. Some 75,000 Italian soldiers had been in Italian East Africa at the beginning of the final phase of the war there and almost all of them were sent into captivity, together with a number of government officials like Felice. Many were transferred to India but the greater number went to South Africa and British East Africa. The Duke of

Aosta and General Nasi were sent to Kenya and interned there, and Kenya was also to be Felice's destination. Nine months later the Duke contracted tuberculosis and malaria: near the end he was transferred to a military hospital in Nairobi, where he died.[18]

CHAPTER 7 NOTES

[1] A Fascist Party (PNF) communique of 25.7.38: 'Colla creazione dell'Impero la razza italiana è venuta in contatto con altre razze: deve quindi guardarsi da ogni ibridismo e contaminazione. Leggi razziste in tal senso sono già state elaborate e applicate con fascistica energia nei territori dell'Impero (With the establishment of the Empire the Italian race has been brought into contact with other races: it is accordingly essential it be safeguarded from all hybridism and contamination. Racial laws to this effect have already been drawn up and are in force with fascist diligence in the Imperial territories).' 'Gentile, S. (2010), *Le Leggi Razziali: scienza giuridica, norme, circolari, Milano:* EDUCatt, pp. 178-179.'

[2] Antonsich, M. (2006), *Addis Abeba caput viarium. La rete stradale del Duce in Abissinia* Limes Rivista Italiana di Geopolitica, 3, p. 139: the hazards on the Via della Vittoria included 'pericoli di imboscate da parte dei ribelli etiopi (the risk of ambush by Ethiopian rebels)'; Cecini, S. (2007), '*La realizzazione della rete stradale in Africa orientale italiana (1936-41), Dimensioni e problemi della ricerca storica 1/2007.*

[3] Podestà, G.L. (2009) '*Le città dell'impero. La fondazione di una nuova civiltà italiana in Africa orientale', Lo sguardo della storia economica sull'edilizia urbana,* Michela Barbot, Andrea Caracausi & Paola Lanaro (eds), Università Roma TRE, pp. 126-129.

[4] 'Stefania' – DVD interview produced by Personal Documentaries op.cit. Also *Point Lenana,* pp. 448-449.

[5] See Ion, A.H. & Errington, E.J. (1993), *Great Powers and Little Wars: The Limits of Power,* Greenwood Publishing Group, p. 192 for an account of conspiring by Cavallero and Cerulli against the viceroy, Cavallero's failures in the field and the Duke of Aosta's success in having both men replaced.

[6] Ion op. cit p. 192-193.

[7] Sbacchi, A. (1997), *Legacy of Bitterness: Ethiopia and Fascist Italy, 1935-1941,* Red Sea Press, pp. 128-129; Sbacchi, A. (1977), '*Italy and the treatment of the Ethiopian Aristocracy 1937-1940',* The International Journal of African Historical Studies, Vol. 10, No. 2, p. 216.

[8] MFA archives: Franca file of 20.1.1948: '...fu destinato nel febbraio 1939 come Volontario di Governo all'Africa Orientale e prestò' servizio in Addis Abeba alla Direzione Superiore degi Affari Politici, ove fu incaricato delle pratiche relative ai grandi capi che venivano allora fatti rientrare dal confino in Italia (in February 1939 he was sent to Italian East Africa as a base-grade officer and served in the Political Affairs Department in Addis Ababa, where he was given the task of processing the tribal chiefs who were at that time being repatriated after confinement in Italy) .'

[9] On the Gruppo Bande (in Eritrea) see O'Kelly, S. (2002), *Amedeo: The True Story of an Italian's War in Abyssinia,* Harper Collins, pp. 147-148 and (in Ethiopia) Arreguín-Toft, I. (2005), *How the Weak Win Wars: A Theory of Asymmetric Conflict,* Cambridge University Press, p. 128.

[10] In the MFA archives is a copy of order 6895 from the Ministry of Italian Africa dated 18.3.1941 that declares the award to Felice for his effort in the Ankober region in June 1939; it was attached to Felice's application.

[11] The dates of all Felice's promotions and movements are listed in MFA archives, in Fascicolo C.D/2 Archivio Riservato.

[12] Felice in a letter to his parents in 1958 recalled that a congratulatory telegram had arrived from General Nasi, in Hargheisa, British Somaliland, which he had reverently kept.

[13] The document, from family archives, is typed with a number of corrections in hand and is probably not a final draft: written partly at first in the present tense, it has been amended to the past.

[14] MFA archives: Franca file of 20.1.1948.

[15] *Il Piccolo* 13.10.71 : *Il solo modo di governare è quello di mostrarsi buoni.*

[16] 'Henze, P.B. (2000), *Layers of Time: A History of Ethiopia,* C. Hurst & Co., p. 234.'

[17] Del Boca, A. (1982), *Gli italiani in Africa orientale: La caduta dell'impero,* Laterza, pp. 461-474; Shinn, D.H. & Ofcansky, T.P. (2013), *Historical Dictionary of Ethiopia,* Scarecrow Press, p. 426; Bocca, G. (1997), *Storia d'Italia nella guerra fascista 1940-1943,* Mondadori, p. 315.

[18] For Aosta's last resting place, in Kenya, see chapter 22, note 8.

<u>Volo di notte</u>

Era ~~passat~~ ^l'ugo^ ~~sempre la~~ mezzanotte ed eravamo ormai
sulla via del ritorno. ~~Sotto a~~ ^mar arrivavo^ i burroni della Valle del Nilo Azzurro.

Il liscio tavoliere che orla il Goggiam, con la sua
trama sottile di campi a scacchiera finiva bruscamente nel
vuoto.

Nella luce lunare l'orlo appariva netto, a separazione
di due mondi, uno ~~s~~chiaro, coltivato, abitato, orizzontale,
l'altro nero, orrido, verticale, che s'in ravvedeva a malap-
pena.

In alcuni punti ~~lingua~~ l'altipiano si protendeva~~no~~ in
aeree ~~lingue~~ ^lingue^ a limitare valloni senza fondo, in altri ~~lingue~~
~~intricatetricerente~~ si staccava~~no~~ in creste ~~aeree~~ a denti di
sega, con pause di ombra fra dente e dente, così profonde e
paurose da mozzare il fiato. Sulla sommità ~~della cresta per fra~~
di qualche, torrione sventolavano brandelli di nebbia sopra i
baratri, gonfaloni di Lucifero."Vexilla regis prodeunt inferni."

Nel più fondo dei burroni (per qualche attimo) il rifles-
so della luna sulle acque tortuose del Nilo guizz~~ava~~ ^ava^ come ba-
gliore d'argento colato. Più a valle, verso occidente, la vista
era sbarrata da banchi di nebbia di fantastiche tonalità di colo
re: da indaco pallido alle gamme più cupe del violetto.

~~Stavo~~ Seduto presso il marconista, ~~e~~ mi sgranchivo i polsi,
poveri polsi da ~~combattente~~ tavolino, che evade per i cieli
notturni, polsi ~~stanchi ed~~ indolenziti per il lancio di pacchi
di migliaia di manifestini. Una volta riconosciuto nel chiaro~~re~~ ^di^
lun~~are~~ ^la~~~^ ^strada^ controllata dall'avversario, avevo lanciato i pacchi con tutta la mia forza, per staccarli nella caduta
dall'apparecchio ad evitare che, assorbiti dal risucchio d'aria,
qualche ~~foglio~~ ^Poff~ ^Poff-Poff^ rimanesse attaccato sotto la carlinga o impiglia
to nei piani di coda. "Ploff" facevano i pacchi ad uno ad uno
e venivano inghiottiti dalle ^fauci della^ notte.

Eravamo sulla via del ritorno e non avvertivo ormai più il
rombo dei motori ch'era diventato musica ritmata col batter del
mio sangue nelle vene e ^di^ l'acre, ~~incobeissibile~~ odore dei lubri-
ficanti avio ^di^ era diventato un profumo.

L'aria sottile dell'alta quota, l'ora tarda, la stanchezza,
m'avevano provocato uno stato di tensione nervosa e di lucidità
mentale straordinaria, per cui sentivo più acutamente l'entusiasmo
del volo di notte ed il fascino magico dei panorami intravvisti.
E quando ad un cenno del pilota aprii il tetto scorrevole della
cabina dell'apparecchio ^L^, insieme ad un freddo intensissimo,
entrò un fulgore tutto tropicale di stelle ed un chiarore soffu-
so di luna, mi pareva che l'aereo fosse lanciato con tutto l'im-
peto dei suoi motori e di una mia arcana gioia, verso gli abissi
ultrastellari incredibilmente cupi, e si avverassero i versi

Draft by Felice of his account of the night sorties dropping propaganda
material

8

STEFANIA

Stefania, scared and angry in a group outside the hotel in Dire Dawa, had to watch while her husband, an Italian government official, was being ordered about by foreigners.[1] They were treating as defeated enemy scores of Italian men, all civilians, moving them over to one side and making them line up in threes. The new prisoners were turned to face down the long straight road, and were given the command to march off. With the other wives she stared as the column got smaller in the dusty distance, their end point apparently a temporary camp three kilometres away, beyond the town perimeter.

There was no way of even guessing when she might see Felice again. It was important that he was young and healthy. But what she was mainly telling herself for reassurance was that at least he was in British hands. For that reason she felt sure he would come back eventually. It would have been very different if he had been a captive of Germany, because nothing good was now coming out of that country she had fled from. Though shaken she remained dry-eyed. A new determination took hold of her. To face the reality that from now on she would be on her own, and that without anyone's help she must look after their baby just six months old. Both of them had to get through the hard times ahead, and that meant her taking full responsibility, from this very moment.

Next it was the turn of the women and children to be sent somewhere else. Armed African soldiers under British command took them in groups to one of three camps in Dire Dawa for the families of the prisoners of war. Out at the airport was Campo Avio, by the far the largest of the three, and in practice it was part of the airport installations. The smallest was a cluster of French-built structures and so became known as the French camp. The third, on the road to Djibouti, had been purposely built by INCIS, the Italian public agency that provided housing for state employees.[2] It was a compound of low-cost accommodation for workers whose projects had not yet commenced. The new home for Stefania and Daniela would be the INCIS camp where all the structures were new and had never been occupied and so were clean, and relatively comfortable. But it was exposed, without a single tree, and the heat bore down relentlessly.

She was directed to a house designed to be shared by two families. In the other half was a woman from Milan who called herself Baby, and who had a twelve-year-old daughter. Water supplies were strictly limited and for a bath or shower water had to be pumped. It promised to be a tedious existence of long hot days with practically nothing for the women to do. In the camp there was a small hospital run by the Red Cross, and before long both Stefania and Baby were able to work there, while Baby's daughter looked after Stefania's little Daniela. In all three camps there were problems with health, with malaria a constant threat. And then at the Avio camp a serious epidemic of measles broke out and caused the death of many of the children there. All the hospital staff including the new volunteers needed to deal with the emergency, doing the best they could to prevent the disease from spreading. A major task for them, too, was to comfort the mothers who had lost their babies and calm those who feared their own child might be taken next.

One day while she was at the hospital Stefania caught sight over in the camp kitchens of a man she recognised. It was a major in the carabinieri, Enrico Genova, who back in Addis Ababa had been in charge of the governor's personal security detail. A number of days passed, however, before she and the major were able to do more than acknowledge each other's presence. Enrico and his wife Lidia had been among the Benuzzis' best friends in the Italian community.[3] Seeing him now doing menial work told her he must have used some subterfuge to conceal his status as a military officer, or else he would certainly have been sent to a POW camp. It turned out that three or four more of those cleaning and cooking were also officers who had demoted themselves with the same intention: to get close perhaps to their wives and children. Lidia Genova at this time was in the Avio camp, where she, too, had been taken sick. Perhaps as a result she was moved across to the INCIS camp, fortuitously close to her husband.

The weeks passed slowly. A break in the monotony came when a girl knocked on Stefania's door with a note from Enrico Genova. In it he wanted to know if she would take a message over to the French Camp. Clearly he had discovered that, as one of her duties with the Red Cross, she made regular visits to deliver supplies to the French Camp which had few facilities, and no kitchen. Each morning and again in the afternoon she would go there in a truck with a driver and an African guard, taking a consignment of baby food and seeing to its distribution.

Genova's request was that she make contact with a certain person and pass him a map and other details of what was in fact an escape plan – and bring back his reply. She had no hesitation in agreeing to be a go-between, and was soon caught up in the thrill of it. The toing and froing with these messages went on for some days, after which Genova asked if she could give shelter to another man who had joined their escape plan. Again she agreed, and tried hard after that to behave as if everything were perfectly normal, including with her routine visits to the French camp.

It was not long before disaster struck. Arriving home one afternoon she found Baby greatly stressed, with the news that camp security officers had just come and seized the man Stefania had been sheltering. Apparently a girl in the camp had heard about what they were doing and denounced them. Soon a senior camp officer appeared and both women were taken away for questioning. Stefania was formally charged. The incident received wide publicity in British-occupied Ethiopia, and there was no doubt she was going to be dealt with severely, and made an example of. In court she admitted her guilt. She was sentenced to five years imprisonment.

Since there was no female prison in Dire Dawa it was directed that she be moved to Eritrea, and held in the capital Asmara. The order came that she should leave her daughter Daniela with her friend, who would be allowed to return to Italy taking both girls with her. At this Stefania demonstrated the strength of will that was a hallmark of her character: she absolutely refused to be separated from Daniela. The authorities gave in, and mother and daughter were put on a bus for Asmara, under guard.

The cross-country journey was arduous and exhausting, taking a week with travel also at night. One other woman accompanied her on the bus, as well as three British officers. While the youngest of them was never other than rude and unpleasant to her, the other two showed some sympathy for her plight, with a one-year-old baby. When they at last arrived in Asmara Stefania was taken by the young officer to the prison, and put in a cell with six women already in it who were evidently prostitutes. The iron door clanged behind her, and an awful dread descended on her. That night she was unable to sleep at all.

The officer who came to check on her in the morning had, she thought, a likeable face. She confronted him, hoping he would see reason: was it not totally inappropriate for a child to be in this situation, and was there not some other place they could be put? To her relief the officer said he could quite understand, and within the hour she was moved to another room; it was still a cell, but she and Daniela could share it undisturbed. She tried to make it as comfortable as possible with the few things she had in her suitcase, and propped up a photograph of Felice. Each morning she was allowed to go outside into a small yard with her baby and walk around. On top of the wall around the yard were African guards: Daniela saw them and waved, and one waved back. Nuns also came to the prison to visit the inmates, and that was a welcome distraction.

One morning, a week or two after their arrival in Asmara, Stefania was shocked to find that her little girl though awake was unable to open her eyes, and had gone down with a really bad case of conjunctivitis. She called for help and the friendly-faced officer, who it seemed was in charge, at once agreed that Daniela should be taken to the camp hospital for treatment, and that Stefania should be with her. Here everything went well. Daniela was given a bed in the children's ward, and her mother was able to stay in a decent sunny room beside it. The officer came by each day to see that they were all right, and having done that left them alone.

Within a few days Daniela had recovered, and had no after-effects. Stefania told the officer when he visited that her little girl was better. He said he was glad, smiled and left – making no mention of their having to return to their former cell. This went on for more than a week, and it was obvious that mother and daughter were being left alone at the hospital on purpose. Stefania began to get bored. On one of his visits she asked the officer if she could do some work in the hospital, helping the Red Cross in any capacity, perhaps as an orderly or a nurse. He reflected for a moment. If he agreed, he wanted to know, might she not leave the hospital, or take advantage of the situation in some way? She promised earnestly that she would stay right where she was.

The months after that were fulfilling ones for her. She was assistant to a charming and elderly Neapolitan professor whose responsibilities were for African patients only. She learned the use of all his surgical instruments, and followed his instructions closely. To be a doctor one day had always been a dream of hers, and this was the closest she ever got to realising it.

***

The tens of thousands of Italian women and children left behind in Africa after the downfall of the Italian empire were an embarrassment for all concerned. The Allied side saw no advantage in holding them, and it was a substantial cost and inconvenience to do so. For Italy their absence and imprisonment was an ongoing laceration to national morale, when in any case the war was going from bad to worse. The Italian Red Cross negotiated a solution with the British through the International Red Cross, and chartered four ocean liners – the *Saturnia*, *Vulcania*, *Giulio Cesare* and *Duilio* – to be reconfigured and properly equipped, painted white and marked prominently with the red cross, and used as hospital ships to ferry the refugees home. Three convoys were organised, between March and June 1942, September 1942 and January 1943, and May to August 1943; for each convoy, two of the ships would leave on a given date and the remaining two would follow eight days later. Because of ongoing war in the Mediterranean, with the Suez Canal a key point in the theatre of operations, the convoys were required to take the long way round from the Red Sea to Italy, via the Cape of Good Hope. Some two and a half thousand people – including a number of soldiers wounded in action – would make the journey which took six weeks.[4]

The first Stefania heard about these arrangements was early in 1943, a year after arriving in Asmara, when a visiting inspector told her about them, and said it might now be possible for her and her daughter to be sent home. They could be in the next convoy on one condition: that she formally request a pardon for the offence for which she had been sentenced to imprisonment. Her immediate reaction was to refuse. She insisted, yet again, that she had committed no crime, and did not want to accept the terms of the offer. She was given a chance to think it over, and she asked the Neapolitan professor as well as the nuns what they thought about it. All of them said that of course she should go home. Her signature on a document was meaningless. What was the point of staying in these prison conditions a minute longer than she had to? So she agreed, and preparations were made for her departure.

The officer in charge brought his jeep over to pick up Stefania and drive her to the office where she was to sign the request for pardon. It was a chance for her to ask him something that had long been on her mind – why he had always treated her so well, especially in not sending her back to prison when Daniela recovered at the hospital. We're in the middle of a war, he told her, smiling, and anything could happen. He had a wife at home and a child of more or less Daniela's age. He just hoped that if he did the right thing, they, too, might come out of it all right. His words and his whole attitude – a man in uniform, with all the power he had over someone so defenceless, treating her with compassion – made a lasting impression on her. It was one of the most important human experiences she ever had. Many years later she and Felice were briefly in Britain and tried, without success, to trace him.

Since their separation two years earlier, she and Felice had had intermittent correspondence through the Red Cross. Letters between them took six to eight months to get through. Under international agreement to which all European countries were party, mail went to and fro, with any wording that seemed controversial blacked out by the censors in Switzerland. Stefania knew that Felice would be worried about her – more so than she was worried about him, once she knew he was safe in Kenya.

Stefania and Daniela boarded the *Vulcania* on what turned out to be the last convoy made by the White Ships, as they became known because of their distinctive markings and the uniqueness of their mission. They left Massawa on 29 June, 1943. They headed south down the coast of Africa and after rounding the far tip of the continent came back up its Atlantic coast to the Canary Islands, before entering the dangerous waters of the Mediterranean at Gibraltar. On 10 July, while they were sea, British and American forces landed in Sicily.[5] Two weeks later, on the orders of the Italian king, Mussolini was arrested.

Everything in Italy was in tremendous confusion as the *Vulcania* headed for home. In Gibraltar they learned that in a change of plan they would dock in Brindisi instead of Taranto. When on 12 August, after a detour through Malta, they finally made landfall the trains that were supposed to be ready for them had still not come from Taranto. There were shortages of everything in the town, but they were given food from the ship's supplies. On board the train there was nothing for them, not even water, and the train repeatedly stopped for no apparent reason. And Daniela had developed whooping cough.[6]

Stefania had to decide where they should go next. One option was Rome, where her sister Lily was. However, she chose against going to the capital, whose status was ambiguous and which was coming under heavy Allied bombardment. There was probably a German military presence there, and as Lily had a clandestine existence the arrival of a sister and niece might well make things tricky for her. Instead Stefania opted for Trieste, where Felice's parents were. It was far from easy to get there, travelling north from territory under Allied control into an Italy still not yet liberated.[7] But they made it, and Giovanni and Berta were delighted to see their first grandchild. Although Stefania had arrived penniless and with virtually no possessions, they made her welcome, too, in the barracks-like building they shared with other staff members of the state railways.

For the Allies, the tide in the war had turned and it would end within two years. But for the Benuzzi family, who would also have six years of war over a slightly different span, their time of strife and family separation was only half way through.

CHAPTER 8 NOTES

[1] This chapter draws heavily on the detailed account in 'Stefania' – DVD interview produced by Personal Documentaries op. cit.

[2] see Zagnoni, S. (1993), *'L' attività dell'Incis. Le case degli "uomini bianchi"*

Architettura italiana d'oltremare 1870-1940, G. Gresleri, P.G. Massaretti and S. Zagoni (eds) Venezia: Marsilio, pp. 231-241.'

[3] In 2012 Genova's grand-daughter Lidia published the family diaries of the period: Genova, L. (2012), *Cieli d'Africa,* Pubblicato dall'Autore.

[4] Novello, M.G. & Zamboni, D. (2010), *Sotto un'unica bandiera: la Croce rossa italiana nella Seconda Guerra mondiale,* Marvia; http://digilander.libero.it/casellidomenico/le__bianche__navi.htm.

[5] Several of those repatriated in the 1943 convoys have given their account, including: http://www.maitacli.it/ricordi/62-era-una-volta-il/230-lavventura-africana-; http://www.youkali.it/favole/Archivio2007/pop-up5/2.htm; http://notizie.radicali.it/articolo/2013-05-23/editoriale/le-navi-bianche-maria-gabriella-ripa-di-meana-ricorda-l-epopea-del-ri.

[6] Stefania on 12.10.2012 told the author the story of the White Ships, their arrival in Brindisi and the onward journey.

[7] The arrest of Mussolini on 25.7.1943 precipitated tremendous confusion within Italy. Hitler promptly gave the order for the implementation of Operation Alaric, planned two months earlier, for seizing full control of Italy. 'See Rodogno, D. (2006), *Fascism's European Empire: Italian Occupation During the Second World War,* Cambridge University Press, p. 409 and Roggero, R. (2006), *Oneri e onori: le verità militari e politiche della guerra di liberazione in Italia,* Greco & Greco p. 207 on Operation Alaric.'

Zuc del Boor

9

Nanyuki

Felice and all the other Italians detained in the temporary camp in Dire Dawa were soon moved on. They were senior officials but were being treated with none of the deference they had become used to, now shoved about by grimly satisfied soldiers – the white officers aware how this win in Ethiopia was a rarity and the Africans at their command pleased to have to carry out these particular duties. Trucks took them first east to Jijiga and then the convoy bounced across rugged country into British Somaliland. They halted at Lafaruk, a cheerless camp in the desert. Here, according to an Italian soldier held there in May 1941, around ten thousand prisoners found themselves in a baking sandy plain with scant protection from wind and sun, with a night-and-day queue for water at one of the two tanks.[1] Another, deposited there two months later, described how the prisoners having been provided without any canvas for shelter had to resort instead to troughs in the sand dug by hand for protection against the fiery granules blown against them from the desert.[2]

Their next stop was thirty kilometres further on, at the port of Berbera on the Red Sea coast, where this group of prisoners waited for transport for their next destination. Italians were being sent to prisoner of war camps around the world including India, Australia and the United States but these from Dire Dawa were mostly going to South Africa, the Rhodesias and Kenya. In a television interview in 1987 Felice recalled the unpleasant experience in Berbera where 'the head of the camp sold off our food rations to Indian traders and as a result we all but died of starvation.'[3] Fortunately their stay there was a brief one; the prisoners were transferred to Aden from where shortly afterwards they boarded a ship and headed south, across the equator.

More than a thousand men disembarked at the port of Mombasa in Kenya. There they boarded a train for what they were told, and it gave them no comfort, would be their final destination. Thirty-six hours later they pulled in to Naivasha, northwest of Nairobi, in the middle of a vast plain. From the tiny station they saw the corrugated iron roofs of hundreds of huts shimmering in the mid-day sun, the barbed wire that enclosed them and the guard-towers. Lined up in fours, the column of prisoners began to march slowly and in silence through the dust and in terrific heat towards the camp. There was no vegetation to soften this depressing scene. For Felice the poles that held up the fence and stuck up into the sky were for all the world like scaffolds waiting for condemned men. The column halted at the gate to POW Camp 352 and the prisoners entered it one by one.

Naivasha in the Rift Valley lay at 1600 metres, and here the year-round climate was quite mild. Once they had settled in, the Italians could see that conditions were not bad. But what became immediately obvious was that life here for all of them would be monotonous, devoid of purpose and tedious in the extreme. For the ten thousand or so prisoners there was nothing to do except wander about. The monotony dulled their spirits, and led to indifference and sheer banality. Since the only interesting thing was the activity of each individual prisoner, it meant that no one had any privacy. Some inmates became fitness fanatics or obsessed with poker or baccarat, everything became inevitably exaggerated. For Felice, this packed-together existence was soulless in the extreme: people here were not actually living, but were vegetating. They had no control over time and indeed time here seemed to have a different meaning: all one could do, to avoid going mad, was to wait for time to pass.

In due course work was found for the prisoners and a good number of them were employed building a road from Naivasha to Limuru, something of an engineering feat as the route ran up the side of a steep escarpment. Along this road, at Mai Mahiu in 1942, the POWs also built a beautiful little church. Father Angelo Tarantino, a Comboni missionary, at one point visited the Naivasha camp having heard that there were a number of prisoners there from his native Veneto region and was warmly welcomed by them.[4] Life at the camp must have been altogether unremarkable. Felice wrote nothing about it except to complain of the boredom, and neither apparently did any of the other prisoners.

In April 1942 Felice was transferred to another camp, also in the central highlands of Kenya but requiring a journey to the capital and then out on another line. A carriage with POWs aboard was attached to the regular run down to Nairobi and then having been uncoupled was left there for six hours sometimes mysteriously being shunted from one siding to another. Under the guard of sentries with rifles and sheathed bayonets the Italians had the novel experience, after many months in captivity, of watching or rather gawping at ordinary people going about their business, men in suits buying newspapers, getting into cars and driving away, women with children, girls young and beautiful, all of them miraculously free.

The idea of escaping was naturally on the mind of every prisoner, and Felice had from the very outset studied the possibilities. From time to time he would hear of attempts made to escape, attempts that were always unsuccessful. The distances to cover were immense: Portuguese Mozambique, the nearest neutral territory, was two thousand kilometres away. To have any chance of making it the escapee would need a considerable sum of money, clothes, faked documents, maps and perfect English. Probably the greatest risk was that of the conspicuousness of a white man in flight, strangely dressed, seeking to cross the great emptiness of Africa;

apparently the authorities had offered a reward of ten shillings for every escaped prisoner brought to the nearest police station by their captors, and that was a tidy sum in East Africa in 1943.[5]

Eventually the transferees arrived at their destination: POW Camp 354. It was outside Nanyuki, a small market town of fertile land and lush vegetation, on a plain in the highlands, right on the equator. It was humid and misty, the rainy season had set in. The newcomers could vaguely discern hilly country around them but the heights were shrouded in clouds. The wind whistled and the whole camp was a quagmire. They made their way to the usual barracks, the rain drumming down on the corrugated iron roofs.

For several days there was no change in the weather and Felice was growing impatient: he knew very well that outside and close at hand was Mount Kenya, at 5000 metres a mountain higher than any he had ever seen. So far all he had been able to make out through the mists was the huge rounded and forest-clad pedestal of the mountain, riven with deep rocky gorges. Then one morning he was shaken out of his sleep by one of the others in his hut: he had to come and see this, have a look at Mount Kenya before the clouds covered it over again. In his desperation he got tangled with his bootlaces, and then he was outside splashing in the mud. There, framed between two dark barracks, was a massive blue-black tooth of sheer rock inlaid with azure glaciers, almost floating on the horizon. Felice gazed at it until banks of clouds shifted, and the vision disappeared. 'For hours afterwards I remained spellbound. I had definitely fallen in love.'[6]

CHAPTER 9 NOTES

[1] Bertone, E. (2004), *Quegli anni del Novecento: storie di partigiani, soldati, contrabbandieri e frati,* BLU Edizioni, p. 88.
[2] Corazzi, P. (1984), *Etiopia. 1938-1946: guerriglia e filo spinato,* Milano: Mursia, p. 75.
[3] Quoted in *Point Lenana* p. 487. See also http://www.wumingfoundation.com/giap/?p=12567.
[4] Gaiga, L. (2002), *L'Africa di Angelo: Angelo Tarantino vescovo d'Africa e missionario*

colombiano, Editrice Missionaria Italiana, Capitolo IV.
[5] *No Picnic on Mt Kenya* p. 52; *Fuga sul Kenya* p. 66.
[6] *No Picnic on Mt Kenya* p. 23.

10

MT KENYA

Felice had always loved mountains. Love was the right word for what he experienced, in every classical sense. From his parents and their parents in Austria he became familiar with snowy peaks, grew accustomed to slopes and heights, and found happiness there. Later he regarded mountains as his friends and companions, more dependable in many ways than their human equivalents. As he grew into a man he felt an almost erotic urge to tackle their beauty, changeability and even cold cruelty: because the exhilaration that came with the conquest or with the endeavour made any pain worth it. And always, to the end of his life, he would look for and find something transcendental, mysterious, spiritual and near-divine in mountains.

After that first enthralling sight, the vision of Mt Kenya receded like the memory of a dream. Day after day the mountain remained blanketed under a pall of mist and cloud. Prison life as ever clamped down with its depressing dead weight of tedium and triviality, with underneath a stratum of uncertainty. POWs had absolutely no idea how long they would stay confined – different from sentenced criminals who might at least count down the days. Word from outside via the Red Cross mails was unreliable. Months passed for Felice without any news of his family, and adding to his anxiety were reports of a deadly outbreak of measles among children in the camps in Dire Dawa.[1]

It was the idea of the mountain out there and for the time

being hidden that sustained him, and gave him hope. Every morning he would stand outside his barracks and stare south east, through the barbed wire, past the township of Nanyuki and the forests on the foothills. Late one evening, after losing three games of chess, he heard as headed back to his hut the sound of hammering coming from somewhere and envied the prisoner who had found something useful to do: for that man at this moment the future existed. Then all at once, just as he reached the spot where he had first had his vision, the clouds shifted and there it was, the magnificent summit against the black sky. In the starlight the white glaciers gleaming, like a challenge. And then a thought flashed across his numbed mind. What if I dared? To break out, get up there, come back afterwards? All of a sudden the future beckoned, and it was within reach.

The clear and simple idea of climbing the mountain fired him. After it came the sparks and smoke of other notions, good ones and bad ones, hopes raised and dashed, chances and impossibilities. Perhaps he was like any other prisoner who gazed from the window in the barracks and dreamed of being free, or patrolled the yard outside thinking up crazy plans for escape. In here everyone rambled on about liberty as they did about banquets and beautiful women and how they could picture themselves now back with their families. Such fancies were marvellous, plentiful, meaningless. But for Felice that first idea was giving him no peace, and he had to act. It had taken on a hard edge. He had to act because something truly solid was out there, those rocky heights were summoning him and would go on doing so. And he could not stay still for another equally powerful reason: the excruciating boredom of prison life was driving him mad and he could bear it no longer.

All manner of problems immediately presented themselves. To attempt a 5000 metre peak, must there not be a long period of acclimatisation to adjust to the thin air? How many days would it take to get up and back? And the equipment: ice-axes and crampons would have to be specially made, and in secret, bearing in mind that gossip thrived in prison like nowhere else on earth. He could not do this on his own, he would need at least one and preferably two companions to climb with him, and how would he find them? Some sort of proof or signature would need to be left up there, why not a flag! How would they actually get out of the camp, and how would they get back in? There was so much to think about and decide upon. Far from feeling daunted by the range of difficulties, Felice was actually excited by them, and determined to solve them.

He started making preparations. He drew up a list of things he had to do and of things he would need. He wrote to his family asking them to send boots and warm clothing. He stopped smoking, since cigarettes were currency in the camp and he would need to acquire items of equipment. For ready money he sold some shirts and underwear that he had got from a friend in Italy, and through another inmate with connections outside he was able to convert this cash into tins of jam, beef extract and a torch. And on the days when the visibility was good he studied the mountain looking for possible ways to the top.

But how feasible was it, this proposal of his? What he really needed was some expert advice. He heard there was a man with a great deal of alpine experience including several impressive first climbs, and the chance to approach him came one evening when the mountain was looking glorious in the setting sun. Felice wandered up to him and with a nod towards it asked nonchalantly: Ever thought about getting out, and climbing it? The man dismissed the idea, retorting: They'd have to start feeding us steak first. Felice asked if that was the make-or-break issue. Not exactly, he was told, although poor quality camp food meant a climber could neither train nor carry any weight into altitude. A lot of food as well as equipment would be needed, and only a lunatic would consider doing it without guides and porters. The changeable weather would anyway make it impossible. Felice chose not to take the discussion any further. There would be no meeting of the minds here, because this man was a hard-headed realist. What Felice needed were other dreamers, others like him who were indeed a touch mad, who would be happy to go with him.

He turned next to someone else with mountain experience, a former *Alpini* soldier he knew from Ethiopia and could absolutely trust: he was in this civilian camp because of injuries from a road accident that had kept him out of the fighting. They discussed who among the inmates might be worth considering for the team. They also made a detailed list of essential equipment, and the ex-soldier had a friend who had an Italian flag concealed in the camp.

From his own experience Felice was fully aware of the crucial importance for any climbing endeavour of having top quality information. One always needed a detailed map and some knowledge of practicable routes to the top; one also had to have a good understanding of weather conditions, and of any special hazards. At the outset, however, he knew virtually nothing about this mountain, its topography, previous ascents or attempts, or paths through the forest. Worryingly, he had read somewhere that there were wild animals in the forest on Mt Kenya and some of them were occasionally seen out in nearby farming country. Finding out more about the mountain became a top priority.

In August someone brought into the barracks a book written by an Italian missionary on the folklore and country of the native population of central Kenya and in it Felice discovered a wealth of valuable material. First, that Mt Kenya had two peaks, the higher one being Batian of 5195 metres and the subsidiary Lenana of 4970 metres: only Batian was visible from Nanyuki, blocking Lenana from view. Second, the lesser rains in that part of country ran from early November to late December while the main rainy season was from April to the beginning of September. Seemingly for this reason the month of January had been chosen by members of the missionary order to make an ascent of Lenana in 1933, setting off on the other side of the mountain.

Felice noticed that a new member of their barracks, Giuàn Balletto, was showing a lot of interest in the book. He turned out to be a doctor, and also someone who knew about mountains. The two of them chatted at length about their mountaineering experiences. Felice told him what it was that he planned to do, and invited him to be a part of it. He was delighted in Giuàn's reaction which was first to be cautious then to ask a thousand questions and finally to approve of the plan and to accept Felice's offer.

A visit to see a dentist at the nearby POW Camp 359 at Burgaret, also on the foothills of Mt Kenya, gave Felice a welcome opportunity to study the terrain between his own camp and the edge of the forest as they passed by in an open truck. At Burgaret, however, he was told that the forest not only had a dense undergrowth but that all manner of wild animals roamed in it. He found more bad news in an article in the *Nairobi East African Standard* of 16 September which reported how a British major had gone up on the northern slopes only to be forced back by a blizzard; moreover on the return journey his porters had had to use rifle fire to drive away a herd of buffalo that had approached the camp, and had shot two of them

Felice and Giuàn, now joined by a third member of their party, Mario, moved into a more active phase of preparations. A tailor helped them fashion some mountain clothing from grey woollen camp blankets. A blacksmith was able to convert into a reasonably good ice-axe a hammer that Felice had purloined from the storage shed used by Indian workmen whose job it was to look after maintenance work in the camp. Prisoners were allowed to take short walks along a track outside the camp under the watchful eye of the guards and this passed by a refuse tip, of old metal: here they found material they could use for crampons. Beds in the barracks had nets fastened to the frames with sisal cord some eight millimetres thick, and they could take some of this with them. Felice was able to make a thinner rope by unknotting the mesh that supported the mattress, although with fifty or more knots to untie this took an eternity and cost him any number of broken nails.

They would go in January, the month chosen by the missionaries. And they would follow the Nanyuki River, for it would surely have its source high up on the mountain. It was a pity that the scale of the map in the missionaries' book was so small and gave only a rough indication of the geography of the mountain. Also sadly lacking was any clue as to the routes taken by those who had successfully climbed it, or any reference to huts or shelters that there might be on the way to the top. There was so much they would only find out about later, when it was too late. One such matter was the fact Mt Kenya had, in addition to Batian and Lenana, a third peak, Nelion. Far more serious was their ignorance of the peculiarity of this mountain almost exactly on the equator: when the sun is in the northern hemisphere, the north face is in summer conditions and the rock is dry, while the southern face is in winter conditions. That meant that from October to March the north face was always covered in ice and snow: and it was their intention to tackle that north face. They were unaware of the fact that to date no one had succeeded in climbing Batian in winter.

One day they were able to add to their information about the mountain when a tin of Kenylon meat was distributed in the camp for the first time: the label on the tin carried an image of Mt Kenya seen from a different angle, and they presumed it was from the south. The slopes of Batian from that side, however, seemed equally difficult with more glaciers than the north.

Not long afterwards there was calamity. Mario, the third member of the group, had made a last-minute decision to escape with some other prisoners: they walked all night before running into soldiers of the King's African Rifles who brought the whole group back to the camp. They were given the standard punishment of twenty-eight days solitary confinement, but then at the beginning of January some of them, including Mario, were transferred to another camp. The planned date of their own escape was now less than three weeks away, coinciding with the full moon that they hoped would help them make it to the forest.

Felice and Giuàn desperately looked among their fellow prisoners for another candidate for their project. With one week to go they settled on Enzo, mid-thirties, no athlete, a heavy smoker and with no mountain experience whatever. But he was reliable, and happily described himself as someone who loved taking on the impossible.

Oddly enough it was not difficult to escape from a POW camp in Kenya. Prisoners were allowed to work in vegetable gardens just outside, in an area watched over by the guards. Giuàn had an allotment there where he had sowed a variety of plants and had also erected a lean-to which gave protection from the sun and was a place to store his tools. During January they dug a hole in this shelter and buried in it their food stocks and equipment, all wrapped in hessian sacks, smuggled out there item by item. What they needed now was a key to the gate to the gardens, normally kept in a nearby office. When the British officer in charge was one day making his rounds of inspection in the camp and happened to leave the key on his desk, Felice sneaked in and in a matter of moments pressed the key down into a wad of tar that he had in his pocket. From the imprint one of the mechanics in the camp obligingly made him a metal key, and did not question what he wanted it for.

***

They chose a Sunday for the breakout because there was no afternoon roll call on that day. At midday the prisoners in the compound were all having lunch and the officer in charge also went off to eat. Felice and his companions crept through the gate into the garden while the sentry's attention was diverted, and hid in the lean-to. Enzo was feeling ill and confessed that he had in fact had a fever for the past two days. Giuàn urged him to give up on the project altogether but Enzo insisted they let him come with them all the same. They stretched themselves out, and waited hour after hour for the sun to set. When it was too dark to see anything they dug up their gear. They donned their mountain clothes, picked up their weighty rucksacks and set off. It was ten to eight p.m. on 24 January 1943.

They crossed open country and reached scrubland, doing their best to avoid tripping in holes and being scratched by the prickly thorn-bushes. At times they struggled through waist-high grasses, stopping every twenty minutes or so to regather their strength. Enzo was clearly unwell. Twice they had to drop to the ground, first to let a train go by and then some military vehicle. After an hour they reached a flat plain and then came to some native huts. The summit of Mt Kenya, its glaciers shining in the starlight, helped them set their bearings. They crossed a freshly ploughed field, stepping between clods of earth. Then when after journeying for four hours they came to the shelter of a clump of trees they decided to stop for the night. They were now on the edge of the great forest that encircled the lower slopes of the mountain to a depth of thirty kilometres. The human danger zone, they thought, was now safely behind them; ahead lay the danger zone of the animals.

Just before 5 a.m. they were on their way again. Enzo had lost his fever and seemed to have regained his strength. They entered the forest but the undergrowth was almost impenetrable and they made slow going. Around dawn they saw a cow up ahead and realised it might be one of a herd. It would be risky to proceed in daylight if there were people about. It was agreed they should lie low for the rest of the day. It was a wise decision. When in the early evening they moved forward again they heard dogs barking up ahead of them. They followed a different track, but after a time came to a junction with a signpost: after peering at it in the darkness Felice eventually made out the words NANYUKI SAWMILL. Then carried on the wind came some rhythmic chanting, bursts of female laughter and a medley of sounds that seem to come from a native village close by. They kept going and at midnight reached the river that had been their objective all along.

For a whole day the river helped them find their way through the forest. They often saw paths trodden by animals whose droppings proved they were of a fairly large size. They stuck as close as they could to the course of the riverbed even though there were easier paths that ran along nearby. When that evening they came to a grassy area in the bend of the river they pitched their tent, collected and stacked up a quantity of dry wood and lit a big fire. During the night they listened to the sounds of the forest which included uncomfortably close rustlings in the foliage. Towards dawn they were disturbed by the crashing of branches, followed by an angry grunt ending in a high-pitched snarl. Felice furiously stirred the embers with a stick causing a flurry of sparks, Giuàn threw a burning branch towards the noise and Enzo clanged on the empty cooking pot with an ice-axe. The invisible beast, which Felice took to be a leopard, answered by growling, hissing, and grunting and then with a final resounding snarl it withdrew. As soon as they were able to, the three men set off again on their journey.

The river led them through bamboo thickets that progressively became stouter and more compact. At times their feet did not actually touch the ground but landed instead on a carpet of forest rubbish, and it was so hard to squeeze between the bamboos with their rucksacks that often one of the others had to give them a shove to force them through. At a place where the sun shone down on the river bank they paused for a bite to eat and the chance to dry their soaked boots and socks. Just as Felice was dunking a piece of dry biscuit in the water he looked up and saw emerging from the forest a magnificent, solitary bull elephant. He shouted and the others swivelled round in surprise. The elephant, perhaps more startled than they were, stopped in its tracks, and considered the three nervous men. Then it lifted its trunk almost vertically, dropped it in a disdainful half circle and turned about with impressive agility; with a nonchalant waggle of its tail it trotted back the way it had come, disappearing into the heavy foliage.

Felice, Giuàn and Enzo sat stunned for a while, having witnessed something that few people ever get to see. In high spirits and with a new sense of purpose they resumed their journey, and left the forest behind them. After an uneventful night they found themselves in a valley too narrow and rugged for large animals. Enzo was unwell again and, with frequent stops, they were only able to trek for four hours. The river changed direction and they followed it between sheer walls of rock fringed with creepers and strawberry-coloured orchids while bamboos formed a roof overhead like the nave of a cathedral. Next day it was Giuan's turn to become feverish. Nearly a week had passed since their escape. They had reached 3500 metres when a tropical storm hit them. It lasted for two hours and thoroughly drenched them, making them miserable. From their tiny tent they could see the barren plains of Nanyuki stretching all the way to the horizon. With his binoculars Felice could make out POW Camp 354. It seemed very far away indeed.

Next day they climbed higher in a strange landscape dotted with lobelias with cylindrical trunks, as high as a man. They reached a valley like an amphitheatre with steep sides and all of them were having difficulty breathing. Felice's rucksack, now carrying an extra two litres of water, weighed a ton. They moved forward in short steps, and pitched their tent in the lee of a granite rockface. When it proved impossible to light a fire they all squeezed into the two-man tent, having put on every item of clothing they possessed.

They woke fresh and rested. It was the first of February and extremely cold. Rounding an outcrop of rock they had before them the peak of Batian, a vision of such dominance that they gaped at it open-mouthed. They followed the course of the river and Felice saw tracks and excrement which he was sure must be those of buffalo. In the afternoon unfortunately Enzo began suffering from mountain sickness and Giuàn insisted it would be unsafe for him to go any higher at all. They stopped there and decided that this had to be where they made their base camp, even if it was not nearly high enough or close enough to where they ought to begin the final climb to the summit.

The following day Enzo was in better condition but was under strict instructions from Felice and Giuàn not to leave the base camp. They set off to scout out the best way to get to Batian, scrambling up screes above the camp. For Felice it was a wonderful feeling as they did their first actual climbing to have his hands on good granite. Around the other side of the mountain they saw Lenana appear for the first time, on the far side of a valley, bathed in light and looking surreal. They came to hard frozen snow and could see that there was more of it on the north face of Batian. It would without any doubt be formidable, but it ought not to be impossible. From different vantage points they examined what might be the optimal way to the top and then returned to the camp. They planned to devote all of the third of February to resting up and making their preparations for the final assault, or what was intended to be the final assault.

Felice and Giuàn were up at 2 a.m. on D-Day, and after a breakfast of two biscuits each and a brew of Ovaltine, powdered milk and plenty of sugar they set off. In a biting wind they scaled the screes and continued up the slopes for three hours until they got to the furthest point they had reached the day before. It took them a further hour to arrive at the wall that marked the beginning of the actual climb. They began traversing more or less along the contour and although the rock was exposed the holds were good ones. The sisal rope with which they were now linked became too rigid and kept getting hooked on any jutting rock. Both of their ropes were too short to make a double rope. By 11 a.m. they were at last on the very body of Batian which was covered in snow, and managed to climb several rope-lengths up it. Giuàn who was in the lead had to swipe the snow clear of handholds in the crumbly rock that were now hard to find; this snow landed on Felice below him, much of it going down his neck and under his clothes, with more of it coming as the man above wielded his ice-axe. A little higher up and the rock turned into smooth slabs, so that even if they had had pitons there were no cracks where they could be driven in. Just after midday Felice noticed rags of mist swirling around the summit above them, and then the temperature plummeted. Giuàn seemed unable to advance, and called down that he could find no handhold whatever in the wall of smooth rock. Soon there were clouds all around them. The wind began to howl, and Felice, his fingers frozen stiff, was shivering.

It began to snow. In a short, shouted conversation in the gathering storm they decided to give up, go back down, make an attempt the next day at the lesser peak of Lenana, if they were fit enough for it. The descended very slowly, with numb fingers having to scrabble for each grip on the snow-covered rocks, in snow that was coming down harder than ever. Not until 5 p.m. having got to the easy rocks at the base of Batian, was it possible for them finally to take off their ropes. It was nearly 9 p.m. after eighteen hours with hardly any stops and none that gave them any real rest, when they struggled back in the dark to the base camp. They shouted his name and Enzo replied with a low grumble from inside the tent.

Next morning they rose late and by silent agreement the day was devoted to recuperating. They made a swift inventory of their remaining food supplies: a mug of rice, a dozen biscuits, some pieces of chocolate, a smidgin of beef extract, tea, coffee, salt. It weighed less than half a kilo and would have to keep them going for at least four days. They stretched out in the tent hoping to pick up enough strength for a final effort. It took Felice a long time before sleep overcame the cold, and his hunger.

They left on February the 6th for Lenana one hour earlier than they had for Batian. At Nanyuki they had observed how bad weather on the mountain one day could often follow the same pattern the next. The previous day the storm had commenced at

10 a.m. and so they needed to be atop Lenana by then. By 8 they had reached the ridge that separated the two peaks, and there were no technical difficulties ahead to be overcome. But the condition they were in meant that even the relatively easy ascent was a struggle. They advanced slowly up to the cairn that marked the highest point, sat down and savoured their victory. It was at the very least a victory over the humdrum daily reality of prison. They were painfully aware of having been defeated by Batian, which rose opposite, 250 metres above them. Then they saw, on the slopes below, a corrugated iron refuge: that therefore was the standard way to the top. There other climbers, having come up helped by porters, might spend the night, warm and well fed. All they could do was shrug. It was time to hoist the flag. They stuck the lower pole into the stones of the cairn, and into its tin sheath they fitted the upper part onto which the flag had already been fastened. A breeze arose from the south and soon the flag, the three colours of Italy, began to flutter then fly, free, against the blue sky, in the direction of the camp. Felice feeling quite emotional did a quick sketch of this crowning moment of their adventure.[2] They left a message with their names in a bottle at the bottom of the flagpole. The weather was getting worse and it was time to begin their descent. Two hours later mists closed around them, it began to snow and they sought shelter beneath an overhanging rock. They decided to leave up there all the gear they no longer needed like crampons and ropes, and as soon as it stopped snowing they were on their way again. Through drifting clouds the sun shone on the surface of a small lake. They caught sight of a dirty towel fluttering like a banner from the base camp tent, and then Enzo emerged between the boulders to greet them.

At dawn on the 7th they began the descent of Mt Kenya. It was bitterly cold but the much greater discomfort was hunger: their food stocks were practically all gone. It was crucial that they move quickly. Once again they followed the course of the little river. Some of the time they slithered, lost their balance and fell. Again they were forced to go via the bamboo thickets, their hands became blistered with the giant nettles, twigs thrashed against their faces, they got covered in mud, but they were glad at least to see they were on the same route they had used coming up. On the 8th their only meal was a cup of sugarless tea and the last biscuit, which Felice had secreted away. It was Enzo's task then to divide it up with a knife, after making the most precise calculations, everyone getting a piece the size of a postage stamp. They carried on, sliding and stumbling all the while. In the afternoon they saw a local man ahead of them, khaki-clad, barefoot, holding up both arms in greeting. He had a companion and for a while it seemed that the Italians would have to follow them to the sawmill. With the smattering of Swahili that they had, Felice and Giuàn tried to get a friendly conversation going, and offered them cigarettes. Incredibly, after an hour or so the Africans left them. Not wasting a second the three prisoners shouldered their rucksacks and shot off like marathon runners in the direction of the POW camp. They followed a road that took them into the forest but by now they had lost all fear. What they did have was hunger.

For the whole of February 10th they trudged on and on, with cramps in their stomachs and an overwhelming general sense of feebleness. At the railway line they paused to ready themselves for a last great effort. They could see the barbed wire, and now at the end of the eighteenth day since they broke out they were finally back in the vegetable gardens, at Giuàn's little hut. All they felt then was a pure, total sense of exhaustion.

It was late when they woke in the morning, to the sound of work parties coming in to the gardens. Once they had removed their mountain clothing and donned the prison uniform it was an easy matter to slip out and mingle with the others. At midday they re-entered the camp through the main gate with one of the work parties, three of whose original members had agreed to stay behind until evening. Back inside the first thing they did was read their mail, and then they attacked the meal in the refectory like those who have truly been starved. Some fellow prisoners wanted them to hand themselves in straightaway but Felice would have none of it. All three of them needed first to clean up, and be allowed to sleep in a proper bed.

Next morning, fresh, shaven, with shoes shining and shirt and shorts carefully ironed, they fronted up at the assembly. The officer in charge had evidently been alerted to their presence. Felice saluted him and gave him a breezy 'Good morning!' They were marched off, meticulously searched, questioned at length and put in a cell. They were to receive the standard punishment of twenty eight days in close confinement.

CHAPTER 10 NOTES

[1] this chapter draws entirely on Felice's two accounts, in English and Italian.
[2] See chapter 11, note 2.

PRIGIONIA

sua città aperta 10 aprile
Capitolazione Abe 29 aprile '41
partenza per Diu Deuo
La Ferry   3 settimane
Berbera   1 settimana
Aden   port 13 meggio '41
Mombasa   attacco all'URSS
Nairobi
Londiani   off Ara Dayal
             Natale uccisione S.Ten ? Edi
Nanyuki   meggio 42   — 24/5/42 partenza da
Londiani   11 giugno '43   Berbera prima nave
Sceret   inizio 44   branda
Kedausa foreste   6 mesi?   8 luglio da Mombasa
Glaneza   3° convoglio

caso problemi fine 44 — fine 45
Londiani   uff. amministrazione
figlie   giugno 46 mia settimana fino 11/6
Mombasa   luglio
sbarco Napoli   2 agosto '46

List made by Felice of where and when he had been incarcerated in Africa

11

ARMISTICE

Far from being severe, the punishment meted out to the escapees was no ordeal at all but more like convalescence, despite the midday heat in the narrow corrugated iron cells, and the fleas and occasional rat that kept them company. Felice and Giuàn were in one together, and Enzo shared a cell with another prisoner who had been caught trading with natives. Smoking was forbidden but others in the camp managed to get plenty of cigarettes to them, enough to pass some on to the guards who in exchange turned a blind eye to the supply of daily necessities. Nor were they allowed books, but these too arrived with the help of friends, during their twice-daily exercise periods.

They were also blessed with an amiable camp commandant. Captain Robin Roberts was a tea planter in Kenya who had volunteered for the King's African Rifles in 1939 when the war began. He had seen active duty in Ethiopia and been impressed by Italy's front-line troops. At the end of that campaign he returned home and was assigned to the camp at Nanyuki, still well-disposed towards Italians. With characteristic humour he told Felice, Giuàn and Enzo that he appreciated their sporting effort on Mt Kenya, and reduced their sentence from four weeks to seven days.[1]

On the very day they started their period of close confinement, word of the escapade leaked out. A British group rambling below Point Lenana spotted the flag and brought it back down.[2] On 20 February the Nairobi *East African Standard* reported the story, under the headline Escaped Italian Prisoners Fled to Mount Kenya! It became an international news item and was picked up by the Italian media: subsequently a weekly magazine gave it front page prominence, with a dramatic sketch of two soldiers on a mountaintop hoisting the national banner in a fierce wind.[3] It was manna for the fascists, this saga of patriotic valour at a time when the war was beginning to take a heavy toll on Italy. The unwanted publicity had repercussions for the three adventurous POWs who were thereafter moved to Londiani, a camp with a tougher regime.

A comfort and joy for Felice during those seven days and nights was the clear view he had had of the mountain they had climbed. One night while half asleep he felt a draught and imagined a wind was blowing. He got up to check, and there was indeed a breeze. He looked out through the bars of the small window, towards the peak of Batian on the horizon, with its halo of stars. A doubt crept into his mind: had they really been up there, or did he just dream it? What followed was something akin to a mystical experience, and it was as if he heard the wind from the mountain speaking to him, murmuring in a language only he could understand. No, you didn't dream it, it was real. And now you are back behind barbed wire, guarded by the bayonets of black sentries, among the other prisoners with nerves jaded by war and captivity and dreadful news from home. But you are not like them, you have been given added strength, and the gift of self-reliance. Up there you learned humility and gained a sense of proportion, riches of immense value which can never be taken from you. Felice wrote two accounts of this experience, one in Italian and a later one in English and the two are slightly different. The former, more immediate and passionate, has the wind telling him that the trio who had gone up the mountain, previously mere ciphers, had been turned back into human beings. The wind in that version told him the flag they left at the summit was not just a symbol of their fatherland but also of the triumph of will over suffering, and of action over inertia. In both versions the wind urges him to tell no one about the wonderful secrets of the mountain, of what they had learned up there. Felice ends his story: "I, obstinate as I am, have written a book about it."

***

The two accounts are in the books *Fuga Sul Kenya* published in 1947 and *No Picnic on Mount Kenya* that came out five years later. The idea of writing the story of their escape had come to him early, while still a prisoner, and may have been partly due to the fact that so much useful information about the mountain that he and Giuàn gained while preparing for their adventure came in the form of stories rather than reference material. During the ascent itself he kept a diary and jotted down all sorts of details, including on the weather, the topography and the flora and fauna of the mountain. When afterwards he researched into who had scaled the mountain before them, his quest often led him to lively tales in books with titles like *Through Masai land: a journey of exploration among the snowclad volcanic mountains and strange tribes of eastern equatorial Africa.*[4]

For Felice books, like mountains, were wonderful things, and especially wonderful were books about mountains. In *No Picnic on Mount Kenya* he has a chapter in which he digresses to reveal information contained in books about the mountain which was simply not available to him at the right time. It is for him such an important point that he inserts this chapter in the very middle, when the climbers have first reached the base camp; in *Fuga Sul Kenya* it comes as an appendix. All that we now know, he wrote, we learnt afterwards from books:

> They were our best companions during our long imprisonment and later through the period of semi-liberty when we were doing work of one kind or another in Kenya. They, unlike other companions, very seldom disappointed us, very often comforted us, always helped us to forget.[5]

The chapter, whose title is 'The Unknown', gives the Kikuyu

origin of the names of the mountain and its main peaks, adding some tribal lore about them. It then recounts the arrival of the European explorers, the early expeditions aimed at climbing Mt Kenya and then the final successful attempt. It was in 1899 that Sir Harold Mackinder led an expedition which first got to the very top of Batian; the second to do it was Eric Shipton, in 1929. Shipton, born three years before Felice, later had much success in the Himalayas and was the logical choice to lead the 1953 triumphant attempt on Everest, being passed over however by the British for Sir John Hunt. Felice had enormous respect for Shipton and in *Fuga Sul Kenya* described him in superlatives, as an absolute champion in terms of technical skill, and, just as important, as a likeable and sensitive writer about mountains.

Felice loved reading about the exploits of renowned mountaineers, and drew comfort from tales of efforts to reach the summit that had ended in failure. He had barely descended from the icy face of Batian when he felt the humiliating and demoralising impact of their lack of success. But he recalled almost at the same time the words of a writer who urged that an effort always be made to reach ever further, and if you failed to get there at least you would not have succumbed to empty complacency. Felice also came to terms with the realisation that he would never be a mountaineer like either Shipton or his friend Bill Tilman: both had gone on from Kenya to spectacular success in the Himalayas. These men had that unique opportunity to make first ascents. Within a few decades all the major peaks in the world would have been climbed, by various routes and in the different seasons.

Felice began drafting his book in 1943. From the outset he had in mind to write a parallel English version, and although still a prisoner of war was able to get assistance in refining his text from various English people. One was E. Robson, a Nairobi pharmacist who had been in the party that retrieved the flag from Point Lenana. Felice took a liking to the English, and in particular their habit of understatement. The book that Edward Whymper, the first to climb the Matterhorn, wrote about his achievement was called *Scrambles amongst the Alps*. Felice, who much later chose *More than Rocks* as the title for his personal memoirs, was evidently happy with his own whimsical title of *No Picnic on Mount Kenya*.

***

Felice, Giuàn and Enzo had returned to the camp a week after the German army in Stalingrad surrendered to the Russians; with the German defeat two months earlier at El Alamein in Egypt, the tide had turned in the war. For Italy, 1943 was cataclysmic. Following its military and political debacle in Africa, it was adjusting also to colossal casualties in the regiments it had sent to Russia, where nearly 90,000 of its soldiers died.[6] At home, these setbacks, combined with constant British and American bombing, were causing distress, and disillusion with life under fascism.

In June Felice was transferred to POW Camp 365 at Londiani and a few weeks later, although he did not yet know it, Stefania and Daniela left Africa aboard the *Vulcania*. Shortly before they landed in Italy the British and American invasion of Sicily prompted King Victor Emmanuel to order the arrest of Mussolini. The Allied forces reached the mainland of Italy, and on 8th September the new Italian Government, headed by Marshal Badoglio, formerly declared an armistice. In effect, Italy surrendered. On 12 September Mussolini was freed by German paratroopers and flown to Munich: he returned to Italy on 23 September and announced the formation of a rival government which was in due course set up at Salò on Lake Garda.

Defeat in war is a national catastrophe. In Italy's case some special circumstances magnified the disaster. The fascism of Mussolini had been embraced by Hitler with dire consequences for both their countries. Initially in Italy fascism had found favour, in terms of political stability, economic development and national prestige. Both the monarchy and the church had gone along with it. But by 1943 Italian fascism was in every sense bankrupt, and morally so after the passage of the racial laws; the bankruptcy revealed itself in near-famine conditions in parts of the country. The 8 September armistice took Italy into unknown and terrible territory. For its armed forces, the dilemma of divided loyalty and ambiguous military purpose was brutally resolved: the Wehrmacht moved in as an occupying force and tens of thousands of Italian soldiers were put on cattle trains destined for imprisonment in Germany. For ordinary Italians, including the many who for two decades had served under fascism, the prospect now was of civil war. Meanwhile the land of Italy became a bloody battleground fought over by the advancing Allies and the retreating Germans. [7]

At the time of Italy's surrender, more than half a million Italian servicemen were prisoners of the British, in disparate and far-flung locations. The 1929 Geneva Convention governed the status of POWs, and the British respected their international obligations and treated their prisoners relatively well. But they offset the burden of having to look after so many men by viewing them as a useful labour supply, within its enormous empire. They got round the narrow interpretation of the Geneva Conventions, once Italy was no longer a declared enemy, by classing those they held in captivity as 'military internees.' In most cases these unfortunates were employed in agriculture; in Kenya many were engaged in forestry and road building. In due course Italy became a 'co-belligerent' of the Allies whereupon the range of work expanded greatly, along with pay and improved conditions. While the outcome of the war against Germany and Japan was still in doubt, the POWs were seen as a huge asset for the British as a docile labour force, and London was keen to hold them as long as possible. [8]

The Duke of Aosta died in Nairobi in 1942. He was succeeded as the senior Italian officer in Kenya by General Nasi. Felice in a newspaper article in 1971 recounted how a month or so before the Sicily landings a senior British figure had asked Nasi whether he was prepared to lead a contingent of Italian troops as part of the invasion force. Nasi refused point blank to take up arms against other Italians. After the armistice the British sought his help in separating out those POWs on whose cooperation they could count from the others still beholden to fascism. Nasi had to take into account the wellbeing of his fellow countrymen, and also their confused state of mind at this particular moment.[9] Most of them felt both relief and joy to learn that hostilities were over, and had some hope that collaborating with their captors might increase the chances of their being sent home soon. But all had made significant sacrifices for their country which had now turned through 180 degrees. It was natural also to feel a degree of rage and shame, of respect for their fallen comrades as well as to reflect on military dignity and patriotic loyalty. For a minority that included those dedicated to fascism it was unthinkable to collaborate: for them a prisoner who did so was a traitor.

In Kenya over 25,000 prisoners of war cooperated after the armistice, while barely five thousand refused. Felice told a television interviewer in 1987:

> The 8th of September was a trauma for us. Because, far from Italy as we were, we weren't physically ready for such a transformation. Naturally most of us POWs stuck by the pledge of loyalty we had sworn to the King, not least because just at that moment when Mussolini established his regime at Salò we in the camps were learning for the first time how the Germans had set up extermination camps. Those who stood by Mussolini's new republic were in a tiny minority. There were one or two suicides and a few people got beaten up. But most POWs went along with it: and we collaborated.[10]

At Londiani, which had a reputation as a punishment camp, there were some 3,500 prisoners, most of them officers: in the wake of the armistice eighty per cent of these agreed to collaborate. By now the British authorities had granted a freedom 'on trust' to Italian prisoners who gave their word they would not take advantage of it by trying to escape or through acts of sabotage. Felice stayed at Londiani until the beginning of 1944, when he was again transferred, this time to Camp 356 at Eldoret, also in the east of the country, with its forested areas; nine months later he returned to Londiani. In both camps he accepted the work that was offered to him.

At the end of 1944 Felice came to the attention of the Assistant Conservator of Forests at Londiani, R.M. Graham, who was on the lookout for a tutor for his eleven year old son. The boy, called Moray, had failed the entrance exam to the Prince of Wales' School in Nairobi; he had never been to school and indeed was the only European boy anywhere in the vicinity; his need was for instruction in the full range of subjects including English, Maths, Latin and History. In all likelihood Graham consulted the camp commandant, who would inevitably have been aware of the singular gifts of prisoner Benuzzi. As a result Felice for a full year not only was tutor to Moray but also lived as a member of the Graham family, in their government-provided house.

Moray Graham, seventy years later, well recalled his time with a tutor whom he always knew as 'Docanuzzi' and who had never been presented to him as a prisoner. He did know that Felice was taken once a month to report to the police at Molo, a township 25 kilometres away, and gathered that he was a trustie. A cousin of his, a Lieutenant-colonel Robin Wilson who came occasionally to Londiani, told Moray later that Felice had not only collaborated with the British but helped them identify the diehard fascists in the camp, which was now reserved for those Italians who chose not to cooperate with the British. Once he took Moray and his father there because he wanted them to see how talented some of them were. They had a workshop in which they were able to make models, as well as a charcoal-powered boiler and a multi-cylinder steam engine and dynamo mounted on an ordinary school desk.

Moray remembered Felice as gregarious, enthusiastic and someone for whom nothing was too much trouble. He was, Moray said, a wonderful role model for a young boy, teaching him to walk long distances, and climb anything that was climbable. Other things that Moray claims he learned from Felice were the tree species that the Forest Department was planting around Londiani, how to preserve bird skins and mount them and how to call a leopard out of the forest. On their outings Felice would take paint and paper that Mrs. Graham had supplied and make drawings of the scenery – never animals or people or events. Felice, he said, was an effortless teacher but one who demanded, and got, diligence. At the end of the school year Moray passed the exam.[11]

***

Among Felice's personal papers is a draft 'Chapter 3' entitled 'Expedition to Kerio' which relates an excursion up the Rift Valley he made with other POWS who by this time had evidently gained a degree of freedom. References to Londiani in it show this must have been during his second stint in that camp in 1944-45. 'Six of us set off,' he wrote, 'the Mt Kenya trio, Giuàn, Enzo and I, and three other fit fellows who were by now our close friends.' A truck took them as far as the Eldama Ravine, to a small settlement of local artisans and Indian-owned stores. Pressing on, they reached a point where they were able to see Lake Baringo shimmering between hills in the distance. This is as far as the draft goes, but it confirms the enduring friendship of the three escapees from Nanyuki camp. It also sheds more light on the character of Enzo Barsotti, who joined their climbing team only at the last moment, revealing him as both witty and knowledgeable about Kerio, describing it as 'a river, a valley, a wild paradise – with rhinos, hippos, lions, the lot.' In *No Picnic on Mount Kenya* Felice paints a brief picture of him:

> Enzo was thirty-five years old, married, a fairly good bridge player and a very heavy smoker. As it turned out, Enzo did not let us down. His endurance, his wit, his true camaraderie can never be praised enough. His health proved to be a serious handicap, but the memory of his cheerful presence remains one of the most pleasant souvenirs of the whole trip.[12]

Felice had a much closer relationship with Giuàn, who was

for him from the outset 'the best companion imaginable for an adventure such as that which was in store for us, but also a friend for life.' The two of them shared the punishment cell in February 1943, and when they found themselves thereafter in the same POW camp, where possible they would make their excursions together. In his memoirs Felice wrote that in 1946 Giuàn had been permitted to practise as a doctor in the public hospital at Londiani, adding that after a time they had both exhausted all the hills within a day's journey.[13]

For his part Felice in 1946 was in the pay office in the Londiani camp, doing accountancy for both the jailers and the jailed. Occasionally he would be sent to Nairobi to close the account of the lucky few who were already able to be sent home. In the capital he would find time to visit the museum or the library, or call on one of the friends he had made. One of these was John Melhuish, a dentist and mountaineer who was responsible for many of the first maps of Mount Kenya.[14] In the preface to his book Felice thanked Melhuish, along with Moray Graham's parents and the pharmacist E. Robson, for their advice and assistance. Although by this time the war was over in every sense, the Italians had to stay on in Kenya because, they were told, there were simply not enough ships, even to get all British forces home. Some who were in the frailest condition were repatriated, but the rest were given work, mainly agricultural. Most hung about in the camps, under the supervision of Italian *carabinieri*.

Some camps were more lenient than others, and at one of them a group of POWs had been allowed to climb Mount Kenya. Felice wanted to tackle Kilimanjaro but was refused. However in February 1946, after a great deal of pestering, he and Giuàn were given permission to spend two nights with friends at a farm. They boarded a train for Nakuru, although train travel for them was off limits. They waited until it started moving and then squeezed into the baggage wagon, only to be confronted by the Indian chief guardsman who asked for their tickets. They said they had only just managed to get aboard, and he told them to buy some at the next station; but given the fact that the train was packed he let them stay on in the baggage wagon where they sat facing the retreating scenery with their legs dangling.

Their destination was Menengai, a crater formed after a volcanic eruption. Next day, with their friends from the farm and two local farm hands, they descended more than 300 metres into it. There was no vegetation and it reminded Felice of the Dancalia Depression in Ethiopia, below sea level and one of the hottest places on earth. The stick they stuck in a crevice caught fire. They climbed an internal rocky peak and found a metal kingpost with a rusty plaque and a 1930s date: in a tin at the foot of it they left their own details, proudly putting below their names the Italian Alpine Clubs of Liguria and Trieste. Next day they rode back to Londiani in an overcrowded ramshackle bus. Tied to its roof were bicycles, baskets of fruit, caged and squawking poultry and all manner of merchandise. The driver careered along, brushing the roadside markers on the curves and skimming the edges of ravines while oncoming vehicles pulled over to the side of the road to let them pass.

Four months later Felice was transferred to Camp 353 at Gilgil, his last one in Kenya, to await his own repatriation.[15] For the POWs preparing to go home after so many years, this was a testing time of impatience and uncertainty, charged emotions and strange obsessions. Rumours flew of shortages in Italy of one thing or another, of meat and coffee and pepper and leather, and the price of these products would accordingly shoot up at once. Currency speculation and gambling took hold in the dining hall each evening. In this frenetic atmosphere, no one dared leave the camp lest they miss some announcement for departees to assemble.

Felice was keen to have a closer look at Lake Elmenteita which he had glimpsed a few times from the road near Gilgil, intrigued by the way the light and the colour of the lake varied according to the time of day. He headed out there with a friend from the camp and was rewarded by one of the most glorious sights of his life. As far as the eye could see were pink flamingos in motion, flapping their wings, skipping on their thin legs, dipping their elegant necks into the water, rising in brief flight, in perpetual movement like a constant shower of rose petals. As a backdrop at the head of the valley were black volcanic rocks against the radiant dark blue sky.

News finally came that he was to leave – on a Monday. It meant he would have one last chance on the Sunday to achieve something he had longed to do since arriving at the first camp at Naivasha five years before, when the outline of Mount Longonot had seemed to him both a challenge and a symbol of freedom. Someone who knew the area now told him he would be mad to go there without a weapon as lions roamed the slopes. Felice was more encouraged by the piece of Masai wisdom someone else passed on, that lions were no problem unless you threw stones at them. He set off in a small truck with the same friend from the previous excursion. The driver seemed quite surprised when they asked to be dropped off in open country, and after they had got out drove slowly off, watching them for some time while they headed into grass up to their waist, lion-coloured grass. They began climbing steeply up under the equatorial sun and reached the rim of the Longonot crater. The spectacle of peaks and valleys all around made Felice wish that Giuàn could have been there, and he recalled a similar moment when the two of them saw Lake Baringo shining on the horizon: Giuàn had remarked that the only missing element that could add to the splendour would be a sung Mass.

Next day the long train with Felice and many others aboard crossed a vast plain populated by antelopes, giraffes, zebras and gnu peacefully grazing. Felice longed for at least a glimpse of Kilimanjaro, which so far had always eluded him. He kept his gaze on the southern horizon, and finally a white breast-shaped blur revealed itself as the highest mountain in Africa. All the prisoners aboard including those least interested in mountains were taken by the vision. After sunset the top of the great mountain still glowed red then became tinged with pink in diminishing shades until finally disappearing in violet. Felice reflected later that this was also the moment in which for those going home the curtain fell on Africa, where they had spent the best years of their youth. [16]

For Giuàn and Enzo, however, Africa would always be important to them. After the war Enzo Barsotti went to live in Mombasa where he ran a construction company. Dr Giovanni Balletto went back for a few months to his native Genoa. Then with wife and children he returned first to Somalia and then Tanganyika, later Tanzania: he settled near Marangu on the southern side of Mount Kilimanjaro, practising as a doctor, until his death in 1972.

CHAPTER 11 NOTES

[1] Captain Roberts' son Glyn exchanged several emails with the author in 2012-2013: he explained that his father died in 1961 when he was 7, and few relevant records survive. *Point Lenana* pp. 103-18 has an extensive correspondence with Glyn.

[2] The flag was retained by the Mountain Club of East Africa and in 1948 was gifted to the Milan branch of the Italian Alpine Clun (endnote *Fuga sul Kenya* p. 294 refers). Further information is available at www.eneafiorentini.it/irecelib/irec01.html .

[3] *L'illustrazione del Popolo* of 14 March 1943, reproduced in *Fuga sul Kenya* (Corbaccio 2012). See also *Point Lenana* p. 11.

[4] See *No Picnic on Mount Kenya* p. 143.

[5] *No Picnic on Mount Kenya* p. 139.

[6] It is hard to determine precisely Italy's terrible losses on the Russian front, but the best data can be found on http://www.campagnadirussia.info/wp-content/uploads/2011/12/I_caduti_del_fronte_orientale.pdf.

[7] In a speech to the House of Commons on 24.5.1944, ten days before Rome was liberated, Winston Churchill said '...here is this beautiful country suffering the worst horrors of war... with the hideous prospect of the red-hot rake of the battle-line being drawn from sea to sea right up the whole length of the peninsula...' German surrender in Trieste was 2.5.1945.

[8] Goodchild, J.M. (2014), *Exploitation of Displaced European Refugees', War and Displacement in the Twentieth Century: Global Conflicts,* Sandra Barkhof & Angela K. Smith (eds), Routledge, p. 109; Moore, B. & Fedeorowich, K. (2002), *The British Empire and Italian Prisoners of War,* Palgrave Macmillan, p. 6. 'Docile' was a word used in this context by Winston Churchill. Also Ferrari, M. (1996), *'Cooperatori e non cooperatori' Italia 1939-1945: storia e memoria,* Carlotti, Anna Lisa (ed), Milano: Vita e Pensiero.

[9] *Il Piccolo* 13.10.71 : *Il solo modo di governare è quello di mostrarsi buoni.*

[10] See *Point Lenana* pp. 487 and 592; see chapter 9, note 3.

[11] This section derives from telephone conversations and correspondence with Moray Graham in 2012-2013. *Point Lenana* pp. 232-236 has an extensive interview with him.

[12] *No Picnic on Mt Kenya* pp. 51-52.

[13] *Più che sassi* p. 76.

[14] Melhuish is referred to in Holman, D. (1978), *Elephants at sundown: the story of Bill Woodley,* W.H.Allen, p. 220 (see also Chapter 20 note 15).

[15] Spadoni, P.S. (1996), *I prigionieri italiani in Africa* in *Italia 1939-1945: storia e memoria,* Carlotti, Anna Lisa (ed), Vita e Pensiero: the non-collaborators from Londiani were the last to be repatriated, and the very last left Mombasa in February 1947, on the *Vulcania.*

[16] *Più che sassi* p. 88.

12

FAMILY REUNION

Stefania had arrived in Trieste at a fateful time, a few days before the 8 September armistice that ended Italy's alliance with Germany and divided the country in two.[1] Two vast armies fought over the territory. Every Italian citizen had to choose between two loyalties, to the new government ordained by the King or to fascism that had ruled the country for a generation. The people of Trieste however had no choice at all. The situation was tense and complicated, not only because that area was strategically vital to Germany and Austria but also because of the Slav dimension, due to the Slav presence in the city and Tito's Jugoslav partisans very close indeed. As soon as the armistice was announced German forces occupied Trieste. Germany annexed the provinces of Trieste, Gorizia, Udine and Lubiana, and the former Italian territories in Dalmatia.[2] Those provinces were collectively renamed Adriatic Littoral, the term used by the former Austrian empire. An Austrian-born Gauleiter, Friedrich Rainer, was put in command there, and Italian prefects, mayors, police and the fascist militias were all directly answerable to him. These authorities were ordered to deal harshly with the increasing challenges the occupying forces were facing from partisan groups, and also to go after the Jews. A former rice-husking mill in Trieste was converted into a transit camp for the deportation of prisoners to Germany and Poland; soon afterwards it was to become Italy's only extermination camp.

For more than a year Stefania had to keep a very low profile, while fearful conditions prevailed in the city. In April 1944 seven German soldiers were killed in an attack and in reprisal seventy-one citizens were shot; later that month fifty-two more were hanged after a further attack. On 10 June Allied air raids began and killed 463, with over a thousand wounded. Aerial bombardment of the city continued until February 1945 causing significant destruction mainly in the port area and the nearby oil refinery and naval shipyards: the Benuzzis lived on the main road along the waterfront.

Nino and Berta were mild people who had close ties with Austria and who had come to like their future daughter-in-law in the early years of her courtship with Felice. Stefania got on particularly well with Berta, who shared German as their mother tongue. Berta had insights out of the ordinary. Stefania related many years later how her mother-in-law was totally convinced that all her four sons would survive the war, and so she had no qualms at all about Felice, imprisoned in Africa. On one occasion she uttered a cry and fell swooning to the floor: the family subsequently established that it was at this same instant that her second son Piero had been shot during fighting in Greece. The bullet passed through Piero's jaws which were open as he was yelling something, and although scarred he was not badly injured.

Once, when Stefania and Berta were out shopping, they saw a copy of a weekly magazine whose full-page front cover was a picture of Italian soldiers hoisting a flag on the top of a mountain.[3] Berta spontaneously said, 'That's Felice!' Stefania objected that there were tens of thousands of Italian prisoners in Kenya, but Berta only smiled, and she was right. The men in the illustration were not named. More than a year passed before Felice made any reference to his exploit, in a letter to Stefania that passed through the censors, and he did it in cryptic fashion. At my last camp, he wrote, I did something really typical – *'ho combinato una delle mie.'* She did not find out what had actually happened until much later.

In the early days she had virtually no money at all. A percentage of Felice's salary was due to her, including back pay for the time since his capture in Addis Ababa, but she could only apply for it in Rome and travel there was out of the question. Luckily for her by now German had become practically an official language in the city, and she found work as interpreter for a trade union leader, a Tuscan who did not speak a word of it. At a certain point the Tuscan had to leave Trieste, and the office closed down. Stefania and Gianni, another of Felice's brothers, grabbed the opportunity, getting into the office and taking away two full sacks of coal. This was welcomed by the family since their rooms were freezing and the only heating they had was a wood-fired stove.[4]

The fighting in Italy raged fiercely on for a year and a half, until the surrender of German forces there on 29 April 1945. On the first of May Yugoslav forces entered Trieste and took control of the city's administration. The following day a New Zealand division, vanguard of the Allied forces, took up positions in the port and held other areas of military significance.[5] The political situation was highly uncertain and the relations between the two armies wavered between formal good behaviour and high tension. The Yugoslavs were set on eliminating any political opposition to their presence and aimed to build consensus for their annexation of the area. For forty days they went after Germans and fascists, but also targeted Italians who were members of the police, the carabinieri, civil servants and people at all levels: the precise number of victims of this period can never be known but after the war a thousand bodies were retrieved from the *foiba* – a mine shaft – at Basovizza near Trieste. One Italian writer described this nightmare as being on a ship going down, with pirates at the helm.[6] On 9 June an agreement between the Allies and Yugoslavia limited the respective areas of occupation within the overall region. This provisional agreement was to last until 1954, when Italy regained sovereignty over Zone A, the western area of occupation which included the city of Trieste, while Zone B was ceded to Yugoslavia.

The Anglo-American presence in Trieste gave Stefania another reason to bless her parents for having put such emphasis on languages in their daughters' education. She was soon taken on by the British naval authorities who had an office in Piazza Unità, the city's main square, but her employers were so unpleasant and their attitudes so demeaning that she quit at the end of the first month. She crossed the piazza to where the Allies had other offices. The first person she encountered, a physically large American major, asked her what she wanted. When she replied that she was looking for work, he invited her into his office, and after a short interview offered her a job.

The major was a colourful *bon viveur* who had taken over a fine villa on the waterfront at Barcola. He had some odd habits. He would sometimes of an evening drive over to where the Benuzzis lived and honk loudly, to Berta's consternation. One of his functions was to grant permits to truck drivers, who had an important role since the only railway line to the city had been all but destroyed by Allied bombing. Stefania's task was to carry out the initial screening of applicants, many of whom came to her with blandishments, including money and poultry.

One day the major sent a jeep for her, summoning her to his villa. When she arrived he produced a letter for her to read. It was from a British security officer, advising all Allied offices in Trieste that she, Stefania Benuzzi, had in Ethiopia been sentenced to five years imprisonment: she was a dangerous person and should not be given employment. The major asked if the information was correct. With her heart in her mouth she told him the facts in the letter were true. He nodded. He said he knew all about her, and for all the past month had been watching her. Then, to her immense relief, he tore the letter up and dropped it in the bin. The matter was closed. Not long after that he left Trieste, someone else replaced him, and she heard no more about it.

***

Felice departed from Mombasa in Kenya on the *Arundel Castle*, in July 1946.[7] On board were many of the non-collaborators among the POWs, whom the British wanted to be the last to be repatriated. Six years later Felice contributed a chapter to an anthology of Italian colonial memoirs, under the pseudonym Arrigo Risano which was the one he always used. In the chapter he gave an account of his journey home. He described the thrill he felt when after passing through the Suez Canal a day or so later he caught his first sight of Italy, with in the distance the mountains of Calabria and Sicily. He was somewhat disconcerted by the final landfall at Naples: to welcome them all back home as they disembarked a town band struck up not the national anthem but the jaunty *Funiculì Funiculà*. Felice called Stefania, and let her know how and when he might get to Trieste.

He travelled together on the train with one of the non-collaborating former prisoners, a diehard fascist, whose family home was in Istria, just beyond Trieste. In Rome Felice shaved off his beard to make himself more presentable to the wife he had not seen for six years. Skirting the lagoon of Venice, they headed north towards Udine and at last there on the horizon were Felice's beloved Alps:

> The mountains soared massive, solid, definitive, timeless, beyond any defeat or victory, beyond the great rupture of 8 September, beyond all human suffering.

They arrived in the Free Territory of Trieste on 17 August. There at the station to meet them were Berta and Stefania. His mother hugged him and said, as always in German, Only now is the war over for me. Felice's ex-fascist travelling companion stayed with the family that night, and next morning caught a ferry down the Adriatic coast to Capodistria, in Zone B now in Yugoslav hands. A few weeks later he was gunned down in an ambush.[8]

The day after his return Stefania borrowed a jeep from the British for whom she was at that time working, and took Felice to find their daughter. Daniela was on holiday for the first time in her life. She had gone on an outing organised by the Trieste city authorities for fifty or so children of prisoners of war, to Forni Avoltri, right on the Austrian border. To find himself so soon after coming home back once more in the Carnic Alps that he knew so well was quite emotional for Felice.

His emotions were about to be stirred much more powerfully. For years he had been thinking about the little girl he left behind in Addis Ababa. While he had from time to time received news of how Daniela was growing up, nothing could have really prepared him for this reunion. He wrote in the Italian version of his book – in a passage he would have drafted before this reunion – how POWs in the monotonous, deadening daily existence in the camps, might once in a while be smitten by a sudden memory. 'It could be a vision of some movement of the tiny creature you left behind, holding her arms out to you: and it stuns you. Then, with enormous effort, you have to pull yourself together, and cope with actuality.' He had last seen and held her when she was eight months old; now it was a week after her sixth birthday.

Stefania, too, was apprehensive. Only a few months earlier she and Daniela had been walking in the centre of town near the post office when just in front of them was a girl her age, holding the hand of her father. Daniela all at once began to cry: 'I want my father, too!' Stefania knew at once that she would have to handle this reunion with enormous delicacy. As the time approached she took care, given that reaction of Daniela's, not to talk much about Felice.

Forni Avoltri was a remote hamlet with no railway. The children had gone down the valley to the nearest station and were playing in a small park at the back of it. Go and find your daughter, Stefania said to him. He circled among them, with an air of desperation. Then he stopped, caught the attention of one little girl sitting on the ground among the bushes, and asked, hesitating, 'You are Dani?' She nodded. Stefania was soon beside her, and picked her up. 'This is your father, you know.' Daniela considered him, shook her head, and said, 'No.' It wasn't possible, because her father was in Africa. Always. She then said, 'You're Uncle Piero.' Because they were somewhat similar. Except Uncle Piero had a war wound on his neck, and this man didn't. With the others contradicting her she shrugged. All right. He was her father. It did not concern her greatly. She had no idea what it was like to have a father. A grandfather, yes: she adored Nino. And she had uncles, including Uncle Gianni who was living with the family then, and she was close to him. But a father – that was beyond her experience. Stefania gently urged her, convinced her. Daniela allowed Felice to hold her. Slowly she put her arms about his neck.[9]

Felice's return was an upheaval in the lives of both his wife and daughter. Stefania remembered, many decades later, the emotional turmoil that it caused and how she had been both excited, and worried. For all the time of his absence she had had every bit of responsibility for Daniela. For the two of them, she had taken every decision herself, without asking anyone's opinion. All of a sudden here was another person necessarily involved. It took Stefania and Felice some time to work out exactly how to get on together.

Daniela resented the disruption to the family caused by her father's return. It could not be helped, this distance that was between the two of them. It remained there, in some ways, ever afterwards, never more so than when he felt he had to be strict with her. It was not until Daniela had her own daughter, and could see what a proper father-daughter relationship was like, that she realised this matter had to be brought out into the open. Then they did talk to each other about it, and things became a little easier.[10]

CHAPTER 12 NOTES

[1] The early part of this chapter draws heavily on the detailed account in 'Stefania' – DVD interview produced by Personal Documentaries op. cit.

[2] Toscano, M. (1996), *Storia diplomatica della questione dell'Alto Adige,* Bari: Laterza, p.215.

[3] The magazine was *Illustrazione del Popolo* – see chapter 11, note 3.

[4] *Point Lenana*, p. 514.

[5] For New Zealand's role in liberating Trieste see Cox, G. (1977), *The race for Trieste, William* Kimber, pp. 89-90, also Stafford, D. (2010), *Endgame 1945: Victory, Retribution, Liberation,* Hachette UK, part three. Felice's appreciation of that role is conveyed in *Più che sassi,* pp. 114-115 and *Sulle alpi neozelandesi* in Alpi Giulie, 67-1(1972) p. 114.

[6] Quarantotti Gambini, P.A. (1967), *Endgame 1945: Victory, Retribution, Liberation,* Mondadori, p. 105.

[7] Felice letter to parents (from Pacific Ocean) 2.2.1959: 'Sul ponte sole c'e' un ammasso di corpi come sul *Arundel Castle*, quando son rimpatriato dalla prigionia (bodies are strewn around the sun deck just like on the *Arundel Castle* that brought me home from Kenya).'

[8] *Point Lenana*, pp. 523-527.

[9] Details of the momentous Forni Avoltri reunion conveyed to author by mother and daughter in interview at Città della Pieve 12 October 2012.

[10] The conversation took place at Punta del Este, Uruguay, in 1975 (from Daniela, Città della Pieve 12.5.2012).

13

MINISTRY OF FOREIGN AFFAIRS

Felice came back to an Italy that was trying hard to bury the memory of the nightmare twenty-year period it had experienced under Mussolini. No one wanted to remember the date of 10 June 1940 when Italy chose to go to war; nor 8 September 1943 when it shamefully and ambiguously sought an armistice; nor 29 April 1945 when fascism came to a dead end, with the body of the Duce hanging on public display in a piazza in Milan. It was better to focus on 25 April 1945 as the day when Italy was liberated, and make that a national holiday; and another would be 2 June 1946 marking the death of the monarchy and the birth of the republic. It was better, too, to view the end of the war as a triumph, even if on 10 February 1947 Italy would have to take its seat at the Paris peace conference as one of the defeated powers, required to pay the price for defeat. Felice was well aware of these contradictions, as he made plain while conversing with the ex-fascist on the train from Naples to Trieste, telling him that the Italian people, after twenty years of totalitarianism, would need to be taught democracy all over again. He added that the Allies had not brought democracy as a gift: it would have to be hard-earned.[1]

Italy was looking for a new way ahead, without having to make a full reckoning with its past. It managed to avoid going through what Germany did, with the Nuremberg trials giving justice to war criminals together with an Allied-supervised purging process of any remnants of Nazi ideology: in the Cold War climate, the Allies were concerned more that communism might prevail in Italy, and were willing to let it resolve its own problems. Italy did in fact carry out a purging process – *epurazione* – although it was a half-hearted one.[2] Very few former fascists actually went on trial. The overwhelming majority of judges and magistrates, those who would have been called upon to apply the purging, had signed up to fascism, and they themselves were never purged. A further difference with the German situation was that fascism was not outlawed, and indeed it continued to be tolerated and to play a part in Italian political life, although never with that name or program. Perhaps the country had, very recently, been simply too divided for a proper purging: in the north there had been a virtual civil war, with the communists emerging as the strongest among the partisans of the resistance, while nothing of the kind happened in the conservative and pro-monarchy south of the country. With the war over, the partisans who had never been part of the regular Italian army tended to be treated as common criminals: the solution, favoured by the political Left, was for a general amnesty for both political and ordinary crimes, including collaborating with the enemy. For the political Right, the focus was on the myth that fascism 'worked' and that public administration was efficient and the trains ran on time, overlooking entirely the repression, the death sentences and long terms of imprisonment for opponents of the regime on trivial grounds, and the racial laws. The consensus seemed to be to treat the two decades of fascism as a parenthesis, as a sick spell endured by an otherwise healthy body. The key thing now was for a return to the normal state of things, for continuity in affairs of the state.

In that summer of 1946 Stefania, after three years in Trieste, would gladly have continued living there. Felice on the other hand, fond as he was of the city, could not wait to get away yet again. He was still formally a civil servant, and he was determined that the family should move to Rome. He intended to pursue the ambition he had always had to be a diplomat. Before the war he did not have the proper language qualifications for entry into the foreign service, but during those years in the POW camp he had mastered English. He discovered that some of his former colleagues in the Ministry of Italian Africa, which was in the process of being wound up, were applying to transfer directly to the Ministry of Foreign Affairs. That idea did not appeal to him at all: he said he wanted to come in by the front door. That would mean applying to sit for a *concorso*, a public exam, to be admitted to the diplomatic career: all the details on how to apply were published in the official gazette. But first and foremost he would have to ready himself properly, and study hard. He knew already how competitive the process was.[3]

With Stefania and Daniela he travelled to the capital across a devastated country of damaged roads and thousands of bridges destroyed, with ports, hospitals and schools in ruins. The aftermath of the war was one of galloping inflation and unemployment, and the country was suffering from an acute shortage of housing. The Benuzzis found a place to live near the centre of Rome, in Via Tagliamento: it was a small flat and they had to share amenities with another family, of five, taking turns for the bathroom, queuing up in the morning. It was far from ideal but it was all they could afford. Felice studied, Stefania did secretarial work, and Daniela went to school near the Spanish Steps, a forty minute walk each day with her parents. They walked everywhere, having no car and saving money on public transport.[4]

Throughout 1947 Felice worked hard at home, but, picking up from where he left off the last time he lived in Rome, he also revealed himself as an author. In August the monthly review of CAI, the Italian Alpine Club, published an article of his with the title 'Mount Kenya.' The article's introduction gives the bare details of Dr. Benuzzi's time in Africa including how, 'as everyone will remember from the reports that were also carried in Italian newspapers,' he and other prisoners of war escaped and planted the Italian flag on the top of the mountain. His story of this adventure, the CAI review noted, would in the near future be published by the Eroica company.[5]

The article, a compressed version of the chapter in *Fuga Sul Kenya* describing previous successful and unsuccessful mountaineering attempts, focuses on the five routes to the Batian summit that had so far been tried. Felice pointed out that even the best English climbers had not sought to use pitons in their efforts on Mount Kenya: in his view, the use of the latest technical means would allow a safe and rapid climb, and this was important because there was only one hut as refuge on the mountain, only twelve hours of daylight were available, and visibility was always limited by constant mists and very frequent storms. Felice made a single reference to his own exploit, in a parenthesis explaining how he and Giovanni Balletto had unwittingly taken the same north-west approach to the summit of Batian as had the famous pair of Shipton and Tilman in 1930, only unlike those two who had done it in August, they had attacked it in winter, and failed.[6]

As an author, Felice's most notable accomplishment in 1947 was the publishing of *Fuga Sul Kenya* by Eroica in Milan, towards the end of the year. In December the magazine *Affrica* published an article of his entitled 'How we obtained Eritrea and Somalia.'[7] In the introduction he explained that he had seen a statement in a newspaper that Italy had seized by force from Abyssinia those two places that had been 'originally Ethiopian.' This was not at all the case. He said Eritrea had only in part belonged to Ethiopia, and it was the emperor who had invited Italy to occupy the other relevant part; Somalia, however, had never been under Ethiopian control. Italy had taken over these territories by classical colonial means through trade and diplomacy, and with the timely offer of protection. Felice's article would have displayed his intelligence and diligence to a potential future employer, possibly the Ministry of Foreign Affairs. In the same shrewd way, his CAI article on Mt

Kenya would have served to promote the publication of his book.

In November the Ministry of Foreign Affairs advertised that applicants were sought to fill twenty positions in the diplomatic service at the base grade level of *volontario* and that these would be filled on the basis of a public exam. Evidently many applicants, including Felice, responded to the advertisement and a process of initial screening took place to reduce the number of candidates. The archives of the Ministry show that in late November and early December various authorities were asked to provide confidential information on Felice Benuzzi, an applicant for a position in the foreign service, and to state whether they would or would not favour his being asked to sit for the exam. On 23 January 1948 Felice submitted a written request that he be permitted to do so.

The initial screening reflects the doubts and uncertainties of public officials who, after two decades of leaden fascist bureaucracy, had to cope with this new era of accountability and transparency in the civil service. The first of four responses was from the Ministry of Italian Africa. In a single sentence it stated that Felice Benuzzi, an official of that agency, had not been the subject of any penal or disciplinary process, or political purging; moreover in the preceding five year period his performance had been rated 'very good.' This assessment was cancelled, with an overwritten 'outstanding.'[8]

The defascistisation purging process had begun back in 1943, almost as soon as the Allies landed in Sicily, and the *commissioni di epurazione* were quickly set up by decree. Official statistics for the previous year show that over 27 million people, sixty-one per cent of the population, were members of the fascist party or its subsidiary bodies. Thorough purging would have brought the state apparatus to the point of collapse: in the event only a limited number of officials, at the higher levels, were removed from their positions. Felice's father Nino, who worked for the legal department of the national railways, was asked to play a part in removing senior fascist elements from that organisation.[9] Felice himself similarly helped the British identify fascists at the Londiani POW camp in Kenya.[10]

Nino's younger brother Valerio was the one member of the Benuzzi family who committed himself openly to the fascist regime. As a young man he engaged in political activities, and was gaoled for his disloyalty by the Austrian authorities during the First World War. At the end of it he worked for Italian military intelligence, and subsequently as a journalist, with close ties to Mussolini's press office. In 1928 he was sent to Vienna, tasked with setting up an espionage network. Over the next ten years he distinguished himself as a fascist undercover operator and a recruiter of agents. During the Second World War he collaborated in Milan with OVRA, the Italian counterpart to the Gestapo, and with the German SS. After the 1943 armistice he was taken on again by the Mussolini puppet government at Salò. He was arrested at the end of the war and tried in 1947 in a special court in Rome set up to deal with collaborators, but his activities were judged not to have been criminal and he was released. He then disappeared from public view. Felice hardly ever spoke of him; Stefania who never met him said he was considered the black sheep of the family.[11]

The other reports received by the Foreign Ministry, by contrast with that provided by the Ministry of Italian Africa, all gave a great deal of detail on the life of Dr. Benuzzi. One of these was sent by the government's representative in Trieste: because that city was not then under Italian sovereignty and its status instead was as the capital of the independent Free Territory of Trieste, the Italian representative office had some of the characteristics of an embassy. Its report outlined Felice's period of residence in Trieste up to 1930, and his time in Rome after that, when he was assigned to the second regiment of grenadiers, and employed by the insurance company Sicuritas before being accepted by the Ministry of Italian Africa and sent on posting to Addis Ababa. It gave full details of Felice's immediate family in Trieste and their address, advising that 'the whole Benuzzi family is of Italian citizenship and sentiment, of good moral and political conduct, and although not property-owners lives comfortably.' Each member of the family was then listed, including Felice's brothers but not his uncle Valerio. His father, former head of the Commercial Traffic Department of the State Railways, was now in retirement after forty years of honourable service; Felice married a 'German citizen of Jewish race,' Stefania Marx, whose parents were Otto and Alice Gotthelft; the report assessed Stefania as of good morality and having come from an honourable and well-to-do family. It concluded that, on the basis of the foregoing and limiting itself to the period of residence in Trieste, its finding was that Felice should be permitted to sit for the exam.[12] The other two reports, from the Rome prefecture and the carabinieri in Rome, both provided details of the family; they emphasised that Felice was of impressive physical appearance, and came down in favour of his being admitted to the diplomatic career.[13]

On 23 January Felice submitted a formal application, in long-hand. Its stilted style may be due to the uncertainty that he along with everyone else felt as to proper procedure in the new environment:

> The undersigned Dr. Felice Benuzzi son of Giovanni, officer level IX of the Italian Ministry of Africa, living in Rome at Via Tagliamento 33, asks to be admitted to and participate in the special examination for twenty places as base grade entry to the diplomatic-consular career advertised in Gazette no. 270 on 24 November 1947, taking into account service rendered by the undersigned as a civil servant employed by the government in Harar as outlined below.

After further flowery official language about possessing the qualifications specified in Article 1 paras a. and b. of the above quoted gazette, as specified in attached copies submitted by the undersigned in response to the notice of the examination in September, Felice then listed the exact dates of his service in Africa. He ended this letter formally asking to be examined in English and German.

Together in the Ministry's files with Felice's letter is a personal information form with standard questions relating to the applicant's family situation and military and civil experience: here the answers have been filled in by hand, by Felice. To questions on religion Felice affirms for himself and his parents as well as for Stefania: Christian Catholic. For her parents his response is: Christian Lutheran. To the question requesting the name of the applicant's previous direct supervisor his response is Dr. Piero Franca, Director of Political Affairs; the next question asking for 'the name of the highest ranked colonial officer in the POW camp where most time was spent' is again answered Dr. Piero Franca.

Among the documents is a one-page 'Note on the period of service of First Secretary BENUZZI Felice' contributed by Dr. Franca, and dated Rome, 20 January 1948. It outlines Felice's political and administrative duties and activities in Ethiopia, first in Dire Dawa and then Addis Ababa. It concludes succinctly: 'He was captured in Addis Ababa as a civil servant on 29 April 1941 and interned as a prisoner of war in Kenya. He declared allegiance to the Badoglio Government. He was repatriated on 2 August 1946. His performance assessment was invariably Outstanding.'[14]

The results of the Foreign Ministry *concorso* for entry into the diplomatic service were published in the official gazette of the Italian Republic on 13 July 1948. The names of the successful candidates were listed in order of merit, together with the marks they had achieved in the exam. Felice was in twelfth place. He was not the only one with an extraordinary background overseas. In ninth place was Amedeo Guillet, whose name was no less famous on account of his exploits in Africa. In 1940, while Felice was a colonial servant in Ethiopia, Guillet was sent to Eritrea in command of a *gruppo bande*, the irregular squadrons that operated independently against the enemy. In January 1941, Guillet led his mounted troops, armed only with swords, pistols and grenades, in a frontal charge on a British armoured column: it was the last cavalry charge ever in Africa. Guillet was not captured when Italian forces were defeated in East Africa, reaching safety in Yemen before returning to Italy as a stowaway on one of the White Ships, a month after Stefania and Daniela. From 1948 on his diplomatic career would run in parallel with that of Felice.[15]

CHAPTER 13 NOTES

[1] *Point Lenana*, pp. 523-527.

[2] Di Gregorio, A. (2012), *Epurazioni e protezione della democrazia. Esperienze e modelli di «giustizia post-autoritaria,* Franco Angeli, pp. 74-76. An article in the *Corriere della Sera* of 2.1.2004 by Loreto Di Nucci neatly sums up the impossibility of an adequate purging: see http://archiviostorico.corriere.it/2004/gennaio/02/Epurazione_missione_impossibile_del_dopoguerra_co_9_040102068.shtml.

[3] This from an interview at Città della Pieve 12 October 2012.

[4] *Point Lenana*, p 402.

[5] *L'Eroica* was founded in La Spezia in 1911 as a quality magazine of art and literature by Ettore Cozzani, and in 1917 was transferred by him to Milan where he developed it into a noted publishing company.

[6] *Rivista mensile* CAI vol. LXVI, 1947, n. 8 pp. 437-440: *Il Monte Kenya*.

[7] *L'Affrica*: from Torino Biblioteca Nazionale: IV.12 dicembre 1947: *Da chi ebbimo l'Eritrea e la Somalia* di Felice Benuzzi p. 217.

[8] MFA archives: Document dated 20.11.1947 and signed 'Martino' under 'Il Direttore Generale'.

[9] From Stefania, May 2012.

[10] From Moray Graham in email of 26.10.12: his source was 'my cousin (Lt-Col ARG Wilson who was the adjutant in Abyssinia of a battalion of the Argyll and Sutherland Highlanders; stayed with us at Londiani once a year for three or four years, liked Felice and talked about him.'

[11] Canali op. cit. 143-144, 193-202, 207-210; Borgomaneri op. cit. footnote 308 on p. 185.

[12] MFA archives: TELESPRESSO N. 133150 From the Rappresentanza Italiana, Trieste to Ministero Affari Esteri D.G.P.A.G. Uff. 1° Roma, signed 'Guidotti'.

[13] MFA archives: Prefettura di Roma Divisione Gab. N. Di prot. 024547-A.1 Risposta a nota 21305/729 del 6.XII.1947. Signed illegibly under 'Il Prefetto'. MFA archives: LEGIONE TERRITORIALE DEI CARABINIERI DI ROMA GRUPPO INTERNO N. 220/165-1-947 di prot. RIS. Dated Roma li 20 gennaio 1948. Signed Aniello Pecorelli under IL TEN. COLONNELLO COMANDANTE DEL GRUPPO.

[14] Franca signs his name under Il Direttore di Governo di 2a Cl. già Direttore Superiore di Governo AA Politici del A.O.I. – indicating that he is currently in a senior position with the Ministry of Africa and was formerly at a higher level in the political affairs department of the government of Italian East Africa.

[15] GAZZETTA UFFICIALE DELLA REPUBBLICA ITALIANA N. 160 p 2524; O'Kelly op. cit. is the

biography of Amedeo Guillet. pp. 262-266: The White Ship on which he was repatriated was the *Giulio Cesare* which left Eritrea on 25.7.1943 (with the *Duilio*), a few weeks after the *Saturnia* and *Vulcania* with Stefania and Daniela. That was the final convoy.

14

PARIS

Normally anyone entering a diplomatic career should expect an initial period of training in political and economic relations and international law, followed by a stint at a desk in the foreign ministry and then the first posting to an overseas mission. The post war period however was not normal and many of the 1948 intake into the Italian foreign service, like Felice, were far from young. The Ministry of Foreign Affairs knew it made sense, in the case of new recruits who had had combat experience and perhaps been prisoners of war, to give them challenging assignments as soon as possible. A fortnight after the gazetting of the names of the successful applicants to the Foreign Ministry, Felice began work in the economic affairs department. He volunteered specifically to join its SET section: it had responsibility for matters relating to the peace treaty signed between Italy and the victorious powers of the Second World War.[1]

He would have understood the importance of what the SET did. The treaty negotiations in Paris had been difficult for Italy which had had to accept heavy economic and military penalties, in addition to the loss of all its colonial territories.[2] In the negotiations France had to all intents and purposes been accepted as an equal among the victors, while Yugoslavia's interests were amply looked after by the Soviet Union. Italy was required to cede territory to both France and Yugoslavia; to transfer a number of naval assets as reparations to the victorious powers including France and

Yugoslavia; and to pay monetary compensation for war damage – $125 million to Yugoslavia, $105 to Greece, $100 million to the USSR, $25 million to Ethiopia, and $5 million to Albania. In terms of foreign policy the Trieste question was of major concern to Italy, and of special interest to Felice: under the treaty the city and its surrounding areas were to be placed under the direct control of the United Nations Security Council, and their future would remain uncertain.

A note in the archives of the Ministry of Foreign Affairs dated 18 October 1948 and addressed to the personnel department asserts that consular attache Felice Benuzzi had provided 'intelligent collaboration' as a member of the SET.[3] This section acted as secretariat of a committee whose members were representatives of a range of ministries as well as of the Bank of Italy; its functions were to study carefully the economic and financial clauses of the treaty and provide advice to the government, and also to assist the Treasury as it sought to make appropriate budgetary provisions in response to the financial burdens being placed upon Italy.

The MFA note also states that Benuzzi had taken over duties as the Italian representative on the Commission for Italian-French Conciliation. There were many territorial, political, military, economic and social issues outstanding between the two countries that needed to be resolved. These included releasing prisoners of war and civilian detainees, matters relating to Italian workers in France and citizens still in Tunisia, questions of border delimitation in the area of the Alps, reparations and economic issues in general, and claims and demands made by France in terms of the army, navy and air force. High priority for the Italian government throughout was to remain on warm friendly terms with France, and build a good relationship for the future with its close neighbour. For its part France was also ready to resume normal relations, to put these difference as soon as possible into the past and look ahead to cooperation with Italy on matters relating to Europe, NATO and the Marshall Plan.

Felice had been anxious to start work as soon as possible in the Ministry. He had also wasted no time in taking advantage of his new employer's recreational facilities. The Foreign Ministry had a pleasant club on the banks of the Tiber, not far from the Flaminio sports complex where he used to swim before the war and where he had first met Stefania. In the heat of a Roman summer it made perfect sense for him to go along to the outdoor pool under towering umbrella pines. Here he made an acquaintance that would stand him in very good stead in his career.[4] Justo Giusti del Giardino was a big man and, in sharp contrast to Felice, an aristocrat. Nevertheless the two of them had a lot in common, and there was an age difference of only two years between them. Justo had been a diplomat in Greece at the time of the Italian Armistice in 1943; he had declared for the king and been immediately locked up by the Germans who were then occupying that country; he managed to escape from the prison train sending him to Germany while it passed through Austria, and once back in Italy joined the partisans. According to Stefania it was her husband's own war time escapades that prompted this senior official while at the Foreign Ministry pool to seek out the new diplomatic recruit.

The name of Giusti del Giardino may well have been already familiar to Felice. It was in the Villa Giusti in late 1918 that negotiations were held to end hostilities between Italy and Austria: the direct consequence of those negotiations was the demise of the Austro-Hungarian Empire.[5] The armistice that was signed allowed Italian troops to replace those of Austria in Trieste, and a week later the First World War formally ended. In 1945, with the Second World War also ending, the Giusti del Giardino family was again involved: Prime Minister De Gasperi sent Justo to Trieste to check on the situation there and specifically to see how well Italian forces were dealing with Tito's expansionist objectives in the city and surrounding area. Justo performed well and the Prime Minister asked that he be included in the Italian delegation to the peace talks the following year. Felice and Justo could have talked about anything from Trieste and irredentism to Italian East Africa (Justo had served in Djibouti) and sport. Most likely they talked about France, and of Felice's role on the conciliation commission. Within a month or two Justo would depart for his next assignment: he had just been named consul-general in Paris.

The Italian embassy in France also needed a deputy vice-consul, and it seems that the ambassador, Pietro Quaroni, wanted the Ministry to fill the vacant position with Amedeo Guillet. On 18 November 1948 the personnel department wrote to Quaroni advising him that they were not able to meet this request of his but that perhaps they would be able to send Felice Benuzzi instead – describing him as 'an outstanding new recruit from the 1948 *concorso*, with experience as a government officer in Africa.' Justo is likely to have been more pleased than surprised to be informed whom it was that Rome intended to send as a member of his staff.[6]

Felice and Stefania planned a visit to Trieste to see his parents before taking up their new posting in Paris. It was not a simple matter of catching a train there. The city was in an area that at this time was not actually part of Italy, and so the formal permission of the Allied Military Government was required for entry into the Free Territory of Trieste. In a note dated 20 December the Foreign Ministry asked the British Embassy in Rome for diplomatic visas to be issued to the Benuzzis who were travelling to Trieste 'for a holiday of about fifteen days.'[7] In mid-February Felice's SET office asked Personnel to delay his departure a little longer, given that his work with them had been 'exceptionally profitable' and to give them time to find a successor.[8] On 2 March another request, identical to the first, was made to the British Embassy for a two-week visit to Trieste by the Benuzzis.

Felice took up duties in Paris on 31 March, 1949, having arrived some weeks ahead of Stefania and Daniela. The city had suffered greater war damage than Rome, and suitable accommodation there was just as scarce. Once again they had difficulty finding an apartment, and ended up sharing with another family. But they were exhilarated to be in what Stefania called the hub of civilisation and were determined to make the most of it. With strong memories of being brought up in affluence in Berlin she took to the diplomatic life immediately, and evidently got on well with Ambassador Quaroni and his Russian wife. For his part Felice was delighted to discover the rock-climbing school in the forested area of Fontainebleau seventy kilometres from Paris, whose boulders had played a key part in the history of the sport. In his memoirs thirty years later he recalled this with an exclamation mark: How many wonderful Sundays did I spend at Fontainebleau![9]

The consular position that he had been appointed to was actually in Lille, but the embassy – most probably in the form of consul-general Giusti – insisted on his staying in the capital. Every month Felice would go to Lille and look after the consular needs of the many Italians who worked in the coal mines in that area and just across the border in Belgium.[10] In June he was promoted from second to first vice-consul.

Another Foreign Ministry colleague who joined Giusti's consular team in Paris that year also had a colourful background. Edgardo Sogno was an aristocrat like his boss, and five years younger than Felice. He had joined the army in 1933, and fought in Spain during the civil war on the fascist side. In 1938 he passed the Foreign Ministry exam but only took up the placement in 1940. On military duties in France in 1942 he was arrested for asserting that now the Americans were on the Allied side they would win the war; he was subsequently released and relieved of his duties. With the Armistice in 1943 Sogno declared for the king; he then joined the partisans in northern Italy, often working closely with British special forces. He was arrested by the Germans and was in a holding camp in Bolzano when the war ended. In 1946 he founded and edited a daily newspaper in Milan, was elected to the *Consulta Nazionale* established to reinforce political representation, and resumed his career in the foreign service. Later, during the chaotic 1970s in Italy, he became deeply involved in far right-wing politics. Sogno and his wife became friends of the Benuzzis in Paris and Stefania recalled a New Year's Eve that they spent together when Felice at the decisive moment, either through his typical quirkiness or else 'because his mind was in the mountains,' wished them all 'Good night!'[11]

In June 1950 consul-general Giusti reported to Rome that after lengthy negotiations with the French Ministry of Justice the embassy had finally been granted access to Italians held in the high security prison at Clairvaux. Giusti said that 'given the importance of this visit' he wished to have authorisation to send vice-consul Benuzzi to check on the incarcerated Italians: the cost of his travel was not expected to exceed 10,000 francs.[12] Doubtless Felice with his keen interest in history derived benefit from the visit. The prison had once been a Cistercian abbey founded by St Bernard of Clairvaux in 1115. Years later Felice would visit other monasteries in France including those at Cluny and Mont St Michel in Normandy, and write articles on them for a Trieste newspaper; after the French Revolution, Mont St Michel, like Clairvaux, was converted into a prison, and remained so for seventy years.

At the end of the year Felice had word that his posting in Paris would come to an early end. Giusti had come back from Rome where evidently he had discussed the career options of this member of his staff. Increasing numbers of Italian migrants were now destined for Australia and the Ministry intended setting up a new consulate there: it had in mind nominating Felice for the position which would be in Brisbane. In January, having just heard that he was likely soon to lose a member of staff who had not been in Paris very long, Ambassador Quaroni wrote to MFA Secretary-General Zoppi, reminding him that Benuzzi had not served even two years and might therefore be required to pay back some of the establishment costs. Quaroni said he would not contest the posting of Benuzzi, but asked that it be at least delayed so as not to 'personally inconvenience an officer who has worked here very well.'[13]

Stefania was stunned to hear this bad news. When Felice rang her to say that the Ministry was proposing to send them to Brisbane she retorted that she had never heard of the place. The idea of a long sea journey to the other side of the world did not appeal to her at all. Nor was she happy to leave what she considered to be the most sophisticated city in the world for something much less than that. But, like Felice, she did not argue.

Felice would have already perceived that the advantages of going to Australia would outweigh those negative aspects so clear to Stefania. He had just turned forty, and was virtually at the bottom of the ladder of his new career. The position he was being offered, as consul, while not a promotion was nevertheless a step up in status, pay and responsibility. The area that would come under his jurisdiction was greater than that of Italy, France, Germany and Spain combined. The new consul would be a sort of pioneer in a country with which Italy was beginning to build a new collaborative relationship principally through emigration.

Australia, with only seven million inhabitants in a vast continent, had faced a threat of invasion from Japan during the recent world war and had emerged with widespread agreement that it must 'populate or perish.' Italy had an opposite problem, of too many people, in a country now impoverished. The two foreign ministers met in Rome in 1949 and discussed the matter, and on 29 March 1951 a bilateral migration agreement was signed in Canberra. Twelve days later Felice formally ended his posting in Paris.

Emigration to Australia commenced at once, and over the next decade almost 200,000 Italians went there to live. All regions of Italy would contribute to this exodus, though no area more dramatically so than the Venezia Giulia region where Trieste was: some ten per cent of the city's population would in this brief period shift to Australia. Most left after 1954, when the Allied military government wound up. Subsequently many of those who had worked for that administration, or who were ethnically Slovene or Croat, or who only half-heartedly supported the Italian character of Trieste or who had favoured its independence, felt they had to leave the city, for fear of losing their jobs or of being transferred to the south of Italy. In an atmosphere of conflict and uncertainty, many preferred the option of Australia.

The symbol of the extraordinary new emigration of Italians was a state-of-the-art ocean liner called *Australia* built in the San Marco shipyards of Trieste, launched in 1950, and about to make its maiden voyage. The *Australia* was of elegant design with a beautiful curved bow, and of conspicuous high performance and stability; the sophisticated technology on board was matched with all the latest comforts of an ocean liner, from air conditioning to comfortable accommodation, restaurants, swimming pool and games rooms. On board would be the Benuzzi family.

In early April Felice unexpectedly received official advice from the Foreign Ministry's Personnel department that he had been appointed government commissioner on board the *Australia* which was scheduled to depart from Genoa on the 19th of the month.[14] He was requested to present himself at the Inspectorate of Emigration in Genoa, one day before departure, to assist with legal matters and to be briefed on the responsibilities he would have during the voyage. At the end of it he would be required to make a full report to the said Inspectorate. His main responsibility was that of broad oversight of the nearly seven hundred passengers. As commissioner he was a person of importance on the ship, and had ready access to the captain. At one point during the journey he was able to take advantage of his temporary lofty status and use the ship's communications to speak with Kimber, his publisher in London, about the imminent release of *No Picnic on Mount Kenya*. Before he left his posting in Paris he had had the satisfaction of seeing the French version, a translation of his Italian original, published there by Arthaud as *Kenya ou la Fugue Africaine*.

As they moved out into the Mediterranean Felice's emotions must have quickened. Twenty-five years later in his memoirs he described his boyhood dream of how when he grew up he would go to sea as a naval officer: it was a career entirely in keeping with everything he had soaked up in the atmosphere of the port city of Trieste. At the age of fifteen he set off full of hope to Venice, for the medical examination he needed to pass for entry to the Naval Academy in Livorno: but he was rejected on health grounds:

> With that shattering disappointment I fell into a state of pain and gloom. The mirage of the life ahead of me had vanished. Even today I confess I can't step aboard the deck of our smallest naval corvette without chasing away vague nostalgic thoughts and suppress the pointless fantasies which like all of our wonderings about the past start off with 'what if?'[15]

From Genoa they headed towards Egypt, and transited the Suez Canal. For Felice it was the third or fourth time he had been through it. They sailed down the Red Sea, with views all too familiar to him on the starboard side of arid lands that ten years earlier were part of Italy's empire in Africa. They crossed the Indian Ocean to Colombo and spent a day ashore. On May 11 they made landfall at Fremantle. From this western side they sailed for a few days in rough seas below the Australian continent, stopping again in Adelaide and Melbourne, where many passengers disembarked. They continued on up the Pacific coast of Australia, and, after Sydney on 22 May, reached their final destination of Brisbane two days later.

It was utterly beyond Felice's experience, this coming to the continent that for him had always been the last page of his childhood atlas. 'What's Australia like?' one of the migrants had shouted down to a relative waiting for him on the wharves at Fremantle. 'It's beautiful, sunshine every day!' was the reply. By the time the ship reached Sydney, as night was falling, there were more specific concerns. 'Is there any work for us?' someone sang out to the crowd of Italians below. 'Do any of you want to work?' came back a laconic singsong from someone in the darkness. All Felice knew about the place was that the seasons were back to front, the swans were black, there were millions of sheep and some truly strange fauna, and the country was rich in minerals, world-class swimmers and tennis players.[16]

The apprehensions that Stefania had long held about this move to somewhere so far away and remote were powerfully reinforced by what happened when they docked in Brisbane. There was absolutely nobody there to meet them. They disembarked with all their belongings and stood on the wharf, looking about them. Stefania and Daniela sat on their luggage and while Felice went off to make some enquiries they felt more like some of the poor and bewildered migrants who had travelled with them than the diplomatic representatives of their country. Fortunately a local Italian resident came up and offered to take them to a hotel in the city. Their troubles were not yet over. To his horror Felice discovered that the Foreign Ministry in Rome had made a mistake and instead of providing him with Australian currency to help the family settle in they had sent Israeli pounds. It was not until he had made an urgent call to the consul-general in Sydney that these matters were properly sorted out.[17]

Things did improve a little after that. The captain had arranged for a reception to welcome the new consul to be held on board the ship that evening. Next morning the *Brisbane Courier-Mail* reported their arrival, under the headline 'Aust. migration news in Italy':

> Queensland's first post-war Italian Consul, Mr. Felix Benuzzi, said yesterday that migration to Australia was front-page news in Italy. Mr. Benuzzi, with his wife and daughter, arrived in Brisbane yesterday in the new Lloyd Triestino liner *Australia*, to begin a three-year term here. A 41-year-old former international swimming and skiing champion, he said one of his main jobs would be to help supervise the expanding migrant flow from Italy. Mr. Benuzzi will make his headquarters in Brisbane.

The *Townsville Daily Bulletin* also carried the story, asserting that an Italian consulate had been established in that city before the war. It added some additional detail:

> Nine years ago Mr. Benuzzi, then a Government official in Kenya, broke out of an Allied internment camp to climb the 17,000 foot

Mount Kenya, 'just for fun.' After he had climbed the mountain — one of the few men ever to do it— he reported back to the camp.

Among the guests at the captain's reception on the *Australia* was Queensland's Attorney-General and he had invited the Benuzzis to come to his home the following evening for a dinner that he and his wife would put on in their honour at their home. When Stefania and Felice arrived they were a little taken aback to see that it was an apartment, overlooking the Brisbane River. It was crowded, and more people were coming in behind them. Stefania wondered where everybody was going to sit and then she noticed a woman in a smart white blouse holding a tray laden with food, and realised that they were supposed to eat standing up. Soon after that a waiter came up with a tray of glasses and wine. She could see that it was going to take a little while to get used to such strange customs. But at least, she told herself, all these Australians that she had so far met had been polite and friendly.

CHAPTER 14 NOTES

[1] Reference to SET in Curti G. (2009) (ed), *Carlo Riccardo Monaco un giurista poliedrico al servizio della pace attraverso il diritto,* Milano: Giuffrè, p. 209. See http://www.edizionieuropee.it/data/html/10/zn29_01_004.html for its official establishment: D.Lgs.C.P.S. 11 settembre 1947, n. 1253 : Costituzione della Commissione consultiva per l'applicazione delle clausole economiche del Trattato di Pace.

[2] Costa Bona, E. (1995), *Dalla guerra alla pace: Italia-Francia: 1940-1947,* Franco Angeli Storia, pp. 37-38; Gilbert, M. & Nilsson, R.K. (2007), *Historical Dictionary of Modern Italy,* Scarecrow Press, p. 339.

[3] MFA archives 8.10.1948: 'APPUNTO PER LA DIREZIONE DEL PERSONALE — Ufficio 1° Ogg: Servizio prestato dall'Addetto Consolare BENUZZI Felice Segnalato a codesta Direzione Generale l'Addetto Consolare Felice BENUZZI, il quale, in attesa della nomina di Addetto, ha prestato volontariamente servizio presso il S.E.T. fin dal 1° agosto U.S., sia col sostituire il Segretario italiano presso la Commissione di Conciliazione italo-francese, in congedo, sia col prestare la sua intelligente collaborazione al lavoro normale del S.E.T.'

[4] From Stefania, 12.5.2012. For Justo Giusti del Giardino (1908-1991 see http://comitatodionara.altervista.org/contejusto.htm.

[5] Lowry, B. (1999), *Armistice 1918,* Kent State University Press, pp. 112-116.

[6] MFA archives: letter to Conte GIUSTI del GIARDINO Console Generale d'Italia PARIGI signed 'Caruso'.

[7] MFA archives: the two notes are from DG Personale Uff 1° and headed NOTA VERBALE.

[8] MFA archives: S.E.T note 45/02600 dated 14.2.1949 is addressed to LA DIREZIONE GENERALE DEL PERSONALE and acknowledges receipt of 'dispaccio n. 61/L1674/6'.

[9] *Più che sassi* p. 92.

[10] From Stefania, May 2012.

[11] *Point Lenana*, p. 404; Sogno (1915-2000) had a splendid name and title: Il conte Edgardo Pietro Andrea Sogno Rata del Vallino di Ponzone.

[12] MFA archives: Message dated 26.6.1950 from Il Console Generale.

[13] MFA archives: letter to Amb. Conte Vittorio Zoppi and signed 'Bibi'. Extract from email to author from Stefania on 21.11.2012: 'Justo Giusti was a great character, big and heavy, full of fun and ready for a joke. Felice said he considered himself lucky to have had Justo as his first boss in the career.'

[14] MFA archives: Note 9162 dated 3.4.1951 from 'Direzione Generale dell'Emigrazione Ufficio 4' to 'DG Personale Ufficio 1' referring to 'telespresso n. 61/63897/C' of 23.3.51.

[15] *Più che sassi* p. 34.

[16] Felice described arriving in Australia in *Più che sassi* p. 92.

[17] Stefania's vivid recollections of this period are in 'Stefania' – DVD interview produced by Personal Documentaries op. cit.

15

BRISBANE

Consul, Brisbane

Brisbane in 1951 was a staid and sprawling town. Its 450,000 residents lived in single-storey houses on either side of the meandering Brisbane River, some twenty kilometres inland from the Pacific coast. Trams and trolley buses trundled along its wide streets. The city lay at the edge of a vast hinterland, dry and sparsely populated cattle country. Its location, however, between Sydney and the top of the continent, had strategic advantages. Ten years earlier, after the bombing of Pearl Harbour, the US chose it as the headquarters of its Pacific operations and eighty thousand American troops then came to the city. Now the national economy was beginning to boom, a major immigration program was under way and further major change was imminent.

Italians had been coming to Australia in dribs and drabs since the beginning of white settlement, as missionaries, political refugees or gold diggers and fortune-seekers. In the late nineteenth century the first of many poor Italian farmers were brought in to replace the Pacific islander workforce in the sugar industry in north Queensland, as part of the 'White Australia' policy. Hundreds more arrived in Brisbane and headed north. Their numbers increased significantly after the First World War as the United States began imposing quotas on its own immigration. These were pioneers of a kind, who after years of toil themselves began to acquire property and take up leases of failed plantations. By 1925 half the sugar cane farms in areas around Ingham and Innisfail were owned by Italians; their presence had begun to make a notable economic and social impact in the tropical north of the state.[1]

There was, however, a downside to this story. Australia at the time was essentially British in origin and outlook, and its policy was one of assimilation, aiming for a society that was stable, homogenous and white. In the 1930s the trade union movement in particular was fiercely protectionist towards labour wages and conditions. Immigrants like the Italians who were ready to work hard and round the clock in areas like mining and the sugar industry were not automatically welcome, and the fear was that their reluctance to fit in with standard practices would harm labour conditions, bring down wages and perhaps even threaten social stability. In the depression that followed the Wall Street crash, there was a degree of discrimination against non-English speaking immigrants, on the grounds that they were failing to assimilate.

The broad acceptance for the need for migrants, and the goodwill towards them, suffered a setback following Italy's invasion of Abyssinia. The Australian press gave full coverage to the rise of fascism and Nazism in Europe, and some articles expressed the fear that the Italian community in Australia could become a fifth column. When Italy joined the war on Germany's side in June 1940 the immediate reaction in Australia was one of hostility and suspicion towards local Italian residents, even on the part of those who had been their friends. The government banned Italians from buying or leasing land or obtaining bank loans, and travel beyond the suburb they lived in required prior formal permission. A general roundup began of Italian citizens, men for the most part; altogether almost five thousand were arrested and interned in camps where living conditions were tough.[2] By 1940 a third of all Italian migrants in Australia were living in Queensland; in 1942 the state premier, fearing a Japanese invasion, sent a telegram to the prime minister demanding a 'complete internment of aliens' including all the Italian canegrowers in north Queensland.[3]

With the war over, things went back to normal, economic activity in Australia picked up and in Queensland the demand for canecutters soon grew. Italy was a ready source of labour, and almost at once a few hundred Italians were recruited. It did not take long however for old prejudices to resurface. Government documents showed initial caution on the basis of the low 'standard of integrity of the intending migrant.' The Returned Servicemen's League argued against recruiting Italians. Nevertheless there was a compelling logic between Australia's shortage of manpower and the surplus in Italy where farm workers made up a good half of the entire labour force. Once the Paris Treaty of 1947 had restored harmony between the former wartime enemies the way was open for negotiations between Australia and Italy. Talks began in 1949 and two years later an assisted migration agreement was signed which led to an increased flow of Italian workers. The six-month season in the canefields began in May, and in 1951 the need for canecutters was urgent.

Unfortunately the economic situation in Australia soon took a turn for the worse. The Korean War had brought about first an economic boom and then high inflation; soon there occurred an unexpected plummeting of the price of wool, vital for Australia.

The impact of the subsequent recession was severe in Queensland where the sugar industry immediately slumped. It was of course impossible to stop or reverse the flow of immigrants into the country. More and more workers with their families were arriving from Europe, and unemployment and social unrest was the inevitable consequence. This was the situation that the Benuzzis were to face in the first years of their posting to Brisbane.

Their first task was to find a suitable place to live, and Stefania took responsibility for this. She chose a 'queenslander,' a traditional wooden house raised from the ground so that in this tropical climate cooling air could pass underneath. It was in a leafy inner suburb, a short walk from the Eagle Farm race course that had been an American airfield during the war. Daniela was to be taught by nuns at Stuartholme, a catholic school which during the war had been transformed into an American hospital.

Like every Italian migrant family arriving in Australia, the Benuzzis found settling in to this strange and often forbidding environment quite difficult. To begin with they struggled with the Australian idiom. Occasionally they faced outright unpleasantness, like the offensive comment made by a man at the swimming pool, overhearing Felice and Stefania talking to each other: 'Can't speak English!' At school Daniela ran into intolerance, including when she used a spoon in a different way to other girls. She made friends, outside school, with a Protestant girl, and had no option but to keep that a secret from her classmates. The family had any number of reminders that while for Italians the war was relegated to the past, lots of Australians saw it as barely over.[4]

But in the social whirl of Brisbane the Benuzzis were a great success. Only a few weeks after their arrival the Brisbane *Courier Mail* reported a reception of theirs with a deal of enthusiasm:

> Spicy continental dishes were the attraction at the first At Home given by the Italian vice-consul, Mr. Felice Benuzzi, and Mrs. Benuzzi, in their Ascot home last night. Mr. and Mrs. Benuzzi arrived In Brisbane from Paris last month— and, aptly enough, their first party was in honour of the Italian maestro, Alceo

Galliera, who is here to conduct the Queensland Symphony Orchestra in a Jubilee concert to-morrow night. 'Strudl' was the name of the fascinating food made with apples. Dainty little biscuit concoctions were 'chifletti.' Others, described in English by Mr. Benuzzi, were strawberry crust and cream, and crab and egg sandwiches. And Italian wines were high up on the menu. Mrs. Benuzzi wore black silk and lace to receive 30 guests in a spacious dining-room, warmed by a blazing log fire.[5]

In October the *Courier Mail* wrote of the clothes worn by Stefania at the informal welcome home party given by Sir Raphael and Lady Cilento for their daughter Margaret: Cilento, whose father had migrated from Italy 96 years earlier, was Queensland's Director-General of Health and Medical Services. A photograph of Stefania appeared in the newspaper in December under a story about how the family would celebrate Christmas.

Felice meanwhile had found suitable premises for the consulate, in Queen Street in the city centre. It was in Heindorf House, an elegant building that during the war had housed the Allied Intelligence Bureau, a group whose mission was to gather 'information of the enemy in the South West Pacific Area... and to weaken the enemy by sabotage and destruction of morale.' As vice-consul he reported directly to the Italian consul-general in Sydney, and they both answered to the head of the Italian Legation there. His day to day responsibilities, looking after migration issues as well as the needs of the Italian community, dealing with trade matters and promoting Italy across the board, were demanding but they did give him a large measure of autonomy which he welcomed.

In September he made his first official visit to northern Queensland. In Cairns, 1500 kilometres north of Brisbane, the local newspaper reported him as saying his main job would be to assist Italian migrants who came out to settle, make their homes and eventually bring out their families to Australia. He warned, however, that there were constraints on the numbers Italy could send out, given its recovery efforts now under way under the Marshall Aid program, and its commitment to rearmament.

Travelling still further north, Felice had his first encounter with the sugar industry. At Mossman a large gathering of locals at a reception in his honour told him of their experiences with the newcomers, and listened to what he had to say. It would have been a strange experience for him, a man of great culture and several languages, fresh from Paris, finding himself in this remote and steamy place where on the one hand the citizens were down to earth, broad-minded and welcoming while on the other were also still unconvinced that Italians, losers in the recent war, were what North Queensland needed. Counsellor Rex of the local Shire regretted that there had been a recent dark period between Great Britain and Italy, but added that history often recorded mistakes, and he was sure that Italy would again be a firm friend of the British Empire. He paid tribute to the hard work of Italian migrants and said they were good citizens and good friends.[6]

The following month Felice went north again, this time with Stefania and Daniela and their car, aboard the liner *Roma*. The *Cairns Post* of 20 October gave full coverage to the arrival of this ship on her maiden voyage:

> *Roma* is the largest passenger liner ever to berth at Cairns... hundreds of people lined the Esplanade to watch her arrival. Hundreds more greeted the vessel from the Cairns wharf. New Australians, predominantly Italians, formed the majority of the welcoming throng on the wharf, and there were many excited reunions when the 18 Cairns-bound passengers disembarked. Last night, the floodlit vessel at No. 2 wharf attracted hundreds more sightseers. The liner will be open for public inspection today between 8.30 a.m. and 12.30 p.m.

The Benuzzis returned home by road, spending a couple of days in the Townsville area. Felice visited a Catholic mission, an immigration camp and cane farms run by Italian migrants. He was back again in Cairns in November, visiting more Italian communities and talking to local authorities about facilities for Italian migration and the prospects for increased trade. Back in Brisbane he dealt with the local response to disastrous floods that had caused damage and loss of life in the Po Valley.

***

Australia, geologically ancient, has mountain ranges rather than mountains and their peaks almost never rise above 2000 metres. Felice however could not help being smitten when he caught his first sight of the McPherson ranges in the far south of Queensland. The Benuzzis had been invited to stay at Coochin Coochin, a 120,000 acre property frequently visited by notables, including the Prince of Wales in 1920.[7] What struck Felice most was the sight of Mt Lindesay whose summit was a mass of rock rising sheer from thick bushland, and he had a great urge to climb it. The local catholic priest, Father Pieter Oudendijk, said he would be happy to come with him. Oudendijk had studied in Innsbruck and also climbed extensively in the ranges.

Some weeks later they set out with three others. The thick bush at the foot of Mt Lindesay was sodden from overnight rain. At the foot of the rock face they came to a gorge and were surprised to find there a pile of rocks and a metal plaque, indicating that in December 1928 Edwin Lyle Vidler had died in a fall and was buried at that spot. They pressed on up the gorge until, just above the height of the treetops, rain started falling and they were enveloped in mist. They reached a great smooth slab of rock and the sight of it amazed Felice: every crack and crevice sprouted tiny clusters of pale orange orchids. 'Don't touch them,' warned the priest, 'they're protected, this is a national park, we'd be in deep trouble if we got rid of any, to make better handholds.' The rockface was too wet and slippery and all they had with them was a threadbare rope, and no spikes. They abandoned the attempt.

Six months later Felice and Oudendijk tried again, this time with Stefania. Their guide was one of Queensland's best known climbers, Bert Salmon, who worked for the Department of Agriculture. When they got to Vidler's grave Felice asked Bert if he knew him. 'I buried him!' Bert replied. They used to climb together, but on Christmas Day his friend had gone out on his own. A day or two later Bert went looking for Vidler; it was his family who agreed this should be his last resting place, at the foot of the rockface with the orchids. With Bert's help Felice and Stefania had no trouble getting to the top of Mt Lindesay, where they found a small jungle of wattle and casuarina at the summit. The descent was easy enough, too, although at one point they did use a rope. They got back to their cars around sunset. The paintwork on the Benuzzi's fine new Fiat had been strangely scarred: a climbing party camped nearby said the damage was done by a cow which had seen its own reflexion and hacked at it with its horns, presumably not liking what it saw. Oudendijk's battered vehicle had not been so graced.[8]

Felice and Bert went a little later to the Glasshouse Mountains, an hour's drive north of Brisbane. These were cores of extinct volcanoes, none higher than 600 metres, rising weirdly from the plain, with equally weird names, like Beerburrum, Tibrogargan, Miketeebumulgrai and Tibberoowuccum. Some of them posed modest challenges to the rock-climber. Felice was curious to know why a spot they reached was called Salmon's Leap. Twenty years ago he had put a plank from the ledge across that gap, Bert explained, to help a fat girl in his group get over. Someone else, who hadn't sought his permission, had given it that name.

In February 1952 *No Picnic on Mount Kenya* was published in London. Felice told his family back in Trieste about it in a letter dated the 24th:

> Kimber has now brought out the English version. Six years after I finished writing it! Anyway he tells me that Shipton spoke at the launch, just one day before departing for Switzerland to make arrangements for the Everest 1952 expedition (which apparently will be Anglo-Swiss, and take the south route up). Kimber says that everything was ready to go when news broke of the death of the king, and he just couldn't put it off. So the book saw light of day at the very moment that crowds in London were off to see the royal body lying in state, meaning that the press had other business to see to. Still the Times and the Daily Mail did mention it. I'm enclosing the cutting from the Times (the DM only had a couple of lines) and ask you to send it me back. It does show good understanding of our effort, only it

doesn't like the style of the book (I blame Kimber more than me for that, he should have checked the English more carefully). Anyway a quarter of a column in the most famous paper in the world ought to be some satisfaction; and actually there has been an immediate follow-up to it.

In Brisbane the *Courier Mail* reported the story, and the volume was duly launched at a bookshop in the city. Consul-general Ciraolo in Sydney made sure the Foreign Ministry in Rome knew about the achievement of their man in Brisbane, reporting on 12 August:

The likeable story and the masterly way in which Benuzzi has told it have found real favour here in Australia, with both readers and critics. Reviews have been excellent. The book's account of a moral reaction to lengthy imprisonment and its spirit of sportsmanship have been understood and widely appreciated. Clear confirmation of this fact has been the offer by the Australian Broadcasting Corporation to put on a radio play of more than one hour, with performances by ABC actors, which went out nationwide yesterday evening. In this country the memories are still vivid in the minds of our nationals of years of internment and they still suffer an inferiority complex as a consequence: for them this book and the positive response it has evoked constitute more than anything the best sort of public relations. In my view Benuzzi's book deserves to be brought – for the reasons just outlined – to the attention of the senior executive of the Ministry.[9]

In October Felice replied to a colleague in Rome who wanted a copy of the Italian version. He regretted he only had one with him; all he could suggest was that his colleague approach the publishers in Milan.

That same month the economic situation slumped and so did Australia's appetite for workers from Italy. Felice went north with the new consul-general, Nicola Simone, who made a public appeal for help in finding jobs for four hundred Italian agricultural workers now on their way to North Queensland. Simone told the *Cairns Post* that the downturn had not been foreseen by anybody, nor its consequence that large numbers of Italian migrants were now unemployed.[0] Felice went to Wacol migrant camp and met dozens of unhappy Italians although it was a government employment officer who bore the brunt of the complaints. The media reported Felice saying the unemployed migrants at Wacol and Colmslie camps were calm, but 'a little crestfallen' at being idle so long. He added that those who had demonstrated in Sydney the week before did so because they had been recruited in Italy for a two year contract with the Australian Government: their only request was that the government fulfil its part.[11]

Matters came to a head early in the new year in an incident that Stefania later described as the worst moment in her life in the foreign service. Mid-morning on 8 January a group of angry migrants tried to force their way into the consulate in Brisbane, and were only held back by firm police action. As the *Courier Mail* reported:

> Three hours later another crowd of about 50 Italians gathered outside the Consul's office and crowded around the Consul's wife as she entered her car. Mrs. Benuzzi drove away but was held up by traffic lights a hundred yards away. About 15 Italians had chased the car, and three then entered the back seat. Mrs. Benuzzi jumped out of the car and ran to a policeman. Police reserves, called by radio, rushed to the scene in several cars and ejected the Italians from Mrs. Benuzzi's car.

The police made no arrests, one police officer declaring that the men wanted to be arrested for publicity purposes. The matter had no immediate consequences, and Felice was able next month to take a break, in New Zealand. It was something he longed to do and had carefully planned. He would go by himself, having told Stefania that he could only do serious climbing on his own. She and Daniela spent this time instead in Tasmania.[12]

***

The mountaineering heroes of Felice's youth were Emilio Comici and Julius Kugy, and later on they were Shipton and Tindal. But he had special respect for Mattias Zurbriggen, a Swiss-Italian alpine guide who first conquered Aconcagua. Zurbriggen had climbed with Kugy and also with English mountaineer Edward FitzGerald whom he met in the Himalayas. FitzGerald wanted to make the first ascent of Mt Cook, the highest in New Zealand, but gave up the attempt when news came that a local team had beaten them to it. Zurbriggen thereupon climbed Mt Cook on his own, and then with FitzGerald made the first ascent of a series of peaks in the Southern Alps. Many years later Felice wrote Zurbriggen's biography; now he wanted to follow in his footsteps. This excursion was clearly of great importance to him because he devoted a good twenty percent of his memoirs to the two weeks he spent in New Zealand.[13]

Arriving in the capital Wellington he was immediately struck by its similarity to Trieste, both cities with their amphitheatre of bare hills above water, buffeted by winds. The first New Zealander he met, at the Tourist Bureau, had been among the Allied troops that captured Trieste eight years earlier, and remembered how gladly the defending Germans surrendered to them at the law courts, rather than to the advancing Yugoslav partisans. Felice took a ferry down to Christchurch, admired the monument at the point where Scott had set sail for Antarctica, and then boarded a bus that would take him to the other side of South Island. Snow-covered peaks rose all around and he asked his fellow passengers to name them: they all shrugged, and replied 'the Alps'. Maybe, Felice reflected, he would have got the same answer if he put that question to those on a bus between Venice and Udine.

Twelve hours later he reached the famed Hermitage Hotel, the stepping-off point for Mt Cook and its surrounding peaks. He went looking for the chief mountain guide, Mick Bowie, and was told that he had gone out that morning with Mr. Odell. 'Noel Odell?' Felice asked. He knew a lot about Odell of Mt Everest and Nanda Devi. Moreover he was familiar with the name of Geoffrey Winthrop Young, who, having had a leg amputated in the First World War, still climbed the Matterhorn: Young had left the Hermitage just the day before. Felice felt luck might not be on his side on this trip, missing these two famous people by so little.

Next morning, however, was the tenth anniversary of his coming down from Mt Kenya, and that could be a good omen. The sky was clear and the glaciers near the hotel were gleaming in the sunshine. He went for a walk and photographed Mt Sefton, which Zurbriggen had described as the most dangerous and most difficult of any he had ever climbed. At a mountain refuge Felice was introduced to Hap Ashurst, who agreed to take him up to the Haast hut on Mt Cook. The view from on the way up blew away the tiredness Felice felt. Over to his right a frozen stormy sea cascaded from the heights, and he felt shrunken and made minuscule by all this majesty. He thought: this is the magic of mountains. In the hut he met two other guides, Harry Ayres and Oscar Coberger, the latter warning him not to hang out on the line the wet jumper he had in mind to – because the kea would tear it to shreds. Felice had never heard of these destructive birds. He ignored the advice, but laid ambush with camera in hand. On cue a couple of the formidable but crafty parrots appeared: they had spotted him. Before turning in for the night he checked on the weather. It was now raining heavily.[14]

It rained uninterruptedly for thirty-six hours. Peering outside Felice was startled to see seagulls up here, but realised Mt Cook was practically on the coast. For long hours he played poker with the others, and talked about mountains. The three New Zealanders all knew Edmund Hillary, who a few months later would be the conqueror of Everest. In fact, Oscar whispered to Felice, it was Harry who introduced Hillary to mountaineering. Only on the afternoon of the following day did the weather improve. Harry had commitments back at the Hermitage so the other three agreed to take Felice up Mt Dixon, which apparently had only been climbed five times previously. They got up early and by 3.30 were trudging along in the dark towards the glacier. Felice climbed with determination and felt good, glad he was able to keep up with the others.

When they reached the base of the summit they stopped to affix their crampons. As they got higher a sudden gust ripped Felice's goggles off but luckily he grabbed them in reflex as they flew away. After a strenuous six hour climb they made it to the top. The view was spectacular and Felice spent some time taking photographs. He took the lead as they began the descent. But even though he was as careful as could be, at a certain point he lost his footing, his flailing ice-axe missed on the bare surface and he was only saved by the rope. For a few seconds he dangled like a sausage before managing to whack in his ice-axe. He hauled himself bit by bit puffing and blowing to where the others were watching him, half anxious, half joking. After that he took his place in the middle of the line. He was furious with himself; because of him they had lost time. Thick mist set in as they carried on down.

That evening Hap invited him to dinner and he met his wife Junee, one of New Zealand's top women climbers. Next day they would try again, somewhere else, if the weather permitted. Hap would lend him some better crampons, and he might perhaps redeem himself for his little fiasco on Mt Dixon. But it was not to be: the barometer plunged and heavy showers were forecast. Felice went off on his own when the weather cleared, with a light rucksack and a heavy heart. In under three hours he reached a hut from where he could see Mt Cook soaring, surrounded by clouds: it was one more unachieved goal, and in fact he not been able even to make an attempt, only marvel at it. He returned to Australia next day, concluding this episode in his diary: 'Farewell alps of New Zealand, the *Ultima Thule* of my restless existence.'

A few months later Felice went on official business to New Caledonia and the New Hebrides, in the South Pacific, to check on the conditions of Italians who had gone there looking for work. His subsequent detailed report was passed on by the Foreign Ministry to Ferdinando Storchi, a former trade unionist, parliamentarian and then head of the Christian Association of Italian Workers. Storchi a few years later would be deputy foreign minister with responsibility for migration. He was much impressed, and wrote a letter of appreciation, adding a special tribute to vice-consul Benuzzi who diligently and with real sympathy 'had looked after and defended our brothers from hateful exploitation and restored to them a dignity that might otherwise have been forfeited for ever.' This letter arrived on the desk of Felice's mentor and friend Justo Giusti del Giardino, now Director General of Emigration in the Foreign Ministry. Giusti sent a telegram congratulating Felice on behalf of the Ministry for his comprehensive account of how Italian workers were faring in those islands and thanking him for taking effective action on the spot to improve their conditions.[15]

It was Bert Salmon's recommendation that Felice get in touch with the climbing club of the University of Queensland.[16] There he found a keen group, including Jon Stephenson who seven years later became the first Australian to reach the South Pole, together with John Comino, Geoff Goadby, Alan Frost and Peter Barnes. Felice went climbing with them several times, once again in the Macpherson ranges. He fondly recalled his last climb with them, up Mount Barney which was the highest in the ranges:

> From the summit in silent contemplation we took in the glorious spectacle of the sunset, whose colours, of a triumphal purity, were clear as though cut with a knife... For a while coming down we climbed and at one point had to make use of a doubled rope. Then, being near the tropics, we were swiftly overtaken by darkness, so that when it came to my turn night had properly fallen. I had to wait until Australia to make a double-rope descent in the pitch black!
>
> At the bottom of the rock wall Peter was waiting for us and together we lit a fine fire. Soon hot water was boiling in the billy, for tea. After the meal we were witnesses to the rising of a gigantic, placid full moon which lessened the ghostliness of the blankets of mist spreading over the valleys. To our amazement Peter took leave of us. He said he had promised to be back in Brisbane by midnight. With the help of the moon he would have no trouble getting down because he knew Barney like the back of his hand. I tried to talk him out of it but the others wouldn't back me up. In fact, as we found out later, he reached Hardgrave's farm in under three hours, got on his motorbike there and was back in Brisbane soon after midnight.

Peter Barnes was the only one of this group with whom Felice later stayed in touch. Sixty years later he remembered Felice as a 'devoted and loving family man. Well educated and versed in the arts with wide and divergent interests. A quiet, unassuming gentleman, polite and considerate. One who enjoyed the company of much younger people, if they also appreciated the finer things of life and the natural beauty of the world in which we live.'[17]

For the rest of 1953 the life of the Italian vice-consul in Brisbane proceeded tranquilly. Italy's Ambassador to Australia, Silvio Daneo, came to Brisbane with his wife, aboard the *Surriento*; with the Benuzzis they flew north and in Atherton were welcomed at a civic reception. Chairman of the Atherton Shire, Councillor Turner, said that the Italians there had been honest and hard-working, and Australia had nothing to fear from their assimilation into the general population. It did sometimes happen that settlers banded together but it was not always the case, and he told Daneo of one local Italian family where all seven children had married Australians. Daneo told an interviewer that he appreciated the warm welcome, adding that Australians and Italians were 'all Christians and all keen to work for a better way of life.'[18]

The sizeable Italian migration to Queensland inevitably caused controversies. In November Felice pointed out that the newcomers would help develop 'large tracts of land' in the state. The president of the Queensland Returned Servicemen's League came out publicly against 'colonies' being set up by some migrant countries that would hamper assimilation. The Italian Government had no wish to see 'Little Italys,' Felice declared in a swift rebuttal, it was merely considering financial help to families wishing to settle on the land. In 1954 he pointed out that it was an Australian priority for more people to come to settle as immigrants. Italy, many times smaller than Queensland, had 47 million people, whereas Queensland had fewer than one and a quarter million inhabitants; the Italians who came were prepared to work hard; of the nearly 13,000 who had come, three quarters had settled on the land. He was quoted as saying how proud he was that Italians had done more than their fair share in the development of the state's primary industries.[19]

The recognition that vice-consul Benuzzi had been performing exceptionally well began to accumulate. He had always had the support of his immediate superior, consul-general Simone in Sydney. As his posting came to an end Simone wrote to Felice saying that he wished to thank him for his collaboration and to put on record how 'you have carried out your duties in a brilliant fashion, under exceptionally difficult circumstances.' This support and appreciation would continue under Simone's successor, Ferruccio Stefenelli.[20]

Felice's posting own posting was set to terminate in 1954, and the eulogies he had been receiving could have done his career no harm as the Ministry considered where to send him next. Turkey was their first choice, with a promotion. A personal communication to the ambassador there in August advised him the plan was to send 'Benuzzi, now in Brisbane – someone who is serious, not in his first youth but who has qualities of intelligence and dedication to duty that have always put him in the best light.' For some reason the plan fell through. Ambassador Daneo advised Rome that Benuzzi had been most depressed to learn he was to miss out on Ankara. Daneo said he deserved proper consideration: he had performed with distinction in Brisbane under trying circumstances. He was also the oldest of all those at his current rank. After more than three hard years in Queensland he should be sent to a diplomatic posting in a milder climate, and soon. Given the added factor of the health of his wife, he should not be asked to have a fourth summer in the tropics.[21]

Instead they posted the Benuzzis to Pakistan. For the rest of the year Felice performed his regular functions. In late August he went to the farthest north, to Thursday Island between the tip of Queensland and Papua New Guinea. In October Daneo congratulated him on the reports he had made about conditions in North Queensland and the possibilities for increased Italian migration to those areas.[22]

On 4 November 1954 the *Townsville Daily Bulletin* reported that it had been 'a non-stop round of farewell gaieties for the Felice Benuzzis, who are widely known in Queensland. They leave this week on their return to Italy on leave and then they will return to take up duty at Karachi. During their sojourn in Queensland they have made many friends right throughout the state.' A photograph showed Stefania arriving at a party during the week 'wearing a very stylish ebony gown with a colourful cummerbund.' The article explained what a cummerbund was, and how it was in fashion, and could be worn with both dark and light frocks.

Felice looking back years later referred to Australia as a country of vast expanses where you never seemed to arrive, where distance was an aspect of every part of life. The mountains there were modest and the landscape in which they lay was sometimes irksome: but they, too, emanated joy and serenity to whoever came to them with an open heart.[23]

CHAPTER 15 NOTES

[1] Jupp, J. (2001), *The Australian People: An Encyclopedia of the Nation, Its People and Their Origins,* Cambridge University Press, especially pp. 489-499.

[2] See Fischer, G. (1989), *Enemy Aliens: Internment and the Homefront Experience in Australia 1914-1920,* St. Lucia and O'Brien, I.M. (2006), *Internments in Australia during World War Two, The Great Mistakes of Australian History*, UNSW Press.

[3] Laurie, R., Stevens, B. & Weller, P. (2001), *The Engine Room of Government: The Queensland Premier's Department 1859-2001,* University of Queensland Press, p. 106.

[4] May 2012 interview with Stefania and Daniela, who said: 'I bore the brunt of it at school, because I learned what prejudice is at age eleven.'

[5] *Courier Mail* articles in the first months of the Benuzzis' posting included 6.7.1951 *Continental dishes at consul's party*; 31.7.1951 *Screening of Italian films*; 20.9.1951 *And in Brisbane yesterday*; 19.10.1951 *Not an early night*.

[6] *Cairns Post* 10.9.1951: *Italian consul welcome at Mossman*.

[7] Shawcross, W. (2012), *Counting One's Blessings,* Macmillan, p. iii. The Queen Mother told Princess Margaret in a letter of 22.2.1958 that she had been 'staying on a station called Coochin with three glorious maiden ladies called the Miss Bells.'

Also Fullerton, S. (2009), *Brief Encounters: Literary Travellers in Australia 1836-1939,* Picador Australia, p. 284.

[8] See *Più che sassi* pp. 93-99 for the climbing with Oudendijk and Salmon.

[9] MFA archives: Felice Benuzzi file 'Encomi' – 12.8.1952 Consolato Generale SYDNEY telespresso al Ministero degli Affari Esteri, Roma 'Libro del dr. Felice Benuzzi: No Picnic on Mount Kenya'. Also Felice's regretful letter of 30.10.1952 to Sg Salvatore BUCCA, Direzione Generale Personale.

[10] *Cairns Post* 29.9.1952: *Italian consul's appeal to northern farmers*; *Townsville Daily Bulletin* 8.10.1952: *An appeal to absorb Italians.*

[11] *The Courier-Mail* 28.10.1952: All they ask for is work.

[12] From Stefania, 12 May 2012.

[13] *Più che sassi* pp. 113-137: *Gabbiani sui rifugi.* In 1972 Felice had published essentially the same material in *Alpi Giulie*: *Sulle Alpi Neozelandesi*

[14] For these guides see Dennis, A. & Potton, C. (1984), *The alpine world of Mount Cook, National Park 1984* Dept. of Lands and Survey p. 75 and Mahoney, M. (1992), *Harry Ayres: Mountain Guide* Whitcoulls, pp. 48, 80. Felice in error refers to 'Hep' Ashurst in *Più che sassi.*

[15] MFA archives, Benuzzi files: Storchi letter 3 agosto 1953 Il Presidente PATRONATO A.C.L.I. per i Servizi Sociali dei Lavoratori, Roma N. 1819 a CONTE JUSTO GIUSTI DEL GIARDINO, DG dell'Emigrazione, MAE; Giusti letter dated 29.7.1953.

[16] See *Più che sassi* pp. 105-110 for the climbing with the Queensland university students.

[17] Correspondence (letters, telephone) Barnes-author in November-December 2012; Barnes made available copies of letters and cards from Felice then in Karachi.

[18] *Cairns Post* 27.7.1953: *Civic reception to Italian, ambassador.*

[19] *Cairns Post* 11.11.1953: *Colonies of migrants reply to State RSL president*; *Townsville Daily Bulletin* 19.10.1954: *Land hungry.*

[20] MFA archives, Benuzzi files: MFA message of 4.8.1954 to Ambassador Pietromarchi in Ankara; 4 settembre 1953 telegram N. 5802 from N.SIMONE Console Generale, Sydney to BRISBANE.

[21] MFA archives, Benuzzi files: message of 13.9.54 from Legazione d'Italia in Australia to Don Pasquale Prunas Capo Ufficio I.D.G.P. MAF commencing 'Caro Uccio' and signed Daneo.

[22] Stefania to author 12.5.2012: 'Felice was not the man who would say, This is wrong, I have a family, a daughter, I don't want to go. He accepted.' *The Courier-Mail* on 20.8.1954 reported from Thursday Island: 'Dr. Felice Benuzzi, Italian Vice-consul in Queensland, disembarked here from the outward-bound liner *Surriento* yesterday morning. He is on a tour of the State, and will leave by plane to-day for Mt. Isa.'; MFA archives, Benuzzi files: 7 ottobre 1954 Telespresso N. 2755 – from Daneo, Canberra to Vice Consolato d'Italia, BRISBANE.

23 *Più che sassi* p. 93 and p. 110.

16

KARACHI

Felice's posting to Pakistan was a strange interlude, although it was an important step in his diplomatic career. It only lasted fourteen months, and was at times stressful for the whole family partly because Felice did not get on well with the ambassador and partly because of Stefania's poor health. It is normal during a diplomatic career to have a posting in a country where security, health and climatic conditions are difficult; these are generally offset by higher pay and allowances, more spacious and comfortable accommodation than one might have at home, and servants. But the mission could well be in a country not high among one's own government's priorities, and for the ambassador it may not be easy to manage staffing and resource questions in a relatively remote location.

In September 1954 both consul-general Stefenelli in Sydney and ambassador Daneo alerted Rome to Dr Benuzzi's fervent desire to take some leave after leaving Australia before commencing in Pakistan. Daneo explained to Prunas, head of personnel in the Foreign Ministry, that Benuzzi had had an exhausting assignment of more than three years in a harsh climate during which he had not taken any leave at all; now for serious family reasons and his wife's deteriorating health it was necessary for him to get back to Italy. In his reply Prunas acknowledged that the climate in Karachi was not good, but he reminded Daneo that Benuzzi was being sent to a diplomatic post where he would have duties well above his present rank, which was what he wanted, and that it was essential that he sort things out with Ambassador D'Acunzo in Pakistan.[1]

Soon after this a message arrived on Prunas's desk from D'Acunzo, who had received from Benuzzi 'the ritual letter' about how happy he was to be coming to Karachi and offering his full and enthusiastic dedication to the task ahead. But, D'Acunzo complained, Benuzzi was saying he couldn't leave Brisbane before the end of October, nor get to Karachi from Italy before the beginning of February. These Lloyd ships, D'Acunzo added, were always late, meaning Benuzzi's arrival would be on February 11 at the earliest. It would be intolerable for him to have to wait another four months for a first secretary: Benuzzi's predecessor had already been gone for three months. D'Acunzo had urged Benuzzi to cancel his leave plans and get to Karachi as soon as possible: if he couldn't do that, the ambassador added, he would have to ask the Ministry to send another officer who was more readily available. A soothing reply from the Ministry said they, too, had been taken by surprise by Benuzzi's insistence on returning to Italy: however it had been an urgent matter, and now it had been agreed to, they would authorise his travelling to Pakistan by air instead of sea.[2]

The Benuzzis left Australia in November, and returned first to Rome. At a function to which they were invited Stefania found herself sitting next to the director general of personnel, who was amazed to learn she was Felice's wife: he said he had approved the Karachi posting believing Felice was single. He told her, 'Signora, if you have difficulties with life in Pakistan just let me know.' From Rome they went up to Trieste to stay with parents Nino and Berta, for some weeks over Christmas. Felice's brother Gianni was also there. Stefania, whose hair went down to her waist, had it cut short in preparation for the heat of Karachi. Felice flew on ahead, arriving on 4 January, and Stefania and Daniela followed by ship.[3]

As the largest city in Pakistan at independence in 1947, Karachi was made the capital of Pakistan; twenty years later the new city of Islamabad would become the capital. Not long before the Benuzzis arrived, Italy and Pakistan had upgraded their diplomatic relations from legations in Rome and Karachi to embassies. Felice, at his new posting, would be deputy to D'Acunzo, whose rank was that of minister. He was about to hand over to Alberto Calisse, who already had the rank of ambassador. In those few weeks Felice developed a good rapport with D'Acunzo, and inevitably would have talked to him about Italy's conquest of K2, the world's second highest mountain, six months before. Controversy surrounded the achievement. As soon as the expedition was over, the Pakistan press launched a campaign of protest against the treatment of one of the porters who had suffered severe frostbite; D'Acunzo carried out an investigation and mediated a solution. The ambassador's report was also brought into a second controversy about the role of the young Walter Bonatti in the final phase leading to the assault on the summit.[4]

The embassy and the house where the Benuzzis were to live shared the same compound in Clifton, a residential area that extended south to the sea. It was not far from Karachi High School, where Daniela, now aged 14, was to go. She described it as an international school with teachers from different parts of the British Empire, not all of them of the highest ability. For her it came as something of a shock after the catholic school in Brisbane run strictly by nuns: her classmates were of every religion, and tolerance was a guiding principle. Her boyfriend – to the extent that that term was valid at the time – was a Moslem of English and Pakistani parentage. For Stefania, having a daughter in this exotic environment who was becoming a beauty was an extra matter of concern.

None of the family liked the new ambassador. He resented Daniela's being the better tennis player. Once, when she and a junior member of Pakistan's Foreign Ministry won a doubles match against him and his partner, the ambassador hurled his racket in her direction but luckily it hit the tennis net on the way.

Felice had a difficult relationship with the ambassador, although his customary self-discipline helped him conceal the antipathy he felt for his boss.[5]

In August Felice wrote to Prunas in Rome, with whom he was clearly on friendly terms. He told him he would like to take up the offer Prunas had made when they met after his return from Brisbane, to let him know if ever the climate in Karachi was becoming too trying for Stefania. Felice had feared the worst then, and now his fears were being borne out. For eight months she had done her best but her health had begun deteriorating in an alarming manner. She was suffering constantly from stomach troubles, insomnia, vitamin deficiency and general weakness. Moreover her eyesight was seriously failing and this, according to the specialist, was as a result of problems with the optic nerve and associated muscles. The doctor had prescribed glasses and some other treatment but his recommendation was that she not stay longer in that climate. Felice said he could not afford to put her on a plane to Italy, and be separated from his family, and so was asking to be assigned somewhere better suited to his wife's health. He apologised for causing any upheaval, but it was only out of pure necessity. In the interests of the service he would readily wait for the arrival of the commercial attaché, whose posting had been announced. The Ministry was quick to respond. Head of personnel Ghigi send a telegram asking the ambassador whether he believed Mrs Benuzzi's state of health was serious, and flagging that it might be possible to get her out straightaway. Calisse replied that Benuzzi considered the situation did not require him to be transferred before the start of the next rainy season, in March.[6]

In the office Felice's work became a lot more enjoyable with the arrival in Pakistan of the noted orientalist and explorer Giuseppe Tucci: from 1929 to 1948 he had carried out eight scientific expeditions to Tibet and from 1950 to 1954 six to Nepal, and now was about to begin an archaeological campaign in the Swat Valley. On 5 December 1955 Felice wrote a long letter to his family in

Trieste describing his encounter with Tucci and the three days that he spent with him.[7]

Felice began with a visit to what he described as the fascinating little town of Peshawar on the threshold of Afghanistan; he toured the bazaar where the colours, faces, customs and smells brought back to him memories of Benghazi and Cairo. He persuaded the director of the museum to take him to a Buddhist monastery eighty kilometres away. There up a track rising 800 metres higher they reached a ridge from where below them in the rays of the setting sun lay the ruins of Takht-i-Bhai.

Tucci arrived that evening. He turned out to be one of the most interesting people Felice had ever met, 'whose conversation ranged with unmatched authority over any historical, religious, philosophical or political subject, from Pythagoras and Lao-Tse to Nehru, Croce and Lin Yutang.' Next morning as they climbed up to the city of Malakand nestling among high mountains Tucci spoke with terrific speed and density of associations, quoting texts and authors, finding Sanskrit or Persian references for the place-names, and telling stories about famous people he knew, like Tensing: it was Tucci who had taken the Sherpa on his first expedition and helped improve his rugged English.

When they reached the Swat Valley they abandoned their vehicles:

> But Tucci was not only carefully watching where to tread and where he was going. His unerring eye could spot a stone against a low wall surrounding a field on the back of which were marks of doorway beams (and bingo! – he knew its period and the style) or else could find among a thousand rocks in a riverbed a pottery fragment, and say to Facenna (the young archaeologist who was in the papers last year after discovering the prehistoric site at Tivoli) 'Look! And we'll have to dig over there, we ought to find over there the corner of a supporting wall' and just a few paces further on, among the roots of a bush, we do find the base of a wall with those characteristics ... Amazing stuff, just putting it down on paper.

The following morning they made a courtesy call on the Wali

of Swat, drinking green tea with him and discussing preliminaries for permission to begin digging next year. The rest of the day was spent examining some ruins on a mountainside; a shepherd showed them in a ditch a Buddha figure that Tucci was immediately able to place in terms of its age and school; in the middle of a field they came across a mound whose passages were used as a public lavatory but Tucci saw it as a ruined shrine which would be excavated next year. On the third day they ranged all over the Swat valley, with its rice-fields, castles, rows of poplars, ferry boats with leather bags, caravans of traders and shepherds on their way down to lower ground. They left it in the early afternoon and headed down a really rough road to Saidu where Felice took his leave of Tucci and returned to Peshawar.

From there, after phone calls to the Kashmir department in Rawalpindi, two days later he boarded a transport aeroplane laden with hospital blankets for Gilgit, up the Babusar Pass. He was the only passenger, wearing every item of clothing he had brought with him, and with an intoxicated feeling watched the sun rise above fabulous mountains in the distance on the Tibet border. His attention was mainly fixed on Nanga Parbat, crowned with a thick layer of cloud lit from below by the rising sun. Its beauty was frightening; then, as they drew nearer, terrifying. Two or three times, when the clouds parted, he caught sight of Rakaposhi soaring sharp and straight: that was the highest mountain peak he had ever seen.

At Gilgit he was guest of the Political Agent, a Pakistani major-general, a most cultivated gentleman, who took him by jeep up the Hunza Valley to Nomai. In the afternoon they watched a game of polo: the whole male population of the valley had turned out for it and barracked like mad. The following morning he departed. The plane was empty. Sitting opposite him were four Hunzas, wrapped in greatcoats with large embroidered sleeves and round berets. At take-off they all held hands. This was the first time they had ever been in an aeroplane:

Frightened eyes peered out from their creased and bearded faces. I dashed from one window to another to look out from both sides, and when we had flown up the pass and the peaks were right above us, and the clouds around Nanga Parbat and the sheer ice on its mighty north face were within arm's reach, through the rumble of the engines I heard a monotonous litany. I turned and drew closer to my travelling companions. *La-ilaha-il-Allah*: they were praying. I smiled at them and they smiled in return. Later, after being invited into the cockpit by the pilot to get a better view, I was gazing out at the wonders of Ladakh when I felt a tap on my shoulder and the whispered word 'Sahib.' I looked round and it was one of the four holding out to me in his brown and grubby palm a handful of Hunza apricots: exquisite. After we landed at Rawalpindi they huddled in their greatcoats in a corner of the airport with their simple belongings and kept looking at me, as if I was their last link to their homeland. Then a Pakistani came with a car and took them away. I have no idea what brought them down to the plains. Perhaps they had to appear in court. But they were people you could love.[8]

Felice in his letter then brought the family up to date with his possible movements. It was unlikely that he would hear about any shift from Karachi before the New Year when Foreign Minister Martino would be coming on an official visit. But he could very well be on the move soon afterwards: his friends in the Ministry had assured him that Stefania's problems with the climate would be taken into account, as would his wish to be posted somewhere that would enable Daniela to keep up her English studies. He doubted he would be sent to the United States or Canada because his rank was too junior for any position of responsibility, but he did not rule out Australia, and that idea had appeal because it would mean working with Daneo, and that was always a pleasure.

A week later he wrote to Peter Barnes, one of the students he used to go climbing with in Queensland the year before. Things have been awful at work, he told him: he had been slaving away for the past ten months, doing the job of four officers. Relief was at last in sight with the arrival of a second secretary and a commercial attaché, and the ambassador was now back after being away. He had however been able to get out of Karachi and into the mountains. It was too late in the year for any climbing but at least he had seen Nanga Parbat, Rakaposhi and some other great mountains. On his return he had got wind of Foreign Ministry plans for another posting for him, but they were shrouded in mystery. Meanwhile over Christmas he would be taking his wife and daughter to India, to Delhi, Agra, Benares and Jaipur, and he hoped things would become clearer when they got back.[9]

Indeed they did. On 26 January Felice informed Rome that he and the ambassador were eye to eye on the work to be done as a result of the just-concluded visit by the trade delegation, and that he had asked Daneo in Sydney if it would be all right for him to start there around the end of March. Felice asked authorisation to come back to Italy for two weeks, essentially to see his mother, who was recovering only slowly from serious injuries in a traffic accident three months earlier, before beginning another posting in Australia for the next few years.[10]

Shortly after that he wrote to his family, giving them the news that he had been chosen for the first secretary position with the Italian legation in Australia, and listing his consequent movements. He would depart from Karachi for Rome at the end of February, for ten days home leave; first he would have to call in at the Ministry; finally he would fly out to Sydney, stopping in Calcutta, Bangkok and Manila 'where the D'Acunzos are waiting with open arms.' While in Italy Stefania would look for a servant to take out to Australia, under some assisted-migration program; she and Daniela would go by sea, leaving Genoa on board the *Neptune* on 23 March.[11]

***

For Felice there were several advantages in his now being posted back to Australia, not least for Stefania's health and Daniela's education. He knew the people and he knew the environment; it was rare for the Ministry to send someone back to where they had been before, and this could mean they saw him as something of an expert on things Australian. There were financial advantages, with the chance of their being able to save enough to put a deposit on a decent house in Rome. He might be able to get to the Olympics in Melbourne. And Daniela would be able to play a lot of tennis. The main drawback was the distance: it was just not possible to get back to Italy for holidays.

Ambassador Daneo had told Felice that a few weeks before his arrival the Italian legation would move from Sydney to Canberra. There were parallels with the situation in Pakistan. Italy had begun by establishing legations in the largest city in each country. Australia had built a new city to serve as national capital; in 1967 the new city of Islamabad would become the capital of Pakistan. Shortly before Felice arrived in Karachi, diplomatic relations were raised to embassy level; the same change occurred for Italy and Australia, shortly before Felice's arrival.

In 1956 Canberra was no more than a country town of 40,000 inhabitants. When the Benuzzis left three years later it had grown to 44,000 and would go on growing rapidly as the Australian government relocated to Canberra from Sydney or Melbourne the head offices of more and more departments, or ministries. But for Felice and Stefania – who noted that the capital's telephone directory only had thirty pages – it was going to be a quiet assignment. They were happy with that. There was harmony in the office, and Felice's career was set to advance, at the rate of one promotion per year. Soon after arriving he was made second secretary but, as in Karachi, acted at the level of first secretary.

As a political officer at the embassy Felice no longer had responsibility for migration issues which had been at the forefront of his activities in Queernsland two years earlier. In any case by this time the Italian presence in Australia was quite normal and indeed had become a key element in Australia's social and political life. One of many immigrants who had settled in successfully was Enrico Taglietti, and he soon became a friend of the Benuzzis.[12] Taglietti had come to Sydney in 1955 to design a promotional display for an Italian art and trade exhibition at the city's leading department store, and his firm decided to set up business in Australia. Next year he came back with his wife Francesca and, invited by the Italian government to submit a design for the new embassy and ambassador's residence, they settled in Canberra. Enrico and Felice, thrown together in any case in the Italian community in the small town that was Canberra, found they had much in common: from 1938 to 1947 Taglietti had lived in Eritrea. Fifty years later Taglietti remembered Felice as a 'complete man – a warrior when he was young, and later an honest and honourable professional.'

Life for the Benuzzis in Canberra's informality was pleasant. They became good friends with British High Commissioner Lord Carrington, and his wife: he and Felice played golf together, despite the great gap between them in rank and social background.[13] Daniela meanwhile completed her schooling at the prestigious Canberra Girls Grammar School, and found a great deal about the wonderful possibilities for a teenager in Australia at this time.

For most of Felice's posting to Canberra his head of mission was Silvio Daneo, a man who consistently supported him. In January 1957 Daneo wrote to the head of personnel, Ghigi, reminding him how when they met in Rome during his recent home leave they had talked about Benuzzi, how he had entered the diplomatic career through no fault of his own at a mature age and how in Daneo's opinion he had reasonable aspirations for promotion. Now, in the latest round, he had been overlooked – in favour of others younger and of lower rank. Daneo hoped that in the next round his experience as first secretary in both Karachi and Canberra would be taken into account. Moreover, Daneo added tellingly, his present remoteness from Italy should not count against him: while the sacrifice of those toiling in the Ministry deserved due notice, so too did that of other officers working in conditions that not everyone envied. Perhaps by coincidence, ten days later another letter arrived on Ghigi's desk from Stefenelli, formerly Felice's boss in Sydney and now serving in Saigon. Stefenelli had heard how

Felice had been overlooked in the promotion round, and gave his opinion that this officer stood out from the rest in terms of his diligence, initiative and sense of responsibility, and deserved every encouragement.[14]

Felice had without doubt brilliantly marshalled high quality forces in his own support. In February Justo Giusti del Giardino also wrote to Ghigi. Justo imagined that the head of personnel's thoughts would be turning to the next round of promotions to grade 7. He wished to advise him that of all those officers currently at level 8 whom he had at different times overseen, the one who in his view absolutely was worthy of promotion was Felice Benuzzi, currently in Canberra. He believed it was altogether in the Ministry's interest to assess this officer appropriately and advance him towards greater responsibilities. Ghigi replied that he had taken good note of what Giusti was saying, and that it accorded with other advice he had been getting recently from colleagues. The final decision however would come via the collegiate processes of the Ministry. On 4 August 1957 Felice was promoted to the substantive rank of First Secretary. His local rank in Canberra was Counsellor.[15]

Then, to general surprise, Stefania again fell pregnant. In January 1958 she drove herself to the Canberra Community Hospital, with Daniela beside her. In the maternity ward she overheard two nurses say to each other, 'the poor thing, having a child at her age.' She had just turned 41. Silvia was born at the end of the month. Felice, absolutely thrilled, sent a telegram to Trieste: I WAS BORN AT 1620 LOCAL TIME PERFECT HEALTH GREY EYES MUM IS FINE SILVIA. In his follow-up letter he described the few days in hospital. The grass had just been mown under Silvia's window, sending up the strong fresh scent of alpine pasture. But too much noise and too much Australian food prompted her to accept at once the suggestion of her doctor that she go home. Felice remarked how amazing it was that someone so tiny should already have a personality, and it was very different from

Daniela's. He remembered how it was eighteen years earlier, when congratulatory messages came in including one from General Nasi, who was then leading Italian forces in British Somaliland.

On 6 February the embassy forwarded to the Foreign Ministry in Rome Silvia Benuzzi's birth certificate, requesting that a copy be sent to the authorities in Trieste so that the birth could be duly registered there. In December the Ministry sent a telegram to Canberra advising that counsellor Benuzzi was being recalled to duties back in Rome.

The Benuzzis left Australia in February 1959 on the *Castel Felice*, a passenger liner converted as an immigrant ship, making the regular run from England, returning to Southampton across the Pacific, via Auckland, Tahiti, the Panama Canal and Lisbon. Felice was in excellent humour when he wrote home, shortly after they had sailed out of Auckland, where they had been looked after for most of a day by Mr G. Anderton, recently New Zealand High Commissioner in Canberra, and his wife:

> Today is Friday once again, and the ship's calendar has made sure yesterday's second of February is not confused with today's by making this one 2 February (2). So we have an extra Friday in our lives and if anyone should tell us 'You're one Friday short' we'll be able to answer smartly: 'Wrong! In fact we have a spare one.' Ha ha ha. The crew are grumbling that they have to work an eight-day week, without any extra pay. Crafty lot, these shipowners![16]

Years later Felice described their approach to Tahiti before dawn, with Mt Orohena soaring more than two thousand metres above the sea and the smooth waters reflecting the brilliance of the stars. After a few hours they glided into the port of Papeete where he could see among the delicious fragrances and the turmoil of happy people, rickety taxis and market stalls a long building with lettering declaring 'Customs' and 'Territorial Assembly.' Bureaucracy had arrived even on this island paradise, where every aspect cried out that it was never too late to do nothing at all.[17]

CHAPTER 16 NOTES

[1] MFA archives, Benuzzi files: Stefenelli message dated 22.9.54; Daneo to Prunas 23.9.54: 'Caro Uccio, Mi riferisco al vostro telespresso urgente del 7 u.s. ed al telegramma di Stefanelli del 22 u.s. ...'; 27.9.54 Prunas to Dr Silvio Daneo, Ministro d'Italia, SYDNEY: 'Caro Ministro, rispondo alla tua lettera del 13 settembre...'

[2] MFA archives, Benuzzi files: 28.9.54 D'Acunzo – Legazione d'Italia Karachi – a Prunas: 'Caro Prunas...'; brief Prunas reply of 14.10.54; D'Acunzo again 25.10.54; final message to D'Acunzo from Maurizio Basso, deputy to Prunas, absent.

[3] From Stefania, 12 May 2012; also *Point Lenana*, p. 412.

[4] Bonatti, W. (2001), *The Mountains of My Life*, New York: Modern Library, pp. 318-320: Chapter 20 has the conclusions of the D'Acunzo report; Lacedelli, L. & Cenacchi, G. (2006), *K2: The Price of Conquest,* Mountaineers Books, p.116.

[5] From Daniela, 12 May 2012.

[6] MFA archives, Benuzzi files: 19.8.55 Benuzzi to Dott. Pasquale Prunas, Vice Direttore Generale del Personale; 9.9.55 Pellegrino Ghigi, Direttore Generale del Personale, MAF, to Ambassador to Pakistan, KARACHI, Alberto CALISSE; 22.9.55 Calisse to Ghigi.

[7] Giuseppe Tucci (1894-1984): eminent Italian orientalist, archaeologist and scholar of religions, considered one of the founders of Buddhist studies. Tucci was an extraordinary linguist, who had taught himself Hebrew, Chinese and Sanskrit before he was twenty. In 1933 he founded Italian Institute for the Middle and Far East (IsMEO, of which Felice became a member upon his retirement). In 1954 Ardito Desio, who led the 1954 expedition to K2, drew to Tucci's attention some Buddhistic high-reliefs of stone in the Swat Valley. It was to these that Felice accompanied Tucci as the first excavations began the following year.

Olivieri, L.M. (2009), *Swat: Storia d'una frontiera,* Roma: Islao, p. 23: 'Nel 1955, Tucci condusse una missione esplorativa insieme a Raoul Curiel, Advisor del nascente Department of Archaeology del Pakistan (bella figura di studioso e gentiluomo cosmopolita), Waliullah Khan, direttore del Northern Circle di quest'ultimo, e Felice Benuzzi, un altro gentiluomo d'altri tempi, grande diplomatico, l'autore di *Fuga sul Monte Kenya*, allora Primo Consigliere a Karachi (In 1955 Tucci carried out an exploratory mission with Raoul Curiel, advisor to Pakistan's embryonic Department of Archaeology, a handsome scholar and cosmopolitan gentleman, Waliullah Khan, the Department's Northern Affairs director, and Felice Benuzzi, another gentleman of a byegone era, a great diplomat, author of *No Picnic on Mount Kenya* and at the time First Counsellor in Karachi).'

[8] Felice reproduced this account almost verbatim in *Più che sassi* pp. 14-15.

[9] Letter dated 13.12.1955 sent from Ambasciata d'Italia 85 Clifton Karachi; Felice apologised for not replying before to Barnes's letter of 17 April.

[10] MFA archives, Benuzzi files: Felice letter of 26.1.1956 to Maurizio Basso-Amalat, Direzione Generale del Personale, beginning 'Caro Basso'.

[11] Letter dated 29.1.1956. He said he was just waiting for confirmation from his new head of mission (Daneo) so that he could sort out the costs of sea and air travel for a March arrival in Sydney.

[12] Charlton, K., Jones, B. & Favaro, P. (2007), *The Contribution of Enrico Taglietti to Canberra's Architecture,* Royal Australian Institute of Architects, ACT Chapter; Favaro, P. (2009), *Drawn to Canberra: The Architectural Language of Enrico Taglietti,* University of New South Wales.

[13] Peter Alexander Rupert Carington, 6th Baron Carrington b. 1919 was British Defence Secretary 1970-1974, Foreign Secretary 1979-1982 and NATO Secretary General 1984-1988.

[14] MFA archives, Benuzzi files: message of 7.1.1957 to Pellegrino Ghigi, DG Personale – 'Caro Ghino...'; message of 17.1.1957 from Saigon to Ghigi from ministro Stefenelli.

[15] MFA archives, Benuzzi files: message of 2.2.1957 Amb. Justo GIUSTI del GIARDINO, Caracas to Pellegrino Ghigi, DG Personale, 'Caro Ghino...'; telespresso of 7.11.57: 'Con provvedimento in data 4.8.57... Ella è stata promossa Primo Segretario di Legazione (With effect from 4.8.57 ... you are promoted First Secretary).'

[16] Written on Sitmar Line paper, this letter is headed T/n 'Castel Felice' and is dated 20 febbraio (bis) 1959, Oceano Pacifico. *Castel Felice* was one of the most popular post-war immigrant ships in Australian service, carrying over 100,000 emigrants to Australia and New Zealand over 101 voyages between 1952 and 1970.

[17] Article by Arrigo Risano in *Il Piccolo* of 21.4.1974: *E il settimo giorno creò Rio.*

17

ALTO ADIGE

In 1959, when Felice came back to Italy for the only posting he would ever have at home, the Foreign Ministry was in the process of transferring its head office from the sixteenth century Palazzo Chigi, alongside parliament in the centre of Rome: Palazzo Chigi later became the seat of government. The new Foreign Ministry building was located in an area between Monte Mario and the Tiber that was once owned by Pope Paul III of the Farnese family. This area had a fascist history. The Mussolini Forum, a vast sporting complex boasting an obelisk with his name engraved on it, was built there in the 1930s, and close by was the Palazzo Farnesina, intended as the headquarters of the Fascist Party. The complex has been renamed Foro Italico and it contains the Olympic stadium. Palazzo Farnesina is a white monolithic structure of fascist style and proportions, the second largest edifice in Italy after the royal palace at Caserta.

In an elegant residential quarter a few minutes' walk from the Ministry is the little street of Via Nepi, where Felice chose a spacious third-floor apartment for his permanent home in the capital. This leafy area is an oasis of tranquillity except during football matches in the nearby stadium. Also close, within a one-kilometre radius, is the Ministry's sporting club with swimming pool to the east, while to the south is the Milvio Bridge where in AD 312 the emperor Constantine won a great battle and as a result converted to Christianity.

One of the first things the Ministry did when welcoming Felice back was to recognise his bilingualism in German, and have him oversee any examinations that new and current officers had to undergo in that language.[1] It also assigned him to Office 10A, directed by Gian Lorenzo Betteloni which had responsibility for the Alto Adige question.[2] The cryptic '10A' name was perhaps given to the office because Italy saw the Alto Adige as an integral part of the country and so it might be best not to advertise that the issue was being handled by the Ministry of Foreign Affairs. Nevertheless the Farnesina was definitely best equipped to deal with the international ramifications of this complex matter. For Italy it was crucial to manage with great care relations with Austria, its permanent neighbour, especially on the issue of territories it once controlled where two thirds of the inhabitants spoke German. The peace treaty that followed the First World War had granted the region to Italy, hiving it off from the northern part of Tyrol; after two years of German occupation between 1943 and 1945 came the Paris Peace Treaty in which the victorious powers returned the region to Italy, at the same time inviting the two countries to negotiate a treaty that would provide for the interests of its German-speaking population. Most of that group believed that under the treaty they had won complete equality of rights with Italian-speakers, together with genuine autonomy – if not for the whole region then at least for the northernmost province of Bolzano. However many differences of interpretation of the Paris treaty in due course emerged.

For Italy it was an internal matter, and it encouraged the region to feel part of the nation with funds, programs and economic development. The situation changed in 1955 when Austria, no longer occupied by Allied forces, became a member of the United Nations and took the initiative on the South Tyrol/Alto Adige question. It sent a note to the Italian government requesting effective equality between the German and Italian languages, equal access to public employment and a limitation on the number of Italian immigrants into the region. It also proposed that a mixed committee of experts be set up to examine the situation and make recommendations for resolving its problems.

When Felice came on the scene the Alto Adige question was at an impasse. A campaign had begun of bombings of railway lines, building sites and monuments carried out by German-speaking extremists, acts of sabotage that were potentially a weapon of blackmail in Austria's armoury. For its part Italy had a trump card: Austria was keen to join the European Economic Community and Italy, as a founder member, was in a position to veto its application. In one sense Felice was the ideal officer to deal with the Alto Adige question in the Foreign Ministry: his family came from Trentino, that southern part of the region where Italian speakers were in a majority, and he himself spoke the two languages perfectly. In practice, however, it was not at all easy for him because with three Austrian grandparents he felt somewhat Austrian himself. 'On the other hand,' Stefania said many years later, 'he was highly disciplined, he knew his role as an Italian official and it was his job to defend certain policies even if he found that awkward, but he always did it loyally.'[3]

Felice made an excellent start in Office 10A. His report card for 1959, signed by Carlo Strano, Director-General of Political Affairs, was extremely positive. According to his report Dr Benuzzi that year worked on the Alto Adige question, as the 'most highly appreciated member of Minister Betteloni's staff,' where he followed assiduously all issues including the state of relations between Italy and Austria. Under all six headings of diligence, initiative, perspicacity, drafting ability, security and tact his rating was *Moltissimo*. Under the three headings of leadership, organisational skills and readiness to accept higher responsibility the rating was Conspicuous. He received unstinting praise for intellectual and linguistic skills (German, French and English all spoken 'extremely well'), and for the regard in which he was held in the office as well as beyond: *Moltissimo*. Under ethics and character he was adjudged as having a deep sense of duty and an exceptional commitment to his work. 'He is disciplined, reserved and loyal,' Strano wrote, concluding 'he is an officer of great professional capability and remarkable moral and intellectual intelligence. I value him a very great deal not least for the balance of his judgement.' The report went forward to the Ministry's evaluation board who gave him the topmost overall rating for the year: Outstanding. He was to achieve an outstanding rating for each of the next three years.[4]

Meanwhile, when not at the office, Felice was having a good time. That first winter he went with Stefania to the Val d'Aosta, somewhere they had never been before. In a letter to his parents he wrote: 'I'd never in my life seen the Matterhorn, although I had seen Nanga Parbat and Daulaghiri.' Giuàn Balletto on the other hand knew the region well: for the first time in many years the two friends were meeting up. Felice fetched Giuàn from Genoa station and took him to Cervinia. For two or three days they skied together; from high up they had fine views of Mt Blanc, the Jungfrau and the trio of Weisshorn-Zinalrothorn-Obergabelhorn. 'Stefi was too cold and so she took the cablecar down,' Felice wrote. 'Giuàn and I, together for the first time in proper mountains since Mt Kenya, headed down to Zermatt... Even now, a week later, I've got blisters on my lips and skin peeling from the dazzle off the snow on that brilliant day.' After that they went to Turin where in the National Mountain Museum they found references to their 1943 escapade that stirred them, but alas not the flag they had taken up and hoisted on Point Lenana. Next day, Felice wrote, they were back home; he went along to a Japanese reception and there met again Giuseppe Tucci, from his Pakistan days.[5]

In another letter dated 7 June 1960 Felice told Nino and Berta that at the end of the month he would be taking his family to Valtournenche, which had become their favourite resort in the Alps. There they would team up once more with Giuàn, with Bert Salmon from Queensland and with Don Soughan, an English mountaineer: 'Fun and games!' he added. Giuàn had sent him a postcard from Zagreb ('I haven't a clue what he went there for') and after Yugoslavia had passed through Trieste just when Felice was there, staying with them. He went on to tell them that Stefania's parents had come down from London and they had all seen the sound and light show at the Forum. On the Sunday they had gone to the beach where Silvia had burned her shoulders and overcome her fear of the 'waves' which were laughable after the Australian ones.

Towards the end of 1960 Austria took the South Tyrol/Alto Adige issue to the General Assembly of the United Nations in New York. Here it had a minor victory, securing the adoption of a resolution that urged the two countries to resume negotiations with a view to settling their different interpretations of the Paris agreement. In January Felice, his language skills increasingly appreciated, was a member of the Italian delegation under Foreign Minister Segni, at discussions in Vienna.[6]

Two months later he went first to Milan where he stayed with his brother Piero and then to Como, for work: he was to be the interpreter for Italian Prime Minister Fanfani in talks with German Chancellor Adenauer. Waiting for him at the hotel was Pietro Quaroni, a senior member of the Italian delegation and formerly Felice's ambassador when he was vice-consul in Paris. Felice reported to Trieste:

> We had a long chat and he told me 'when you're not there nobody understands anything.' He meant that at the Fanfani-Adenauer meeting in Varese last year there was only the German interpreter, and nobody took a record of their conversation. I was to make sure that didn't happen this time ... We waited for a while: Quaroni held court and Fanfani was in great form. Then came Adenauer in a black Mercedes 300, with motorcycle escort. He seemed calm and relaxed and at age 85 doesn't seem a day older than his 84 of last year. Handshakes and photographs. Then he went off for a private meeting with Segni and Fanfani, his interpreter who is a lively bespectacled young lady of about thirty with an astounding memory (no shorthand: she jots down the points in regular writing and doesn't forget a comma), and me. We were in a small room for

more than an hour, and the talk was about everything except Alto Adige (the press have been guessing from my being there that that subject would have come up). They even told jokes. At one point Adenauer said, 'It's a cruel world, the one we're living in.' Fanfani replied, 'Pope John XXIII had visitors recently who moaned that it's like we're in the Bible's valley of tears,' and the Pope said the Bible was right, 'but then he added 'actually we're having such a good cry!' Adenauer, much amused, laughed heartily. All I had to do was monitor the translator (and I did correct her, over a couple of minor details) and take notes. After that came the official meeting. You will have seen reports of it in the papers.[7]

Now that the matter had been raised to the international level the pace of discussions picked up, but at the same time the strain also increased at every level. Felice participated in talks in Klagenfurt between the two foreign ministers in late May, and again in Zurich in late June. However between these two meetings the Alto Adige region was subjected to a *Feuernacht* – a night of fire – when forty electricity pylons were blown up. Further attacks by local extremists followed in July, while the forces of law and order in Italy wasted no time in adopting harsh measures. Dialogue between Italy and Austria became deadlocked; Italy made formal protests over the terrorism but these were rejected by Austria, which had distanced itself from such violence; Italy introduced a requirement for visas for all Austrians wishing to visit Italy. In Rome Felice, for the family's protection, arranged for a secret telephone number at home.[8]

Italy could not make concessions to terrorism but nor did it wish to cut a poor figure at the United Nations. On 13 September an Italian diplomatic initiative led to the creation of a 'Committee of 19' made up of parliamentarians, experts, and administrative and economic representatives of the German-speaking population of Alto Adige tasked to study the region's problems and recommend ways to solve them. A few days later Felice arrived in New York where he would stay for two months with the Italian delegation to the UN General Assembly.

Felice's letters to his parents reported how well things were going at home. Stefania had been doing some translation work and had earned 'enough to pay the dress-maker.' Daniela now was employed by Alitalia and had been put in charge of other hostesses 'we imagine because her English is the best and she knows how to treat the passengers.' On 20 August he wrote that 'Dani is on night duty at the airport and Silvia is asleep. Stefi is reading the newspaper. The beast is washing the dishes. That sums up our situation here.' Giuàn Balletto was now in Rome having climbed the 4000 metre Pollux in the Pennine Alps 'on a cloudless day with people from Trentino he met in the refuge;' Giuàn's leave was now over and he would soon be heading back to his medical practice at Arusha, on the slopes of Mt Kilimanjaro. Felice ended saying Foreign Minister Segni was now back as were Director General of Political Affairs Fornari and his own boss Betteloni, and they were all hard at work. 'There's nothing else I have to tell you. So good night, hugs and kisses, Felice.'

He wrote his letters from New York longhand and Stefania first typed them up and then sent them on to Trieste. One of these, written at midnight on 22 November, reported a strenuous day's work in which Felice had helped draft his minister's speech to the UN. 'When Segni delivered it at 8.10 pm we circulated ninety cyclostyled copies of the English translation done in record time by a UN translator with my constant supervision. I had a sandwich in the office at 2pm and another at 8. An hour ago I went to a drugstore and had a steak.' Stefania added a comment in brackets: 'You can see he's getting thinner, and it suits him!' On 28 November Felice's letter began: 'Darling, it's all over! Hurray, really good... Anyway, I'm leaving on Saturday or Sunday for London – that is unless a speech has to be done for Martino, in response to one by Kreisky.' At the end of the letter Stefania added:

> Dear people, And that's my copying job done. Yesterday morning, Sunday, Dani was on duty as usual and I'd agreed with Gianni who is in town for him to call me around noon so we could go and eat somewhere. So when the phone rang at 11 and

it was a male voice speaking I assumed it was him calling a bit early so I answered 'Hello Gianni, what's up?' The answer: 'You don't know your own husband's voice?' I was flabbergasted, and I rang London straightaway to alert the two old folks who were waiting for Felice to call from his hotel…

Felice's performance evaluation for 1961 was Outstanding. He had organised and directed the office responsible for Alto Adige, and been on the Italian delegation at official talks with Austria in Klagenfurt and Zurich, and at the UN General Assembly. He had 'a deep sense of duty and attachment to the service' and he was 'collaborative but resolute.' In the section on the regard in which he was held by those outside the Ministry it was asserted that he had 'a great ability with contacts, and a notable power of persuasion in regard to foreign diplomats.' Summing up, Director General Fornari said Dr Benuzzi 'has an unlimited capacity for work and the constructive contribution he made to the work on Alto Adige was of the highest order and has been greatly appreciated by all senior officers with whom he has had dealings. A first class officer from every point of view, displaying exceptional performance and absolute reliability.'[9]

A junior officer in the Italian embassy in Vienna in 1961-62, Marco Vianello-Chiodo, recalled in his autobiography the brief dealings he had at the time with Felice, who worked in Office 10A. It was headed by Gian Lorenzo Betteloni whom they affectionately called 'Bibo': he was the only senior colleague who played volleyball with them at the Foreign Ministry sports club. Betteloni pretended to be grumpy, but was a very nice man. He died of cancer at a young age, and Vianello-Chiodo recalled how at his funeral at the church of Ponte Milvio the church was full and everyone was in tears. He remembered, too, how Felice Benuzzi, Betteloni's deputy, had been of tremendous help to him when he sat the Foreign Ministry entry exam: he was about to be rejected, but Benuzzi had been the examiner in German and had argued persuasively that the Ministry needed people who could speak the language well. Half a century later Vianello-Chiodo recalled Felice as 'a tall and handsome man, a very hard worker, kind, lively and with a good sense of humour. I was very fond of him.'[10]

On 9 August 1962 Felice was promoted to the substantive rank of counsellor. The Ministry of Foreign Affairs had found the right man to send as Italian consul-general in West Berlin.

CHAPTER 17 NOTES

[1] Felice's official career record was among his private papers, passed to the author by the family in May 2012: MINISTERO DEGLI AFFARI ESTERI – DIREZIONE GENERALE DEL PERSONALE E DELL'AMMINISTRAZIONE INTERNA – Matricola e Documentazione – STATO MATRICOLARE. It shows, under MISSIONI ED INCARICHI SPECIALI: 'Membro Agg. Comm. esaminatrice concorso dipl. cons. per la lingua tedesca 22.8.1959.' The same entry – indicating his temporary assignment to the examining committee in German language for applicants for the diplomatic service – is made for 1960 and 1961.

[2] For Betteloni and Office 10A see Curti G. (2009) (ed), Carlo Riccardo *Monaco un giurista poliedrico al servizio della pace attraverso il diritto, Milano:* Giuffrè, p. 96.

[3] *Point Lenana*, p. 415; Stefania to author 9.5.2013, on the Alto Adige question: 'It was hard for him to defend a hundred per cent the Italian point of view. And that put him very much *a disagio.*'

[4] MFA archives, Benuzzi files: RAPPORTO INFORMATIVO PER L'ANNO 1959 - BENUZZI Felice Diplomatico-Consolare Grado: Consigliere di Legazione. Strano dated his report 18.1.1960; the board signed off: 'Roma addì 14 ottobre 1960'.

[5] Letter dated 30.4.1960, on old letter paper with their Australian address cancelled: '65 Dominion Circuit, Canberra ACT'.

[6] For the complex Alto Adige, South Tyrol question see Toscano, M. (1975), *Alto Adige, South Tyrol: Italy's frontier with the German world,* Baltimore: Johns Hopkins University Press and Alcock, A.E. (1970), *The history of the South Tyrol question,* London: Michael Joseph: for these years of Felice's direct involvement see Rossi, M. (2011), *Tutela dei diritti umani e realpolitik. L'Italia delle Nazioni Unite (1955-1976),* CEDAM, pp. 162-175.

[7] Letter dated Roma, 26.3.1961.

[8] *Point Lenana*, p. 415.

[9] MFA archives, Benuzzi files: RAPPORTO INFORMATIVO PER L'ANNO 1961 BENUZZI Felice Diplomatico-Consolare Grado: Consigliere di Legazione; signed ROMA addi ' 16.1.1962 Ambasciatore G. Fornari Direttore Generale degli Affari Politici.

[10] Vianello-Chiodo, M. (2012), *Under-Soldier,* AuthorHouse.

Mt Barney 1954

18

BERLIN

It was not surprising that the Italian Foreign Ministry, fully aware of Felice's good work on the Alto Adige question and his effectiveness in the language, should consider him for a posting to Germany. That country still after seventeen years remained split in two under arrangements made by the victors of the Second World War. The Italian embassy was in the small town of Bonn, while the old capital of Berlin, also divided, was in an enclave in the communist East. A posting to the consulate in Berlin was not one avidly sought by Italian diplomats, because all knew of the claustrophobic atmosphere and the many constraints on living there. When the head of personnel came up to Felice at a diplomatic reception at the Quirinale, the palace of the President of the Republic, and asked him if the post of consul-general in West Berlin appealed to him, Felice replied at once and with customary wit: No thank you, I've already done my time in prison.[1]

Stefania on the other hand was attracted by the idea of revisiting the city in which she was born, even though it would surely have changed almost out of recognition. That evening she asked him to think further about it not just because Berlin was better than Frankfurt but the work would be interesting, too. Felice could see that taking on this posting would be good for his career and so two days later he went back to the office and told them he was in fact willing to be sent to Berlin.

It was a good decision, proving them both right: the six years he and Stefania were to spend in Berlin were for them the most rewarding of the twenty-five they had in the foreign service. For most of the time Felice's rank was that of counsellor, but in many ways his role in Berlin would be comparable to that of an ambassador. The uniqueness of this isolated but hugely important city, cut off from the rest of the country and the world at large, meant it was logical and indeed necessary for the representative of a foreign country there to report directly home. Italy had an ambassador in Bonn but the Foreign Ministry in Rome wanted a direct line to its consul-general in Berlin. Felice would have to stay in constant contact with the ambassador but for practical purposes would run his own office and send his reports to Rome on the political and economic situation in Berlin.

Felice, Stefania and Silvia arrived in February 1963. Silvia was not quite five, and already at that young age was looking forward to the chance to learn German. Daniela, now 21, stayed on in Rome where she had a job with Trans World Airways. Because the previous consul-general was a bachelor and had stayed in a hotel it was Stefania's early task while Felice was at the office to find a suitable house for them. She chose a fine villa with a garden in the quiet suburb of Zehlendorf, near the Wannsee, the lake with woods and beaches that was one of West Berlin's main recreation areas.

The building housing the consul-general's office was remarkable: it was huge, and partly in ruins. Located near the zoo at no 1, Graf Spee Strasse – the street name was changed to Hiroshima in 1990 – it was opposite the also imposing but much-damaged and empty Japanese embassy. It had been donated by Hitler to the Mussolini regime; opened in 1941 it was partially destroyed by Allied bombing and ceased functioning as an embassy in 1943. In 2003, after a complete restoration of this neoclassical palace, the *Corriere della Sera* wrote: 'The dimensions tell the whole story. Ten thousand square metres on five levels, including the basement; five hundred rooms and four hundred windows; thirty pillars and an uninterrupted sequence of salons, dining rooms, ballrooms, conference rooms, terraces, loggias, conservatories, an internal courtyard and even a bunker.'[2] In 1966 an American journalist reported: 'After the war one wing was restored for use by the consulate-general. The other wing was walled up from the outside while inside debris and ruin remain. Wild plants grow from rooftop wreckage and a battalion of pigeons make camp in the king's dining room. A great reception room looks like a shattered railroad station.' He added the lament of consul-general Benuzzi: 'So massive, impressive and yet so sad.'[3]

Stefania recalled the devastation all around: their street was like a desert and apart from the two embassy buildings nothing remained standing. Inside the former Italian embassy were some huge and beautiful rooms suitable for receptions. The rest was completely abandoned, with holes in the walls through which birds came and went. Silvia remembered wandering around those strange spaces with her father, salvaging bits and pieces, and at other times playing there with the son of the janitor. Her parents warned her not to stray into the rubble in this neighbourhood because of the risk that something there might explode.[4]

The Cold War was now in full swing. Just over a year earlier the Berlin Wall had been erected, splitting the city in two and marking in brutal fashion the divide between freedom and consumerism in the west and harsh, gloomy communism in the east. The Benuzzis could hear gunfire on a regular basis, and read reports of the deaths of those shot in their attempts to flee from east to west. The stifling and dangerous environment for them was all the more depressing because the sun never seemed to shine, and they feared it was their lot to remain forever under grey skies. Their spirits were briefly lifted when four months after their arrival US President John Kennedy visited and in a passionate speech at the Wall told a vast crowd: '*Ich bin ein Berliner*!'

While it was hard for West Berliners to get permits to cross over to the eastern side of the city, it was not a problem for diplomats to pass through Checkpoint Charlie, and Felice and Stefania often did that. On the eastern side of the wall was a small Italian community and every Sunday a priest held a Mass in a basement there. Stefania recalled one particularly icy day when, after the service, they went into a shop and asked for hot milk, for Silvia. The woman there could tell at once from their good clothes that they had come from the West, and refused them. They persisted, offering to pay in deutschmarks which were double the value of east marks, but that only made the woman angrier. Stefania took her visiting parents to where the family used to live, at Budapesterstrasse 3: it had been levelled by bombing. A hotel had been built on the site, but across the street was the old hospital with its chapel.

One citizen who was allowed to make the crossing from west to east once a month was Archbishop Alfred Bengsch, who in 1967 was made a cardinal. For Felice he became an important contact. Only four months after his arrival in Berlin he received high praise from Fornari, director general of political affairs in Rome, who wrote to Felice saying that he had read with much interest his excellent report of his conversation with the Archbishop, and he wished to congratulate him also on behalf of Ambassador Cattani, the secretary general of MFA, for the excellent work he was currently doing in Berlin which was such a sensitive political observation post.[5]

On 14 October Felice wrote to his parents apologising for a long silence, because this last period for them had been very intense, or rather unbelievably extremely and intensely intense. It was not only for work: Stefania's parents had come for a two-week stay, in a hotel – for their first visit to the city in thirty years. Felice could only guess at the emotional impact of it on his father-in-law, but Otto was visibly pleased with several unexpected encounters he had with people who genuinely respected and liked him and from whom he had heard nothing in all that time. Stefania had taken them all over the place, including to East Berlin, and they had seen a number of performances at the new Philarmonic.

Stefania's sister Lily had also visited, 'as guest of the Senat for a women's conference whose exact scope I've forgotten.' Felice had recently been to the embassy in Bonn: there he had met the conductor Fernando Prevaliti, who remembered well, as a guest of the Benuzzis in Brisbane, the calloused hands of very rich Italian migrants who had started out in Australia as cutters of sugarcane. On his return to Berlin Felice and Stefania went to a sumptuous reception at the Charlottenburg Palace:

> The Mir of the Hunza, whom we knew from Karachi, was among the guests and of course I chatted with him about Gilgit and Karakorum. He invited me back to his mountains – I'm ready to go right now! A group of Germans saw me buttonholing the Mir and asked who that chap was, in leather beret and wearing medals, so I told them. They were astounded: 'From the Himalayas?' They wanted to know what the decorations were for. One of them was a German one, I told them. 'What, did he get it today?' No, I had to explain, he got it in 1956, from your Ambassador Podeyn, and do you know why? No! Because he provided the guides and porters for your expedition up Nanga Parbat. The poor fellows had never heard of Hermann Buhl.

Felice invited Nino and Berta to come and stay with them over Christmas. He offered to come and get them, and take them home at the end of January, when he and Stefania went to the winter Olympics in Innsbruck. If they agreed, he told them, they could save themselves a cold month in Trieste and enjoy the Berlin chill instead.

In his letter Felice mentioned how he was caught up in a big way in the preparations for an 'Italian week' in Berlin with trade, cultural and promotional elements. It must have been frustrating because he complained of the differences of opinion among his own people and how, only ten days out from the start of the event, the final program had still not been agreed upon nor could any invitations yet be printed. He would give a radio interview in a few days' time but would have to stick to generalities because he couldn't afford to talk about things which might not go ahead. But he need not have worried. In November Ambassador Guidotti in

Bonn reported to Foreign Minister Piccioni that Italy had had a stunning success in Berlin. Credit should go to the Italian Institute for Foreign Trade, ICE, which had organised the show. He continued: 'However I want to put on record the valuable contribution made by Consul General Benuzzi who for many months with great diligence and forethought took care of every local aspect.'[6]

This was a strange period in a city formally divided into American, British, French and Russian sectors. Felice spoke good English and French, and without doubt his fluent German with its melodious Viennese accent made him stand out among the diplomats in Berlin. His Italian rank was not a high one but in due course he became the dean of the consular corps. One of his key tasks was to find out as much as he could about the international situation in a place where the interests of the major powers clashed so conspicuously. At times Soviet troops made difficulties for the transit of American military convoys along the autobahn corridors linking the city with West Germany. In 1965 the Wall, which had been quite modest to start with, was substantially fortified. Felice made regular visits to the east, especially for trade reasons, visiting the Leipzig Fair, once with Stefania. He had a personal motive for that: his camera was a Leica, and the part of the fair that interested him most was the section displaying cameras and photographic accessories.

In April 1964 Felice received another burst of praise from the Ministry in Rome, first from a friend who wrote to him: 'My Dear Benuzzi, Let me tell you how rare it is to come across an officer of your efficiency. The Kühen case, your analysis of the Berlin media on the South Tyrol question, the steps you took to protest against the Radio Free Berlin program etc – all this marks you out as one of the best in our business. I hope Fornari, who is back from Brussels tonight, will put his name to something congratulatory which he will send on to Personnel and to Bonn.' A telegram did duly arrive soon afterwards advising Felice that the Ministry had noted and approved the line he had taken against the Radio Free Berlin's program on South Tyrol which had revealed a built-in hostility towards Italy. Deep appreciation was also expressed for Felice's 'extensive and intelligent information activity on the South Tyrol issue and the impact it had made on public opinion in Berlin and in the German Democratic Republic.'[7]

In a letter home in March 1965 Felice told his parents that he was drinking a wine sent him by Piero Marinari: they had been soldiers together in 1936 and then as POWs. He had met an American at a cocktail party whose wife was from Lucca: he'd asked her casually if she knew Marinari and she said yes, he always lets us use his garage! Then Felice related how he had been at a truly memorable dinner during a recent visit to Bonn. Before going there he knew that Mussolini's daughter would be among the guests, but when the lady with dyed blond hair turned to him as they were introduced he could not help collapsing into a chair:

> Edda Ciano Mussolini shot a look of her father that went right through me. She must have been aware of the impact she had made (it would have happened to her ten thousand times) and she was irritated by it. My God, I was sitting next to the Duce reincarnated. And to think (I couldn't help it) that this father she mentioned from time to time ('No, don't talk to me about opera, my father took me once in Milan, I was four or five and I was so sleepy and a man there, he was the prefect, kept me awake with sweets, I've loathed the opera ever since.' 'Even Wagner?' I asked, the devil in me as always. 'Even Wagner' she replied, staring at me just like her father and making me shiver again) had killed her husband (him she speaks about with more detachment than about her father, but it's all pretence, her self-control is obvious). We're living in history, in tragic history. She is on tour around Germany (though not to Berlin this time), as with intelligence and curiosity she toured India, and would like to tour the South Pacific (her three sons have all been to Tahiti at different times). At Trier the sight of the Roman gate made her jump. Then she'll see the carnival in Cologne. During the meal whenever she made any reference to politics everyone banked sideways like planes doing aerobatics, and away we go. But late in the day, at the home of the Marquis of Ferrara, I don't know how it happened that she came out with something I couldn't let go by and we fell into a bitter and sharp-edged debate that was never going to end. We wound up vowing earnestly we could never agree: but we became friends. I call

her Edda. She of course is a fascist still, but above all she is from Romagna, revolutionary, intransigent, dynamic and emotional beyond reasoning.[8]

The Italian consul-general in Berlin often operated in a rarefied atmosphere. High level visitors included some of the biggest names in Italian politics like Aldo Moro and Giuseppe Saragat. Felice got on friendly terms with Willy Brandt, then mayor of West Berlin, later Chancellor: he came to dinner, telling Stefania that he never accepted invitations to the homes of diplomats because if he did 'I'd never see the end of it.' Other guests of the Benuzzis included novelist and playwright Guenther Grass, and film stars Sophia Loren and Gina Lollobrigida.

One visiting VIP from Italy was the composer Luigi Dallapiccola, whose wife had been at school with Felice in Trieste. He brought his opera *Ulisse* to Berlin for its world premiere. Dallapiccola and his wife spent a good deal of time with the Benuzzis: they were there for practically every meal, Stefania remembered, drily. She had a low opinion of *Ulisse*. In every other respect, however, the music side of their life in Berlin was what made the posting so wonderful for her. They went often to the Berlin Philharmonic, and after a concert for the victims of the disastrous floods in Florence in 1966 its principal conductor Herbert von Karajan came to dinner. Stefania was on even better terms with Wolfgang Stresemann, director of the orchestra, who had an American wife. He said the Benuzzis were welcome at the opera at any time and only needed to put through a call to his secretary to get seats.

In 1967 Bert Salmon, Felice's old climbing companion from his Brisbane days, came to see them again. Bert, now sixty-eight, wrote a detailed diary of his Europe tour and described his hosts' meeting him at Templehof airport: they both looked wonderfully well and young for their years, though unhappily Stefania had developed some spinal trouble three years before which did not respond to treatment, and limited her activity in things she always liked best, namely mountaineering, skiing and walking. For her part Stefania remembered how it was when in 1960 at Valtournenche

Bert, Felice and his brother Piero had climbed to the top of the Grand Tournalin, often used as training for the Matterhorn itself. She had no option but to look after a girl in their group who had suddenly fallen ill, and so she could not go with them; Stefania was sure she would have reached the summit and as it turned out that was the last chance she ever had to do any proper climbing. Bert had been so appreciative of their kindness back then that he had presented Felice with his two precious Whymper volumes and a massive tome on New Zealand mountaineering: now he was delighted to see them prominent on Felice's shelves in Berlin.[9]

In August Bert caught up again with Felice, Stefania and Silvia at Madonna di Campiglio, in the mountains between Dro and the Austrian border, and they spent four days together. Bert and Felice made their way up to a mountain refuge high above the Val Brenta from where they could see the whole massif and the surrounding peaks:

> Facing the refuge across a shallow valley a great gash seams the mountain wall from top to bottom at a very high angle; it is filled with ice, overlaid with snow in parts, and with a length of about 2,600 feet is one of the longest ice couloirs in Europe. We loafed around this area for about two hours, waiting for the mists to uncover certain points, while my eager eyes scanned every wall and vertical gully in search of possible lines of ascent. Felice hardly needed to assure me that practically every yard of these glorious cliffs has felt a man's hand and known a nailed boot. There were any amount of other walkers coming and going, some of them more elderly than myself, a few almost decrepit, and quite a number carrying climbing equipment. Alpine flowers in scores of varieties laid a crazy pattern of many colours over the ground between the fallen rocks, the Alpine rose (Rhododendron ferrugineum) lying in pinky-red masses on the slopes. Apart from the susurration from lacy curtains of water shimmering down the rock walls, and the croaking calls of a flock of yellow-beaked crows, the mountain silence was solemn and profound.
>
> We left at 4.40 – it seemed terribly late, but Felice knows his mountains and his weather – and started down, retracing the same route for 40 minutes, then turning definitely away from the heights, soon reaching creeping mountain pine and then

larches and firs. The track is a very kind one, relatively smooth and never really steep, so we lost height easily and quickly, our pace slowed to a halt later on by the search for blueberries, which yielded more than we could afford time to pick. In two hours we were down to a rough road above a very fine roaring waterfall, and at 7.40 had reached Madonna di Campiglio, where Stefania and Silvia waited while Felice walked the mile-plus for the car, and I shimmered off to dinner, a hot bath, and bed. The weather remained superb, if hot, all day.[10]

When he was in Berlin in May Bert had met Daniela who had flown up from Rome for a brief visit. He described her as 'now 26, tall, very brown, distinguished, alive, alert and altogether charming and captivating, as one might expect to find the daughter of such fine parents.' The two of them met again in November in Rome near the end of his Europe trip, when Daniela took him first for a meal at a pizzeria that had been a favourite of her parents in the 1930s and then a few days later to the sprawling archaeological site at Ostia Antica, with a Norwegian girlfriend who also worked for an airline. Daniela was now engaged to Alan Ford, an American diplomat; they were married in Rome and at the end of 1967 left Italy for Alan's next assignment, in the Philippines.

In November Giuàn Balletto and his brother Albino who was a chemist came to Berlin and Felice took them to the east. Giuàn had brought photographs that Felice found wonderful, of Kilimanjaro and of his house near Moshi, with mangoes, cypresses and bougainvillea and views from the veranda of Kibo and Mawenzi. Also present that same evening was Giordano Bruno Fabian, who had often climbed with Emilio Comici and who was now deputy head of the Italian national Olympic committee. Giordano and Giuàn enjoyed each other's company, and it made Felice feel his age when he realised he had brought together one friend whom he had known for thirty five years with another he had known for a quarter of a century.[11]

The following year Moray Graham, whom Felice had taught as a ten year old during his time as a POW in Kenya, came to stay with them. In 2013 he still recalled vividly going with Felice and Stefania to a Beethoven concert at the Philharmonic, with Otto Klemperer conducting. Felice had got for them seats in the centre of the dress circle, and they entered the theatre at the same moment as Klemperer. 'I never knew for whom the entire audience stood, in deep and respectful silence, and after a minute sat down. If asked, I would to this day swear it was for Felice and Stefania; many waved to him; many spoke to him at length during the intervals and afterwards.' Stefania scoffed at the Moray story.[12]

Moray went with Felice to Leipzig, where they met Archbishop Bengsch, and they also went together to an exhibition of Queen Nefertiti's mask, on display at the Egyptian consulate. He was delighted to see Felice again, and they maintained a lifetime friendship after that. Moray, reflecting on his time with his hosts in Berlin, commented that Felice 'could be rude, even rough, with Stefania.' He said he meant that in an emotional sense.[13] It is not easy to explain Moray's observations. It seems Felice sometimes resented Stefania's occasional passing on to him information she had got from Wolfgang Stresemann, and, always meticulous and professional, may not have liked to see family concerns intrude upon his official duties.

With no real evidence for it, Moray suspected that Felice once or twice facilitated movement of goods or people from east to west. Daniela thought she had heard a story of a person in the boot of the car. The only incident that Stefania recollected was that of some soap being smuggled to Cardinal Bengsch for his washing machine. She said Felice had never mentioned anything like that to her, but then again wherever his work was concerned he revealed as little as possible.

For Stefania, the posting to Berlin had many complex elements. It was where she had been born into a Jewish family. Under the Nazi threat Otto and Alix had become Lutherans; she herself under fascism had abandoned the Marx surname as well as her faith. That side of her story would have undoubtedly done some harm to her self-esteem, never so much as being back now in

Germany. Nevertheless it was here, even more than in Rome or Paris or in Australia, that she found personal fulfilment, and a new independence. She found strength and gratification especially in Berlin's cultural life, and her memories of their time there were positive. She liked to tell of an incident that had amused her:

> One day we were at a reception at the British Minister's. At one stage he came over to Felice and said he wanted him to meet a colonel, whose name I've forgotten, and who had recently arrived. They were introduced: Colonel, please meet the consul-general of Italy. The colonel said, 'Ah. I just read a book by an Italian chap called Benuz, Benuzzy something. Do you know anything about him?' And Felice, without changing expression, said 'I shave him every day.' The British Minister was rather stiff, got rather a shock. Then of course when Felice revealed that he meant that it was him, well! And he became friends with this colonel, who had come from India, and he read the book, and loved it, and now by chance had met the author. He asked Felice to all his dinner parties. And of course within minutes all the diplomats who were at this reception were informed of it and Felice was the hero of the evening.[14]

Felice's work was always interesting, but at times problematic, for example if politics intervened. On one occasion he was called by someone on the Prime Minister's staff in Rome who said national elections were coming up: it was important for parties on the Left to have certain people from East Germany over for the campaign, and so would the consulate-general please issue the appropriate visas. Felice asked what these visitors might do in Italy and was told that they would speak during the election campaign. He explained that this sort of behaviour fell outside what had been agreed to among NATO members, and so he would not be able to oblige. His caller getting annoyed said that the consul-general failed to understand the political situation at home and should issue these visas. Only with written instruction from his own minister would he do it, Felice retorted, and the caller hung up. Recalling this, Stefania said the three individuals, party officials from the German Democratic Republic, nevertheless went to Italy, apparently getting permission to enter at the airport. Of course the Americans found out, and took Felice to task: he explained that he had given the East Germans no help whatever.

In July 1967, in recognition of his good work in Berlin, he was promoted to 'Envoy extraordinary and Minister plenipotentiary second class.' This ranking, immediately below that of ambassador, qualified him to be sent abroad to head a diplomatic mission. In September 1968 he wrote to a friend referring to the immense amount of work he was faced with due to the Soviet invasion of Czechoslovakia, a further indication of his finding himself in a location and at a time of major international significance.[15]

At Easter 1969 Felice ended his posting as consul-general in Berlin and perhaps after six difficult years this came as a relief. But virtually his last letter home, on 9 April, was as positive as all the others:

> Dearest people
> As I told you on the phone we're grandparents and very happy ones, too. At 5 am local time on the third (12 in Manila) Dani rang to tell us of the birth of Livia. All we know, summing up, is that she weighs 2.95 kg and that mother and daughter are fine. Nothing else, not even if she's fair or dark. Knowing how much Dani has always loved kids and what she picked up during Silvia's first years we're sure she'll be a wonderful mum. But given the distance we can't be wonderful grandparents, as we'd want to be. We'll just have to wait for the first letter.
>
> Meanwhile spring has sprung. It snowed just last Tuesday and even yesterday there were piles of frozen snow here and there, but at least the temperature has now suddenly gone up (it gets to zero only at night) and flowers and leaves are sprouting miraculously. We're spending hours working in the garden, you wouldn't think we were off in four weeks. But we want to leave everything tidy...
>
> ... Yesterday I met the youth water polo team here for an international tournament: chats and drinks (fruit juice for the athletes, aperitifs for their minders) and what useful things I could tell them about Berlin. This evening at the Schoenberg pool we saw our boys draw with the German team 4-all, even though they were technically the better team. The Yugoslav referee was terribly finicky. But it was just wonderful being able to barrack like mad at a swimming pool. Even Silvia had a lot of fun.

Next Sunday we'll pop over to Paris to look at a few apartments and maybe pick one. We hope Frau Leupold can come with us for a couple of months until we're settled in. Her daughter and grandson need her too much for her to leave them any longer.

So Happy Easter again to everyone, lots of hugs and kisses
Felice Stefania.

CHAPTER 18 NOTES

[1] 'Stefania' – DVD interview produced by Personal Documentaries op.cit. Also *Point Lenana*, p. 417.

[2] Corriere della Sera 10.6.2003 p. 37.

[3] *Pittsburgh Post-Gazette* 16.11.1966.

[4] Author's conversations with family May 2012.

[5] For the significant figure of Alfred Bengsch see Schäfer, B. (2010), *The East German State and the Catholic Church, 1945-1989,* Berghahn Books, pp. 87-90. MFA archives, Benuzzi files: message of 9.5.1963 – Ministero degli Affari Esteri a Felice Benuzzi: 'Caro Benuzzi, ho letto con molto interesse il Suo rapporto n. 3378/497 del 23 aprile u.s. relativo al colloquio che Ella ha avuto con l'Arcivescovo di Berlino Est... (Dear Benuzzi, I read with much interest your report of 23 April on your meeting with the Archbishop of East Berlin).'

[6] Letter from Berlin to parents of 14.10.1963.

[7] MFA archives, Benuzzi files: 20.11.1963 Italian Embassy BAD GODESBERG N. 21863/3319 to On. Sen. Attilio PICCIONI, Minister of Foreign Affairs.

[8] Letter among family archives, dated 19.4.1964, on letterhead of Direzione Generale degli Affari Politici signed by 'Francesco Bellin.' His final point is to commend to Felice work being done by Mario Toscano on Alto Adige (op. cit.). Telespresso N. 10/A00686 dated 22.1964 and copied to Italian Embassy, Bonn 'Attività del Console Generale in Berlino in merito alla questione altoatesina'.

[9] Extract from the obituary in *The Independent* 11 October 2014: 'When Edda Mussolini was born in Forlì in 1910, her father and her mother, Rachele Guidi, had not yet married. At that time, the man who would become Italy's Duce was just one of the many Italians listed as a "political agitator" by the police. Edda was Mussolini's first and favourite child. She was followed by four other children: Vittorio, Bruno, Romano and Anna Maria.'

[10] Stefania on 9.5.2013 related these events. In her view Piero was the better climber: 'Piero era più bravo nell'alpinismo, aveva più tempo di lui, era più allenato (Piero was the better climber: he had more time for it, and he was fitter).'

[11] Letter from Berlin to his parents dated 26.11.1967.

[12] Email from Moray Graham of 26.10.2012.

[13] Telephone conversation with Moray Graham 27.10.2012: He made the point twice: 'They were an unusual couple. Stefania admired him. He was quite rough with her.'

[14] Related on 12.10.2012; see also *Point Lenana*, p. 419.

[15] Letter dated 5.9.68 to Mario Fantin (1921-1980), a noted climber who was the official photographer on the successful 1954 K2 expedition, see Lacedelli op. cit. pp. 55-56. In 1967 Fantin set up and presided over the Centro Italiano Studio Documentazione Alpinismo Extraeuropeo (CISDAE) to gather material on Italian mountaineering exploits.

With Silvia at Puy de Dome in France, 1973

19

FRANCE

On 29 April 1969, after a period of home leave and consultations with the Foreign Ministry in Rome, Felice arrived in Paris on his next posting, as minister counsellor in the Italian delegation to the OECD, the Organisation for Economic Cooperation and Development. It would be the only posting he would ever have that involved him fulltime on multilateral and economic affairs: both these elements form essential parts of any diplomatic career, and for that reason alone he would have welcomed the assignment. Still, after having enjoyed a wide measure of independence in his six years in Berlin, and four in Brisbane, he would find it challenging to be a member of a team directed on a daily basis by an ambassador.

The OECD had been in operation for just eight years. Its predecessor body was the OEEC, also with headquarters in Paris, made up of a group of European countries who in the aftermath of the Second World War and boosted by the US Marshall Plan tried out the novel idea of working together for their common good. By 1960 the time had come to create a bigger organisation, with as members the United States and other developed countries sharing a democratic system of government and a market economy, to coordinate their approach and resolve common problems and set international trade standards. These were important matters for Italy, a member of both organisations. The Italian office was at 50 rue de Varennes. The ambassador, for all of Felice's four years there, was Francesco Malfatti di Montetretto who fought with the partisans during the war and went into politics after it. He was ten years younger than Felice, and the two of them got on well.

Felice, Stefania and Silvia had brought their dog Dingo with them to Paris. Their apartment in rue du Bois de Boulogne was close to one of the main gates of the great park, and that was handy for walking their dog. The apartment was large and comfortable and Stefania liked it a lot: especially after the constraints of Berlin she was glad to be back in this city that she knew and loved. On the other hand she was not particularly fond of the French, whom she did not consider friendly.[1]

Stefania also knew that she might well have some problems ahead in the social life in this fascinating city. Twenty years earlier the police report provided to the Foreign Ministry in Rome said of Felice that he was of fine physical appearance, with distinctive bearing and features: this was still a fair summary of the nearly sixty-year old diplomat in 1969. Those close to him noted that he only had to enter a room and heads would turn. He was charismatic, cultivated, dignified, witty, and attractive to women; perhaps inevitably Felice was drawn to some of them. And he had more time on his hands in Paris where his duties were less demanding than at other posts, and the day to day work interested him less. However, in everything he did he was professional, self-disciplined and devoted to Stefania.

Someone who knew him at this time was Sergio Romano, minister-counsellor in the Italian embassy in Paris although they did not work together – Felice's office was in the consulate across the street from the embassy. Romano ended his career as Italian ambassador in Moscow and thereafter became an author and a noted columnist for the *Corriere della Sera*, in Milan. Writing about Felice forty years later, Romano described him as being tall, athletic in the way he moved, quite at home in the polyglot world of international organisations, fluent in French. Asked to elaborate on this in an interview, Romano said Felice had a great naturalness about him, with absolutely no snobbery or hauteur: he knew how to put his interlocutors at ease, and in Paris, as everywhere else in his career, he performed with elegance and sensitivity.[2]

On 8 July 1970 Felice sent a letter from Paris addressed to my 'Darling four little ladies' who were together on the Italian riviera: evidently he had slipped away from a holiday by the sea, leaving behind Stefania, Daniela and baby Livia, and Silvia. He hoped to be back within a few days if he could get the ambassador's permission for a long weekend, and if so would get the night train to Nice and Ventimiglia on Saturday and return to Paris next Tuesday. He told them about a minor hearing problem that had made him go and see a specialist, and about chaos in the office and far too much work. A young member of staff had had a heart attack but Felice was unsympathetic because young people have to work. Elsewhere the newly-arrived were clueless, and refused to do anything outside their narrow spheres; no instructions had arrived from Rome, nor any funds; only a small amount of his salary for June had come through. Total disaster. Nevertheless he went on to describe a merry dinner at the ambassador's. One of those invited, a lady Stefania knew, was wearing something:

> which gave full view of her bellybutton (not a pretty sight) and when she turned to her neighbour on the right (Mario Tedeschi) she showed me an expanse of bare back which made me cross-eyed. The ambassador's wife at this moment, with a naughty smile, asked me 'Are you a vegetarian?' 'Meat-eater from way back,' I told her, 'but only of the best cuts.' I won't pass on the snide comments Antonini made about the commercial attaché's wife's hairdo.

Felice had flown back to Paris via Trieste, and wrote a whole paragraph on what he felt about his home town which was 'more Balkanised than ever, really sad.' The small yard in front of the station was now a bazaar full of stalls where nobody spoke Italian. In the 1960s Italy underwent great change everywhere because of the booming economy, but Trieste changed for special reasons: as relations with Yugoslavia improved, Slovenes, Croatians and Serbs flooded in to buy things they could not get at home. Many stayed and settled, and hundreds of small Slav-owned businesses popped up, and the quality of goods fell. Felice had not lived there for a long time and was struck by what he saw as chaos from across the border; before his very eyes the city he had grown up in was vanishing.[3]

It was France, rather than the work in Paris, that most stimulated Felice. In 1971 he began to write again, and for the rest of his life would contribute articles for publication in magazines and journals on things – mountains, cities, museums – he had seen and that interested him. It was logical he should look to place his articles first in Trieste, and on 15 July he wrote to Chino Alessi, the editor of the daily *Il Piccolo*, hoping he would remember him from the time when he was consul-general in Berlin; he told him of a recent visit he had made to Nuremberg where he had seen a lavish exhibition commemorating the five hundredth anniversary of the birth of Albrecht Durer; he had scribbled something on this, and hoped his piece might be published before the exhibition closed at the end of the month, enabling readers possibly to see something really worthwhile during the holiday period. If Alessi agreed, Felice said he would like the article to go out under the pseudonym Arrigo Risano, one that he had used in other writings. Alessi did agree, and the article was published a week later.

The Trieste paper published more than twenty articles during the time Felice was in Paris, under the same pseudonym.[4] It was an interesting choice of name: the Risano was a little river, one of several that flowed beneath the Carso, the limestone plateau that hugged Trieste, near Val Rosandra where he had learned rock-climbing. As he wrote in his *Più che sassi* memoirs, he found these rivers strange and fascinating: one of them, the Timavo, 'swells with the waters of the forest... and disappears under the rocks by the castle ruins... but it resurfaces below a chasm a little further on into the wan light of caves and grottoes ... before again plunging into the depths and then reappearing briefly in the Abyss of Serpents.' Elsewhere 'the impetuous crystalline sources of the Risano... gush out of the rocks at the head of a valley... springs of clear water bursting with secret energy that well up into the flat landscape, among the trees and fields.' The territory that the Risano flowed through when Felice was young was Italian; in his later career it was Slovene. But this name may have another significance, for in his memoirs he explains how:

> not far from the sources of the river a small and ancient church marks the place where in the time of Charlemagne the Istrians held a protest gathering that history recalls as the *'Placito di Risano'* (*Placitum of Rizana*), to lodge a formal complaint against the introduction of Germanic laws, the abuse by bishops and immigration by Slav peoples. As we were taught at school, the document of complaint was forthwith accepted by the emperor's messengers: it was an event of much importance.[5]

Felice's pseudonym, adopted to mask the identity of a government official, seems at the same time to reveal some complex and even contradictory aspects of his character.

The next article was, like the first, about an artist – Georges Rouault – and about a current exhibition of his works. Similar ones followed from time to time, including one in November on Venetian art on display at the Orangerie. All were substantial, around 2,000 words, and were colourful as well as scholarly, and conveyed Felice's enthusiasm for the matter in focus. An article on Monet began:

> When the police hurried to an incident on the Pont de Vernon on 3 February 1966 they were surprised to discover that the reckless driver of the mangled car there was Michel Monet, killed on the spot at the age of eighty-eight. I am told he was stone deaf. He was then one year older than his father, the painter Claude Monet, had been when he died: he was laid to rest alongside him in the peaceful cemetery at Giverny which was where he had gone, as he often did, on that fatal day.[6]

At the beginning of 1971 Felice's own father Giovanni Benuzzi died, and he, too, was aged eighty-eight. From that moment Felice stopped writing his weekly letter to the family recounting his and Stefania's various activities. Thus was brought to an end a story that had begun twenty years earlier – some four thousand pages detailing their diplomatic life from its beginning, in Paris.[7]

Death, or the anniversary of a death, often inspired Felice to put pen to paper. In August of that year he told his readers how in a London newspaper forwarded to his mountain hotel – he and Stefania and Silvia were holidaying at Sölden in Austria – he had read how author and explorer Frederick Spencer Chapman had just been found dead, with a double-barrelled hunting rifle alongside the body. Felice summarised the extraordinary life of this man who had so long been a hero of his. It was while he was a POW that he had read Chapman's *Memoirs of a Mountaineer*, having no means of knowing that exactly then Chapman had been officially declared missing presumed dead in Malaya, although he was in fact alive and carrying out improbable exploits behind Japanese lines. Felice had other heroes and wrote obituaries, including of the palaeontologist and naturalist Louis Leakey, General Nasi who had been in Ethiopia and Kenya, and the mountaineers Shipton and Tilman.[8]

In November 1971 Felice contributed an article to *Lo Scarpone*, the magazine of the Italian Alpine Club, describing how he had made it to the top of Mont Ventoux in Provence, without getting out of his car. He had wanted to reach this place with its fine views of the Mediterranean coast and the Alps because of its connection with the Italian poet Petrarch. In April 1336 the poet had climbed the mountain with his brother Gerardo, and the account of that feat, in a letter to Father Dionisio of Borgo San Sepolcro, was according to Felice unique – nobody before had written in the first person singular about climbing for the sheer pleasure of being able to admire the view from the summit. The letter was in Latin and Felice, having translated it himself, quoted extensively from it in his article. Apart from that ancient precedent, Petrarch's experience must have resonated with Felice in a number of ways. He would have found an echo of his own exasperation as a POW when the idea of climbing the mountain occurred to him because Petrarch also had had a hard time finding the right person to go up the mountain with him: 'First one person seemed unsuitable for this reason and then someone else for another reason, and I ended up choosing my own younger brother.' The modest, self-deprecatory style of Petrarch may echo, too, in *No Picnic on Mount Kenya*:

> We set off again only this time more slowly. While I was having to take it easy on the steep track, my brother found a shorter way up across a ridge. Feeling weak I went even lower, and when I heard him calling advice on the best way up, answered that my way around the other side was hopefully easier and I didn't mind if it was longer. It was only an excuse for my own laziness, there was I wandering about at the bottom while everyone else was at the top... In the end, rueful and annoyed with myself, I decided to go straight up; and when, worn out and hungry I caught up with my brother who was thoroughly rested after waiting so long, soon afterwards I continued on with him, and kept up.[9]

In the spring of 1972 Felice returned to that part of southern France near Avignon where Petrarch had lived. Now he was writing regularly about his excursions out of Paris with Stefania and Silvia, without ever naming them: an article in February for *Il Piccolo* began 'The guide who showed us around the ruins of Cluny Abbey...' In May 'wondering if the place would meet our expectations, we set out' for the town of Fontaine-de-Vaucluse, for the house of the poet. There was disappointment straightaway: in a small square shops and booths were awash with Petrarch memorabilia in an 'orgy of shoddiness' to meet the latest tourist tastes. Fortunately the house itself was moderately interesting and the garden delightfully peaceful. By the time they were required to leave, Felice was more or less resigned to the junk and kitsch they would have to walk past again on the way out: 'The price we have to pay for a consumer society, for mass tourism! Just part of everyday life!' He could see why everyday life was what the poet loved escaping from.

***

In March 1972 Felice wrote to his daughter Daniela and husband
Alan a letter which brought out the frustrations felt by practically
every government official in mid-career:

> I want you to know straight away that I understand your
> disappointment on missing out on that promotion and seeing
> your hopes for Athens go up in smoke. Believe me, there is no
> one who would understand that better than me, who have had
> a great many disappointments in my career. I know through
> experience how soul-destroying it is to see the laurels go to
> spectacular fools (believed to be so not by me but rather by
> people in general and probably by God) solely on the basis of
> their ability to warm themselves in the sun of some political
> luminary. You console yourself after that, as you must, knowing
> you can sleep easily at night because you won't have anything
> on your conscience to disturb your sleep. And after all, being
> able to sleep peacefully is good for the health...

Ever since he joined the foreign service at almost forty years
of age Felice had always been conscious of that initial age
disadvantage, and had kept a keen eye out for the progress made
by his colleagues, especially those who were in the same intake
as him. Too often he had seen some of them move rapidly ahead
in this competitive process, and not always because they were
more talented. Finally on 22 December he did get promoted, to
Minister Plenipotentiary, level 1. Among his personal documents
is one handwritten just after this which lists all those who were
in the 1948 intake, together with their present rank; four of them
however had died, and nine had retired. In this list he put himself
in fourth place, behind three distinguished Italian diplomats
one of whom was Amedeo Guillet, the hero of Eritrea and now
ambassador in India.[10]

In May Felice told Daniela and Alan that Stefania had just
come back from the United States on a visit that had been a great
success. On her return to Paris they had both gone to Rome for the
national elections. In a few lines, which were brief and for him very
rare, he spoke of politics. He said the elections had hardly changed
anything at all but overall the outcome was a positive one because
the communists had made almost no progress and their allies

the PSIUP had disappeared altogether; the Christian Democrats had held their ground whereas in the 1971 local elections they seemed to be slipping; the neo-fascist party had not improved their position as much as had been feared; and the youth vote had mainly gone to the centre. The only negative factors he saw were the over-abundance of spoiled or blank ballot papers, and the very poor performance of the Socialists and Liberals. This all showed Felice as very much a man of the centre.[11]

Felice had also met Giuàn Balletto one more time, and the two of them paid a surprise visit on Enzo Barsotti, at Lido di Camaiore, his home town just north of Pisa. And so, Felice reported to Daniela, the 'three madmen of Mt Kenya' were together again, for the first time since 1948. They had all dropped in on a local health worker whom Enzo said had come into a fortune, and had gone with him after dinner to his fantastical Fellini-like house in the mountains. Felice said that Giuàn intended to go to London but would spend two or three days first in Paris. He had written a book about his life as a doctor in Africa which was due out at the end of the year: Felice had read most of the manuscript on the train and found it really interesting for lots of reasons, and it was seasoned with Giuàn's dry humour.[12] The following month Felice wrote to Mario Fantin, a friend who collected and published accounts of Italian mountaineering exploits and who had always been interested in the achievement on Mt Kenya. Felice told Fantin that Giuàn Balletto was with him in Paris, and that the secretary of the French Alpine Club, Maurice Martin, had handed over to them some of the things they had taken up the mountain which were recovered by a French expedition in 1953, including their sisal rope and one of their four crampons. They had not especially wanted them, so they passed this material on to the Alpine Museum, in Chamonix.[13]

Giuàn's book *Kilimanjaro: Montagna dello splendore* ends with these words: 'Tomorrow I'll go back to my work and I believe it is this that gives me strength. Work among simple people who in the everyday struggle are able to forget: work has for me, too, been a blessing, a gift to forget the sad toll of a life that has not always been easy and not always joyful.' Evidently Giuàn had for years been suffering bouts of depression. In December 1972, before his book was published, Felice received the sad news of his suicide in Tanzania. He later had the opportunity to honour his old friend in the preface of his book on Kilimanjaro.[14]

In 1972 Felice, perhaps with the encouragement of Mario Fantin, had published in *Alpi Giulie*, the prestigious magazine of the Italian Alpine Club, a long illustrated article about his experiences twenty years earlier in the New Zealand Alps.[15] He told his readers that although no mountains in New Zealand reached 4,000 metres, many soared up from the sea and glaciers went down to that level, far below any in these parts. Moreover unpredictable weather was such that the famous Swiss climber Marcel Kurz believed that any climber would be lucky to scale one major peak in a week. Felice's account was essentially the same as the one he wrote in his memoirs a few years later, but it had a quite different final paragraph:

> In the afternoon, after bidding my companions farewell, I went for a wander near the Hermitage Hotel and took some photos. Around the summit of Mt Cook, which had suddenly made an appearance and where it would been quite impossible to stay on one's feet, a great battle of clouds was raging this way and that, fascinating, exciting. But on the nearby tennis court people were running after a white ball and it seemed that that titanic struggle up there meant absolutely nothing to them. But on the other hand, why should everyone be infected as I am by mountain fever?[16]

Two articles in 1973 for *Il Piccolo* in Trieste bring out Felice's singular character. He had been to see an exhibition currently on in Paris of a unique, rich and surprising collection – *Les Sorcières* – of witches, and witchcraft in art. He concluded his article saying of course we could only shake our heads at these mediaeval aberrations, but should reflect on how superstition was alive and well today, and ask ourselves how many ideological witch hunts this very generation had witnessed. A second article described the Paris metro and its underground world, and notably its special smell whose components were mould and dust and airlessness but also the heat of overcrowding which was a human heat. Felice was particularly struck by the precedence given in signs indicating specially-reserved seats: first to the war-wounded, then to the legally blind, then those with work injuries and only after that to pregnant women and people minding children under four. He had seen Italians who disapproved. 'But here the past has precedence over the future. These are people who are not burdened by the past. Quite the opposite: it gives them strength.'

Felice travelled to Rome to seek news of where they might be sent next. In the Ministry he discussed the options before him, ruling out embassies like Washington that were too lofty in terms of rank, and those in tropical Africa, Indonesia and elsewhere with an absolutely impossible climate. He expressed a preference for Oslo, with Lima his second choice because the work there would be interesting, as would the archaeology and the mountains. He wrote to Daniela telling her how all of this distressed her grandmother, and it grieved him to think of her left behind at Malnate, north of Milan.[17]

During their final six months in Paris the Benuzzis toured the country and Felice continued to write articles for *Il Piccolo*: one about Cambridge after a visit to England, another about William the Conqueror, the Bayeux tapestry and the D-Day landings after a visit to Normandy. And then in high summer they left Europe, and from Lisbon Felice contributed an article on Belem, its monastery and its monument to the great discoverers, shaped like the prow of a ship with at the forefront Henry the Navigator and behind him Vasco da Gama, Ferdinand Magellan and others. Soon afterwards, like those travellers, they set out into the Atlantic. Felice's next assignment would be the high point of his diplomatic career.

CHAPTER 19 NOTES

[1] Stefania conversation 12.10.2012; email of 22.11.2012: 'the first time we had a flat in rue de Prony connecting Place Wagram with Park Monceau, the second time we moved to Neuilly, rue du Bois de Boulogne.'.

[2] *Corriere della Sera* 20.6.2010: *Con tre prigionieri italiani sulla vetta del Monte Kenya*; Telephone conversation with Sergio Romano 10.5.2013.

[3] Italy's economic miracle, and the passage of years, saw an improvement in Italy-Yugoslavia relations, which culminated in 1975 with the Treaty of Osimo that basically confirmed the status quo and the arrangements of 1954. Botta, F. (2009), *Seduzione e coercizione in Adriatico. Reti, attori e strategie, Milano:* FrancoAngeli, especially pp. 23-33. In the 1960s more and more Slavs came to Trieste, seeking commercial opportunities, and this did change the character of the city, as Felice observed when he returned there after a long absence.

[4] The first article of his published by Il Piccolo was on 24.7.1971 and the last was on 8.10.1986.

[5] *Più che sassi* p. 44.

[6] *Il Piccolo* 6.2.1973: *Su le tele del 'tesoro di Giverny' Monet s'è eretto il più bel monumento.*

[7] Letter collection of Silvia Benuzzi, made available for reading April 2014.

[8] See annex C, articles of 17.9.1971; 13.10.1971; 14.2.1973; 20.12.1977; 13.1.1980.

[9] Felice in his article in *Lo Scarpone* of 1.11.1971 noted that a sign on Mt Ventoux incorrectly gives the date of Petrarch's famous climb: it states 9 May 1336 when in fact it was on 26.4.1336.

[10] See Chapter 13, note 15.

[11] Letter of 14.5.1972. The elections held on Sunday 7 May were for both houses of parliament, and for the first time were brought on early; they reconfirmed the governing role of the Christian Democratic Party.

[12] Letter of 14.5.1972. See also *Point Lenana*, p. 425. In a letter to Paolo Caccia Dominioni (one of Italy's most prominent soldiers in World War II in Africa) dated 28.11.1986 Felice reports the death during 1986 of the second of his companions on Mt Kenya, Enzo Barsotti, adding 'dei trei matti resto l'unco superstite' (of the three madmen, only I remain).

[13] Letter to Fantin (note 14, chapter 18) of 19.6.1972: 'Caro Fantin, Poiché ti sei sempre tanto interessato alla nostra gita sul Kenya, vorrei informarti che alcuni giorni fa Giuàn Balletto si trovava qui a Parigi. Allora il Segretario Generale del C.A.F. Maurice Martin ... (Dear Fantin, Since you've always been interested in our Kenya adventure, I should inform you that Giuàn Balletto was here in Paris a few days ago. The secretary general of the French Alpine Club, Maurice Martin...). '

[14] *Più che sassi* end note on p. 90 refers to a full tribute to Giuàn contributed by Felice to *Lo Scarpone* on 16.2.1973, as well as to favourable references to him made by various other writers.

[15] *Alpi Giulie* 67-1(1972) pp. 1-24: one of the end notes refers to the Fantin publication *Italiani sulle montagne del mondo 1967*.

[16] *Più che sassi* pp. 113-141; see Chapter 15, note 12.

[17] Letter of 15.10.1972. In it he says he asked Silvia (then aged 14) which postings she would favour: her choice was 'prima Oslo, poi Lima... Figlia di suo padre!! (first Oslo then Lima – her father's daughter!)'.

Presenting credentials as Ambassador in Montevideo, August 1973 (behind
the document he is holding stands Giampaolo Collella)

20

South America

In the early part of his diplomatic career Felice was prepared to go wherever the Foreign Ministry sent him: to remote Brisbane, to torrid Karachi despite Stefania's poor health, and then back to Australia. Later he turned down Berlin before accepting it, and in 1970 refused a posting to Somalia even though it would have been good for his career, partly because the climate would have been intolerable for Stefania and partly because he felt his past experience in Ethiopia might have been awkward for him and for the Somalis. He explained to daughter Daniela that he could not really afford to refuse any other posting, so close to his age of retirement.[1] When in 1973 the Ministry proposed that he go as ambassador to Montevideo he accepted it. One aspect of the posting disappointed him: Uruguay was the only country in South America with no mountains. The family left by sea in July and crossed the equator: it was freezing when they arrived in Montevideo two weeks later.

Perversely, Felice might have been attracted to the country by its current precarious political situation. No country in South America had a stronger democratic tradition than Uruguay, and in the 1960s it was arguably the most affluent and stable of all, and its army and police force were both remarkably small. But the economy was in decline, and, as in other countries, a rebellious group called the Tupamaro were starting to become a nuisance, robbing banks and carrying out political kidnappings.[2] Under the presidency of

Juan Maria Bordaberry, the authorities began cracking down, with notable success. However, disputes with his deputy and with the military led Bordaberry in June 1973 to dissolve parliament and suspend the constitution. His fierce manoeuvre, suppressing political party activity along with many civil liberties, became known as the *autogolpe* or 'self-coup'. Bordaberry remained in power for the next three years – exactly the period the Benuzzis were to be in Uruguay – until he was deposed by the military. The repression did not end with his departure. It was marked by torture and unexplained disappearances, as in Argentina, in Chile which also entered a period of brutal dictatorship in 1973 and in other countries on the continent.[3]

So for Felice Montevideo was likely to be an interesting assignment. Italy's national hero Giuseppe Garibaldi had lived in the country for seven years and had married there and had three children. He established an Italian legion whose members wore his famous red shirts, and it was in Uruguay in 1847 that he was given command of the small Uruguayan fleet.[4] Italians began migrating to Uruguay in significant numbers after the unification of the nation in which Garibaldi played so central a role, and at its peak in the last years of the nineteenth century more than one hundred thousand emigrants were coming annually. Political, cultural and trade relations between Italy and Uruguay had been excellent for more than a century, and Felice had more than thirty predecessors as ambassador or head of mission. Apart from routine cooperation at the international level the ambassador's main task was to oversee the sizeable Italian community. During Felice's time Italians made up over forty per cent of the population. It was the second and third generation Italians, those who had retained their Italian citizenship, who most often needed the embassy's attention, especially once the political crackdown began.

On Felice's staff was an administrative officer, Giampaolo Colella, who was accredited as consul. Colella was bilingual, and knew the situation extremely well having been a school teacher and long-term resident in Uruguay.[5] It was he who dealt with the routine cases but the ambassador was required to intervene in anything complex or sensitive. The test of special sensitivity was anything that might be reported in the media in Italy concerning the torture of citizens, especially politicians and trade unionists, which could lead to matters being raised in Parliament and a press campaign with unpredictable consequences. Always to be avoided because it raised the diplomatic temperature immediately was the filling-up of the public areas of the embassy by those believing themselves at risk: just such an occurrence involving hundreds of people seeking political asylum took place at the Italian embassy in Chile in 1974.[6]

From time to time Felice would accompany Colella on visits to Italian citizens arrested under the emergency regulations and detained in army barracks. On one occasion permission was given to the embassy to visit eight prisoners and Felice took along some cigarettes, chocolate and *panettone*. To his chagrin he was told when they got there by the relevant military officer that the way gifts were packaged meant they might contain messages for example in invisible ink and so the cigarettes would have to be reduced to loose tobacco and the other items broken down into small fragments. He protested vehemently but the lieutenant told him he had his orders and they could accept them or leave. Felice took the second option, telling Colella it was unacceptable that the detainees should be required to lick up crumbs like scavenging dogs. Such intemperance, however, was out of character. For Colella the ambassador was the consummate diplomat, always exceedingly polite to the Uruguayan authorities, and the good relations he developed with them helped get better access to those being detained and improve the conditions of their incarceration. He could however dig his heels in. He often used to say that those he dealt with had to be civilians, not generals and colonels: in other words the President of the Republic and the Foreign Minister. With the latter, Juan Carlos Blanco, he was on friendly terms, and that proved profitable.

Nevertheless for the Benuzzi family the posting to Montevideo was one they enjoyed. Silvia, the only daughter with them, was at school where she added Spanish and Portuguese to the languages she already spoke fluently. Stefania found it trying to be in a country where she did not know the language.[7] She was not especially enamoured of Uruguay but did appreciate how kind the people were, and their positive response of 'Ah!' when they learned the family was Italian: in Australia that 'Ah' had been guarded, and in France the reaction had been one of indifference. The social life was burdensome, with a diplomatic dinner or reception practically every day. Otherwise her day to day existence was frankly boring. Silvia declared that she found the place scary: once in a while there were reports of bodies being washed up on the beaches they used to frequent. For the family, the real compensation for the various difficulties was the opportunity they had to travel in Latin America and beyond.

***

The chance came early with the arrival on the scene in November 1973 of Giovanni Aimone Cat, whose father had been chief of the Italian Air Force for a number of years late in the Second World War and afterwards. Four years earlier Aimone Cat had been the first Italian to sail to Antarctica, and he was now on his second expedition, once again in his elegant sixteen metre *San Giuseppe II*, with a small team of scientists. This genuine adventurer made a deep impression on Felice. Silvia later believed that her father saw him as a character who might have been created by Karl May – a 19th century German author of adventure stories that he had loved in his youth and which she, too, had later read avidly.[8] At dinner at the Benuzzi home Aimone Cat had described at length the frozen continent and the accessible islands near it, in particular the volcanic Deception Island. All of them including Stefania had been captivated by what they heard, and that evening undoubtedly changed the course of their lives. In January 1974, the Benuzzi family boarded a Brazilian vessel for the first of two visits they would make to Antarctica, which would remain a vibrant element for them ever after.

Felice described that first visit in an article he wrote the following year, published in *Alpi Giulie* under his own name rather than a pseudonym.[9] After a long introduction on the unique nature of the most remote of the six continents he gave an account of the journey which began badly even before they reached Cape Horn, with a fearful storm in the Roaring Forties that lasted for twenty-four hours. After that the sea was calmer and they came to Bransfield Strait where seventy years earlier an explorer had written in his diary: 'Abandon hope all ye who enter here.' Off Deception Island one iceberg towering higher than the ship caused someone of Felice's age to exclaim 'a gothic castle!' but he preferred Silvia's comparison of it to an oil refinery. They continued down along the Antarctic Peninsula with its walls of ice and under the crags and glaciers of Anvers Island which prompted a vision for Felice of the alpine valley at Zermatt sunk below the waves so that only the peaks broke the surface. At a Chilean meteorological station they were told that theirs was the first visit by a passenger ship and by women. At a second Russian base the passengers were able to venture up a nearby hill. There was a trig point at the top and Felice stepped back so Stefania could get there ahead of him and perhaps claim a female mountaineering 'first.' His references in this article to both Silvia and Stefania are the only times in any of his published writings that he used their names: he may have been aware of the significance for the family of this visit to Antarctica.

On their return they had a summer holiday in the seaside city of Punta del Este two hours east of Montevideo, and the following month voyaged to Ushuaia, the southernmost town in the world. It took them three days sailing to reach the Island of los Estados at the very tip of Argentina where the Atlantic and Pacific Oceans meet. Enormous albatrosses flew above them without the least sign of effort as their ship turned west and followed the inhospitable coastline of Tierra del Fuego, Argentine territory, to their right. They entered the Beagle Channel and on their left now, to the south, lay the sizeable Navarino Island in Chilean territory that included Cape Horn. The channel widened and at the foot of a snowy chain of mountains appeared a small town consisting almost entirely of single-storey buildings. They landed on the Argentine side. Ushuaia with its 3,500 inhabitants was strung out along the foreshore and on two or three parallel streets further up the slope. It had a temporary, frontier town feel to it and Felice sensed that this really was the end of the inhabited world. Ninety Italian families were living there, traders, mechanics, dockworkers and airport staff. The Benuzzis took a trip for a hundred kilometres or so due north along a road that rose up a steep pass from where they could see in the heart of Tierra del Fuego a body of water the size of Lake Geneva and named Fagnano after an Italian missionary. Back at the ship they watched the seagulls squabbling for rubbish thrown overboard while a pair of magnificent albatrosses circled disdainfully overhead.[10]

In May they visited Asuncion, in Paraguay, and two months later they were in Bolivia. After admiring the colossal stone monuments and majestic statues at Tiahuanaco, capital of a pre-Incan empire, they went on to nearby Lake Titicaca, the largest in South America. While they were intrigued by both places, undoubtedly it was the Andes themselves that captivated Felice. The moment he arrived in La Paz he was struck by the sight of Mt Illimani which according to Sir Martin Conway, the first to climb it in 1899, was so intimately associated with the city it seemed to look into the windows of the houses. Felice in wonder described the panorama before them as their car took them out of the capital on the road to Titicaca, up on to the Andean plateau:

> How the glaciers of the Cordillera Real are gleaming today! Up there on a rocky point of Chacaltaya the dome of an observatory sparkles in the sunlight and beside it is the highest ski-lift in the world, taking you up to 5300 metres! Beyond them rises

the elegant and jagged 6000 metre summit of Huayna Potosi with its subsidiary Italy Peak, and further along the compact formation of Condodiri, Chachacamani and Illampu, giants all of them, covered in ice.[11]

Stefania and Silvia were not so delighted, when they parked and had to struggle up to the ski-lift. It was high summer and because they had only recently arrived in the country none of them was acclimatised to the altitude. Even the short distance they had to walk was painful, breathing was difficult and afterwards mother and daughter both had headaches.[12] Felice however would be back the following year, for an attempt on Illimani.

Two days later they left Bolivia and crossed into Peru; at Juliaca they took the train to Cuzco – a ten hour journey across the high plains of the Andes. Felice wrote several articles about their visit to Machu Picchu that were published the following year. With Stefania and Silvia he also climbed the Huayna Picchu rocky pyramid that towers above the famous ruins.[13]

***

In September 1974, on his way back to Rome for official leave and consultations with MFA, he went via Africa. He had received an invitation from the Mountain Club of Kenya to attend the 75th anniversary of the first time it had been successfully climbed. John Temple, a noted local mountaineer who had organised the celebratory dinner at Nanyuki, remembered the five days he spent with Felice: 'He was a genuine gentleman – he was charming, controlled, self-possessed, very straight. After thirty years, people in Kenya still had an enormously favourable impression of him.' The ambassador, Temple went on, was the star of the show. At one point Felice told his audience: 'I know that Uruguay does not exist. I have been there.'[14] Temple introduced him to Bill Woodley, warden of Kenya's mountain parks, and Woodley took him up in his two-seater Piper for a nostalgic flight around Mt Kenya and its environs. They flew past the site of the POW camp, over the plain they had crossed in the moonlight with their weighty backpacks and the now-abandoned sawmill, and close to Point Lenana. Felice remembered every detail of the landscape, including the spot where once they had made their base camp, suddenly there before them as they nosedived into the Hausberg Valley.[15]

It was less than two years since the death of Giuàn Balletto. Felice had written an obituary of him for *Lo Scarpone*, and contributed a eulogy in the preface to Balletto's book *Kilimanjaro, Montagna dello splendore*, published in 1974. Now he intended to make a pilgrimage to his grave at Moshi on the southern slopes of Africa's highest mountain and, in honour of the doctor who had worked in Tanzania for decades, he would also climb it. Nearly thirty years earlier he had seen Kilimanjaro on the horizon from the train, as the sun was setting on his last day as a detainee in Kenya. When he got to Marangu, the starting point for the standard route to the top, he had to negotiate with the manager of his hotel, a resolute German lady who had authority for excursions up the mountain. He said he would not need a guide but she exclaimed that it was compulsory to have one, and insisted he have at least four porters. This was because an elderly man like him had recently had a heart attack up there, and three porters had not been enough to bring his body down.

Next morning he set off, with two cooks and two assistants plus a guide called William. Using the Swahili that bit by bit came back to him, Felice learned that William had known Dr Balletto well, and had accompanied him to some of Kilimanjaro's lesser known glaciers. They walked at a measured pace, spending three nights on the way up at comfortable huts, with lit fires as the temperature had plummeted. At 1.30 a.m on the fourth day the group began the difficult final leg up the rocks and black screes to the Kibo crater and he had to keep stopping to regain his breath. The last hundred metres or so to Uhuru Peak at 5895 metres were really hard. Felice, slightly disappointed with that final moment and the view, shook hands with William and they each said what a fine effort they had both made. Felice took some ritual photographs and made an entry in the book kept in a box with a bronze lid at the summit, and then it was time to descend.[16]

On his return from Africa and Rome Felice wrote to Mario Fantin, publisher of accounts of Italian mountaineering exploits, noting that at the end of 1975 he would turn sixty-five and so the end of his career was in sight. Before that happened, however, it was his intention to make the most of the opportunity he had to see the world, and in particular as many of the beautiful mountains in Latin America as he could. One of these was in Argentina: with Silvia and a seventy year old resident of Bariloche who used to climb with Emilio Comici, he reached the high point of the northern ridge of the Pico Catedral near the town.[17]

In June 1975 Felice attended Moray Graham's wedding in Scotland and two months later he was back in Bolivia, this time with ten day's leave, to make an attempt on Mt Illimani. He was welcomed in the capital by a foreign service colleague, Sergio Kociancich, who had recently arrived as Italian ambassador. Kociancich, an able mountaineer himself, introduced him to Alfredo Martinez, the top mountain guide in the country who had climbed with Walter Bonatti. After some days of necessary acclimatising to the altitude and with a third man called Juan Carlos Queiroz, Felice set off in a hired jeep on 4 September, turning off eventually up a steep track:

> The higher we went, the narrower the bends and the more horrid was the abyss to one side of us. Luckily there was no oncoming traffic. On a rockface that jutted out into the 'road' was a written warning: 'Trust in Jesus and you'll get home.' No need to add a comment to that.[18]

They camped on the side of the mountain where some miners were digging for tin, wolfram and other minerals. Alfredo and Juan Carlos engaged three of these as porters and guides. Next morning they turned up befuddled by sleep or coca, but once they got moving it was at high speed. Felice could only go half as fast. Six hours later and exhausted he was the last one to reach a ridge at 5500 metres and found when he got there that the green tent was already up. He woke at 8 next morning when the sun's rays at last touched the tent. After a big breakfast and with the porters no longer with them he and his two companions set off roped together and wearing crampons. Around noon it began to snow, making the rocks slippery. Alfredo recommended they go back for the time being to the tent, and that they remain roped. He pointed to where two years earlier the Italian climber Carlo Nembrini had fallen: he himself had climbed down 700 metres to recover his body. The weather deteriorated further, snow was coming down heavily and Alfredo said they risked being blocked in there for some days. They decided to go back down the mountain while they still could: three hours of daylight remained. Felice was low in spirits with yet another uncompleted climbing experience, and he knew only too well that he would not have another chance to climb that mountain. But he comforted himself with the knowledge that he had reached an altitude of 5700 metres, up to Illimani's dazzling crown of glaciers.

***

From September to December Felice was in New York for the United Nations General Assembly and then he returned to Montevideo for Christmas. In the new year he planned a second visit with Stefania to Antarctica, and in a letter to his mother about it told her they would begin and end the sea journey at Ushuaia in the south of Argentina; he added that the sudden collapse of the Argentinian peso had given them, with their Uruguayan funds, a sense of being able to live like lords in that country. A letter at the same time to Daniela answered a question Felice guessed she had been asking herself: how could they afford this trip? The answer was that they had sold their sporty Fiat 124 for a very good price and in exchange had bought a 128, the sort that pensioners might drive – the difference between the two was the cost of the cruise.

In a final comment to Daniela he said that the current government crisis in Italy was, yet again, of great benefit to them: until it was resolved no successor could be named for him in Montevideo.[19]

They travelled on the Swedish cruise ship *Lindblad Explorer* and their first stop was at Port Stanley in the Falkland Islands. Although the ambassador in Montevideo had consular responsibility for the territory, only a handful of Italians lived there and the Foreign Ministry in Rome never asked him to go. Moreover the British did not want embassies in Buenos Aires to cover it. However Felice made this a semi-official visit, and accepted an invitation to lunch from the governor. They spent three days in the Falklands, where everybody knew everybody and people kept telling the Benuzzis they wanted nothing whatever to do with Argentina: they were British to their bootstraps. Their ship took them to other islands, including New Island on the far side of the archipelago where only two or three ships a year came by. In that remote place they were guests of the Evans family. Stefania never forgot the conversation she had with Mrs Evans:

> I asked her, don't you feel lonely here, is there anything you miss? And she answered, 'It all depends where your values lie.' For her the important things were when a sheep was born, or the first red hen. She didn't care whether there were cars or not, whether it rained or not. She wouldn't change it for anything. She was an amazing person.[20]

A few days later they entered Antarctic waters and anchored in Paradise Bay. Transferring to rubber boats they landed at the Argentine naval base of Admiral Brown. Here twenty five young scientists and sailors welcomed them 'with Latin warm-heartedness', as Felice put it in a long article for *L'Universo*, the magazine of Italy's Institute of Military Geography. In the pages of the visitors book for 1974 they found the signatures of Giovanni Aimone Cat and the crew of the *San Giuseppe II*. Heading south the prow of the *Lindblad Explorer* frequently had to break through a thin crust of surface ice. They dodged icebergs as big as castles and cathedrals, ones that brought to mind the Baths of Caracalla or the Sydney Opera House. For two days they sailed parallel with the Antarctic Peninsula before turning east and then north east, and after visiting a British base they entered the strange circular bay of Deception Island. This crater of an extinct volcano had disappointingly once seemed to offer the safest of harbours but in fact proved vulnerable to winds and storms. A further disappointment for the Benuzzis was the rubbish on the grey ash of the beach and the total absence of wildlife for which the island had once been famous. At King George Island and then again on the mainland at Hope Bay they had better experiences that confirmed the magic pull they had felt from their first visit to the continent. Getting back to their ship had its hazards. The temperature was dropping fast and the surface of the sea was beginning to ice over. They encountered numbers of large leopard seals on ice floes, some wrestling with the penguins they meant to devour and flailing them about in the water, others shooting like dark torpedoes into the water beside the rubber boats or under them.[21]

For Stefania that second trip to Antarctica had been the most interesting and exciting of her life. On board their ship was a team of scientists who every evening explained to the passengers what they would see and do next day and answered their questions. She had been enormously impressed by everything she saw in this ultimate wilderness which became for her a lasting fascination not only up to the time when she lost the companionship of her husband but above all afterwards, for the subsequent twenty-five years.

In April they flew down to Patagonia, landing at Trelew. The Welsh had founded the town and given it its name; they also, the Benuzzis learned, gave the name to penguins, *pen gwyn* meaning white head. The first thing to impact them on arrival, however, was the wind which they were told was the real ruler of Patagonia. At the oil town of Commodoro Rivadivia they saw small boys catching with their bare hands sardines washed in dense shoals towards the beach. From Puerto Deseado further south they headed by bus into this vast and empty territory, where the wide streets and low pioneering structures in the small settlements made them think of outback Australia. After hours on the road they came to a remarkable attraction, a forest of petrified tree trunks lying like gigantic warriors felled on a battlefield, and a sign giving the explanation for tourists: araucaria conifers 80 million years old. They crossed an arid steppe on unasphalted road and after six hours reached the Andes. The small town of Calafate appeared as an oasis beside Lake Argentino: great blocks of ice floated in its waters of every shade of green.

Their destination was in fact the Moreno glacier. Huge masses of ice, fifty to sixty metres high, every so often fell with a fearful roar and thud into the lake; when they reached the glacier they impacted with enough pressure to carve a tunnel down through it. This sight of a mighty struggle between the forces of nature for the Benuzzis was by itself worth the whole journey. A motorboat took them into fjords that cut into the precipitous mountains. In the waters tinged dark violet were mirrored dense soaring forests and shattered glaciers. Waterfalls of Andean proportions thundered down, out of sight. Then all of a sudden they were aware of the flight coming out from a rocky ravine and descending towards them in wide circles of a solitary bird with big black wings. On board all eyes and binoculars and cameras hurriedly turned skywards and many were shouting, 'a condor, a condor!'[22]

***

The family was not done with travelling. In 1976 they also visited Mexico. Felice reported in a letter to Fantin how he had climbed Popocatepetl, an active volcano, to a height that he guessed, due to the mist, to be between 4700 and 4900 metres. Stefania and Silvia came to Mexico with him, but decided against going up the volcano. All three visited the Mayan monuments in the Yucatan, flying first to Merida and going on to Uxmal and Chichen-Itza. After that they flew south to Tikal in Guatemala, in an old twin-engine DC3 left over from the war. As they approached the airport they realised that one of the engines had failed: they had a terrifying landing from which they reckoned they were lucky to escape with their lives.[23]

Ambassador Benuzzi clearly got a lot out of these last three years of his career in the foreign service, not only from the chance to travel that his position provided him. He evidently enjoyed running the embassy, and was liked by his staff. Consul Colella, who held him in the greatest esteem, told an anecdote of his boss's first visit to Bolivia, and its aftermath. In La Paz Felice and Stefania had been fascinated by the national pastime of chewing coca leaves, and bought a small quantity when they saw it on sale in the market. They tried some of it out in their hotel room. Back in Montevideo the ambassador called Colella, the embassy counsellor and others over to his residence and told them he wanted them to help with an experiment. He produced a small box stuffed with strange leaves and asked them to try chewing a few. They all declined as politely as possible but he insisted: he wanted to know if this coca would have any effect. Reluctantly they each put a leaf in their mouth, and then two or three more at the ambassador's urging. None of them liked the taste but they had to keep going under the boss's mischievous eye. After a while their gums began to tingle but otherwise there was nothing. Finally the counsellor protested: 'That was fun, ambassador, but could we now do the right thing and have some coffee!' The ambassador certainly had an idiosyncratic sense of humour, Colella decided. He later asked a Uruguayan doctor about coca who told him that if mixed with saliva for long enough it helped deal with the rarefied air above 4000 metres mainly by warding off the tiring effects of altitude.

In August 1976 as his last act Felice wrote a report to the Italian Foreign Minister, describing how over the past three years the country had shifted from a democracy to becoming a stereotypical

Latin American state. He noted the efforts the embassy had made to assist the Italian community, adding that without false modesty he could take satisfaction from what had been achieved generally. On the issue of the political detainees, however, the task of an ambassador was depressingly arduous and he confessed to having been able to secure the release of just one. When he paid a farewell call on the Foreign Minister he had raised matters in similar terms, wondering aloud about the human rights situation in the country. That had made minister Blanco get hot under the collar, causing him to answer rudely: 'We're at war!' Felice now made a recommendation to his own minister regarding the fifteen Italians still being detained: that the government advise the Uruguayans that until their release no agreement could be given for a new ambassador to Italy. The Venezuelans had seemingly had success in holding up diplomatic credentials in this way. Since he was now also bringing to an end his own career Felice offered a comment for those who might have to read a copy of his report, especially younger colleagues: best to avoid all politicisation. The diplomatic career was not just a profession but a whole life of service to an ideal that transcended politics, a life that, were he to be reborn, he would not hesitate for a moment to live all over again.[24]

Felice and Stefania took the opportunity for one last trip out of Montevideo. They flew via Chile out across the Pacific to Easter Island. Because it had no name until it was finally discovered, Felice reflected that it had to be the most isolated island in the world. They spent several days there, and were naturally fascinated by the monumental stone figures. No less interesting for them was one of their guides, Leonardo Pakarati. They had read in a French text that he had gone adrift in a small fishing boat with three brothers and two children, for thirty six days, living off only raw fish. Eventually the family decided they should eat the oldest brother, Domingo. As luck would have it, before the horrid plan was put into effect, currents drove them ashore on an island of the Tuamotu group. Felice and Stefania did not feel like testing the truth of the story out on the protagonist, but they did regard Leonardo with some curiosity. On their last day they came across an elderly and solitary rider out on the open road. Their guide ground to a halt, jumped down from the jeep and greeted him with great respect. He introduced them: this was Domingo. The Benuzzis shook his hand with considerable warmth, without daring to explain why that was. The perhaps unfathomable mysteries of the island gave them plenty to think about as next day they headed back to normal life.[25]

CHAPTER 20 NOTES

[1] From Stefania 12.10.2012. Felice was offered an ambassadorship to Somalia: 'He declined, saying "I have an African past, which will not be well accepted in the country. It is not in your interest to send me there."' Felice letter to Daniela and Alan 3.3.1972: 'Nel dicembre '70 ho osato rifiutare Mogadiscio ... (In December 1970 I dared to knock back Mogadishu ...).'

[2] 'Tupamaro: Uruguayan leftist urban guerrilla organization... The earliest Tupamaro efforts were a mixture of idealism, public relations, and theft—robbing banks and businesses and distributing food and goods to the poor. In 1968 Tupamaro began more-aggressive efforts to undermine the established order, including raids on arsenals, arson, political kidnappings ... Its success was brief, however; by the time of the June 1973 military coup in Uruguay, Tupamaro had been neutralized by government troops, which managed to kill some 300 members and imprison nearly 3,000 others.' (*Encyclopaedia Britannica*).

[3] See Ros, A. (2012), *The Post-Dictatorship Generation in Argentina, Chile, and Uruguay: Collective Memory and Cultural Production,* Palgrave Macmillan; Kaufman, E. (1979), *Uruguay in Transition: From civilian to military rule,* Transaction Publishers, pp. 34-39; Powers, R.S. (2012), *Protest, Power, and Change: An Encyclopedia of Nonviolent Action from ACT-UP to Women's Suffrage,* Routledge, pp. 149-151. From Giampaolo Colella (see note 5 below): Uruguay had the fewest disappearances, with 1 in every 15,000 of the population – for Argentina it was 1:1600 and Chile 1:1000.

[4] Colella points out that Garibaldi was and is a controversial figure in Uruguay: in the civil war between the two traditional parties Colorado and Blanco he actively assisted the former in the defence of Montevideo, and was resented by other generals.

[5] Giampaolo Colella was of great assistance to the author with this chapter, in an interview in Rome on 23.5.2013 and in a detailed email message on 5.4.2014. He insisted that he not be referred to as consul: he was locally accredited as consular attaché as a way to provide him with protection in the event of diplomatic problems between Uruguay and Italy in this sensitive period.

[6] See De Masi, P. (2013), *Santiago. 1 febbraio 1973-27 gennaio 1974,* Roma: Bonanno

and Barbarani, E. (2012), *Chi ha ucciso Lumi Videla?* Milano: Mursia.

[7] Stefania (12.10.2012) meant that she did not speak Spanish perfectly, qualifying her remark: 'It's not so different from Italian... but I didn't want to pronounce a sentence that wasn't correct.'

[8] Email of 27.10.2013.

[9] Felice's account is in *Alpi Giulie* 69-1(1975) pp. 7-26: *Alle frontiere del silenzio bianco.*

[10] The account of this trip is in *Il Piccolo* article of 18.4.1974 by Arrigo Risano: *Beati loro sulle ali del vento.*

[11] Article in *Il Piccolo* of 5.11.1974: *Nelle acque affume di Titicaca le origini del culto di Vinecoche.*

[12] Email from Silvia of 3.11.2013.

[13] *Il Piccolo* 10.9.1974 and 16.4.1975; letter to Fantin 22.9.1977.

[14] Letter from Temple of 29.7.2013 and telephone conversation on 17.8.2013.

[15] Emails from Bongo Woodley of 16.11.2012, 29.11.2012, 11.12.2012; see Holman op. cit. pp. 220-221.

[16] Felice's account is in *Alpi Giulie,* 72-1(1978) pp. 7-22: *Andare sul Kibo;* Colella says that when Felice told him about his achievement he added: 'Just 37 metres more and I would have scored a 6,000 metre peak, maddening!'

[17] Letter to Fantin 22.9.1977.

[18] Felice's account is in *Alpi Giulie* 71-1(1977) pp. 7-17: *Incompiuta all'Illimani.*

[19] Letters of 12.2.1976.

[20] Stefania 12.10.2012; Felice's account is in L'Universo Anno LXII – n.4 luglio-agosto 1982 p. 641: Viaggio d'epoca alle isole contese.

[21] *L'Universo* Anno LXVII – n. 3 maggio-giugno 1978 pp. 513-576: *Il continente della solitudine.*

[22] *Il Piccolo* articles of 30.4.1976, 23.5.1976 and 25.6.1976.

[23] Letter to Fantin 22.9.1977; email Silvia 3 November 2013; Felice's account is in *L'Universo* Anno LXIII – n.4 luglio-agosto 1983: *Nella terra dei Maya.*

[24] From family archives: Letter to Minister Arnaldo Forlani dated 20.8.1976 and enclosing Felice's final report n. 330 'Rapporto di fine missione.'

[25] *L'Universo* Annata LX, Anno 1980, n. 3, pp. 361-388; and (second part) Annata LX, Anno 1980, n. 4, pp. 545-576: *Diario di Pasqua.*

Climbing Mt Whitney 1984

21

ANTARCTICA

Their return to Italy in the summer of 1976 represented for Felice and Stefania a seismic shift in their lives. Felice went into retirement and for someone as active and restless as he was, the future seemed testing: but he was determined to keep on travelling, writing and climbing. Stefania for her part was not one for a peaceful and static existence. Fortunately as they entered retirement they also had now living in Rome their daughter Daniela, her husband Alan and their seven year-old granddaughter Annalivia. Silvia had completed a year studying in England but had recently moved to California to begin a university degree in anthropology. Within a year Felice's mother Berta would also pass away, seven years after Nino did.

At the northern end of a long valley, the lengthened pyramid of the Matterhorn overlooks Breuil-Cervinia, one of Felice's favourite places in Italy. It was here at Easter 1976, a few months before his foreign service career ended, that he wound up his 150-page autobiographical memoir *Più che sassi*. Its final pages had the tenor of a requiem: 'Gradually, and inexorably, evening is coming on. What time is left is closing in. The breadth of what is possible lessens with each passing season. It is now already late.' He went on to recall how five years ago he had laid his father to rest in the village where the family had its origins, and how more recently the incomparable Giuàn Balletto, to whom he felt bound by much more than the thin sisal rope that linked them in their madness on

Mount Kenya, had also been buried on the slopes of Kilimanjaro. And so many other friends with whom he had climbed were also no more, among them Emilio Comici.[1]

But he brightened then, stating his determination to go into the mountains again, as soon as possible, because the passion was still there, the mountain bug still infected him, and was part of him now, he would probably never lose it. And, writing these pages, he was indeed back in the Alps and hoped to return to them many more times because he still had it in him, he was far from finished, 'and there is always room for hope.' No one knows why Felice did not have this memoir with its valedictory overtones published. He did continue contributing articles to the Trieste newspaper and also for specialised Italian magazines. Now that he had more time at his disposal these articles were longer, and often illustrated with photographs he had himself taken. His articles on Kilimanjaro and Illimani in *Alpi Giulie* were of about 4,000 words while others on Antarctica, Easter Island and the Mayan monuments were of 10,000 words each.

Alpi Giulie at that time was edited by Dario Marini, who well remembered Felice coming the first time to see him: he wanted to look the editor up because the previous year in the book at the top of Kilimanjaro his eye had been caught by 'Alpine Club Trieste' underneath the name Dario Marini. They got on well immediately, and Felice insisted they be on 'tu' terms. The ambassador was a gentleman, Marini said, cultured and elegant – but like any Triestine he was also easy-going, curious and cynical. He had the rare ability not only to put people quickly at ease but, by revealing interesting things from his own experience, to draw out similar things from others. He would often drop in to deliver his articles by hand, and linger at the office to look up old numbers in the archives. For those he would have to go up into the dusty loft and would emerge later in some disorder, quite out of character. He was in fine physical shape which was how he was still able to go climbing in his seventies. He had suggested to Marini that they go on excursions together, but the chance never came.[2]

An article that Felice brought along in 1979 was in the form of a letter which began: 'Dear friends, when you heard that I had climbed Mount Olympus, some of you asked for more information and I'm happy to provide it. In fact I think it is worthwhile spelling it all out for all the readers of our magazine.' Typically, that article had historical and cultural references including to Homer, detail on the features and flora of the mountain, as well as a depiction of how it was for him personally: 'Every half hour or so (at the pace I was going) comfortable benches, invariably situated in some panoramic spot with the scent of thyme and pines wafting, would lure me: but with an effort I resisted and carried on.' The article ended recommending that his readers spend longer than his twenty four hours on the mountain and see more than he did: and he counted on them to send him a postcard from Mount Olympus.[3]

Felice and Stefania had returned to their fine apartment in Via Nepi, close to the Ministry of Foreign Affairs. He had a number of matters to see to there, to do with terminating his nearly thirty years of service, and with his pension. The meetings he had in the Ministry, together with his declared availability, resulted in his being offered a range of assignments, most requiring only minimal personal involvement. He was appointed to the board of the International School for Advanced Studies in Trieste, and in that city, too, he was a founder member of FIT, an international body promoting the peaceful uses of science. He agreed to be president of the Italy-Pakistan cultural centre, and was made a member of the Institute of the Middle East and Far East, whose director was the venerable Giuseppe Tucci whom he had met during his posting to Karachi. In the corridors of the Farnesina he bumped into an officer who had worked for him in the consulate in Berlin, and naturally asked him what he was working on now. Antarctica, was the answer: the government is considering negotiating to become a party to the Antarctic Treaty. Felice, really interested, explained that he had been twice to the frozen continent. His colleague, who regarded this part of his job as tedious and a chore, spoke with his superior. Before long Felice was offered a consultancy, with the task of studying how Italy might join in the negotiating process. He accepted gladly. He would be involved with Antarctica on and off for the rest of his life.[4]

In 1980 Felice contributed an article for the *Rivista di Studi Politici Internazionali*, a quarterly review of foreign relations, which set out in detail perhaps for the first time for Italian readers all the elements of the Antarctic Treaty, including its legal aspects and the territorial claims made by some countries. In a second article on Antarctica that year, for *Il Piccolo* – for the first time it carried his own name as byline – Felice commented on a recent significant development, namely the passing by the lower house of parliament of a bill authorising the Italian government to join the Antarctic Treaty. In the article he explained that Italy had had no prior involvement largely because the government had not been interested and because funds had not been available for scientific programs. He then went on to spell out the advantages of joining the Antarctic 'club' established in 1959. Only by so doing could Italy take part in programs of great importance such as those in meteorology of relevance to the whole planet; research into oil and mineral resources were in their early stages; and the waters around the continent abounded in organic life including krill and algae rich in proteins and antibiotics. It would be another nine months before Italy was formally in a position to sign the treaty, but, as Felice noted at the end of his article, better late than never.[5]

Without doubt Felice was intrigued by the strong connection there had always been between mountaineering and the opening up of Antarctica. The first Italian to set foot on the continent was Pierre Dayné, an alpine guide from the Val d'Aosta, in a 1903-1905 French expedition. In 1957 the conqueror of Mt Everest, Sir Edmund Hillary, led a British Commonwealth expedition to the South Pole. In 1962 Ardito Desio, leader of Italy's successful attempt on K2, was the first Italian to the Pole, courtesy of the National Science Foundation of the U.S.A. Perhaps these common mountaineering experiences played their part in the development in the 1960s of ties between New Zealand's Antarctic Division and Italy's Council for National research (CNR), which for its part worked closely with CAI, the Italian Alpine Club: as a consequence between 1968 and 1977 CNR was able to send to Antarctica, in collaboration with New Zealand, three scientific expeditions whose members included not only geologists and physicists but also mountaineers.

In 1981, as a consequence of the Italian government's commitment to Antarctica and the good results of the scientific expeditions, a national program of Antarctic research was set up and a period of cooperation with New Zealand commenced. Italy was in a position to support joint projects, and had no territorial claims; New Zealand, which had a long history in Antarctica, needed to be able to justify the massive annual expenses occasioned by its Antarctic activities. So far for its program New Zealand had relied heavily on support from the United States with whom it had close links, but these were increasingly coming under strain: in 1984 a Labour government had been elected which wanted to bar nuclear-powered and nuclear-armed ships from entering its territorial waters. The ensuing difficulties in its relations with the US led it to seek greater independence of action and look for other countries ready to cooperate with it. Italy, a major economic power with a substantial logistic and industrial capacity, might well prove to be the ideal partner.

***

Felice now was fully engaged in learning all he could about Antarctica. He began translating Dayné's diary which would be published in 1989, under the auspices of Ardito Desio, text by Felice Benuzzi. Felice and Desio collaborated on *Antarctica: geography, economy, nature* which was published in 1984.[6] In

January that year the two of them called on the ninety year old orientalist Giuseppe Tucci, shortly before his death. In an article for *Il Piccolo* Felice wrote that they had found him as always extremely lucid, and effervescent. He wanted to have a whisky with them and when they toasted the start of a new year he replied 'chairete filoi' – cheers, friends. Then with half-closed eyes Tucci continued in classical Greek, quoting passages from one of Plato's dialogues, after which they talked of recent Italian exploration in Nepal.[7]

The first time Felice heard of the exploits of Mattia Zurbriggen who came from Macugnaga near Monte Rosa was when back in the 1950s he went climbing in New Zealand; the second was in Bolivia when people spoke of the man who conquered Aconcagua. In 1981 Felice wrote an article on Zurbriggen for *Alpi Giulie*. After further research, including hearing tales from old people in Macugnaga, he wrote and had published a 100-page book on the alpine guide, by the National Mountain Museum in Turin, in 1987. One story he told in it was of the fourth attempt made by English mountaineer Edward FitzGerald and Zurbriggen to climb Mount Sefton in the New Zealand Alps. At a certain moment a chunk of rock broke away which hit the mountaineer:

> and sent him into the void, head first, dangling from the rope that Zurbriggen struggled to hold on to for he was also barely able to keep his footing. FitzGerald, with a kick against the rockface, righted himself, checked the swaying of the rope and managed to grab a handhold so freeing Zurbriggen from the near-unbearable weight. Then, still with both ice-axes in his left hand, he climbed back up to where his guide was and together they sat for half an hour to regain their breath and steady their nerves. They saw that the chunk of falling rock had sliced through two of the three strands of their rope so that FitzGerald had literally been hanging by a thread.[8]

Now that he was retired Felice went climbing whenever he could, in the Cervinia area or in the Dolomites. He also climbed in Abruzzo which could easily be reached from Rome, with Sergio Kociancich who had looked after him in La Paz. In 1984, taking advantage of the posting to San Francisco of Daniela and Alan, Felice climbed Mt

Whitney: in North America, only peaks in Alaska and Mexico are higher. His companions on this outing were Gary and Jean Smith, good friends of Alan and Daniela. Gary tells the story:

On September 14 we were to meet Felice at Los Angeles airport. We were told to look for him at the airport arrival gate and he would signal us by holding up a comb. I dutifully scanned the arriving passengers looking for a 72 year old man. As the passengers cleared the gates, I had not been able to recognize any elderly foreign gentleman when suddenly one of the few remaining passengers raised his arm to produce a comb. The handsome gentleman looked twenty years younger than his age.

We picked up Jean from her office near the airport and drove about four hours to stay the night at a campground above Lone Pine California. Early next morning we were joined by the remainder of our hiking party and set out from the Whitney Portal trailhead. We reached our initial destination at Trail Camp after six miles – at 12,000 feet – and set up camp in early afternoon. While we boiled water on a gas cook stove for tea that evening, Felice said 'Please pass the fresh lemon and honey.' To this day we are uncertain whether he was serious or whether it was his dry sense of humour. He was further surprised to find we had mostly dried food that had to be hydrated before cooking. Upon retiring, he mused, 'I wonder how many people on the top of the continent are sleeping in their granddaughter's sleeping bag.'

Next morning, we hiked nearly five miles to the Mt Whitney summit, at 14,505 feet. We had started under clear skies but as the morning progressed, clouds moved in and by noon there was moderate snow and wind at the summit. Jean had partnered with Felice anticipating a slower pace due to the altitude. In the end, it was a younger Jean who was affected by the altitude, with Felice pacing her to the summit. A stone hut there provided shelter from the elements. Unfortunately, the cloud cover and moderate snowing at the summit prevented any view from the top of the mountain. An unknown hiker in the hut offered us boiling water for tea and a rest before returning to the Trail Camp. During this rest, I proudly presented Felice with a small replica of the Italian flag. He graciously accepted it with the comment, 'this flag is for Hungary but if you turn it this way, it is the flag of Italy.' The descent to the Trail Camp was uneventful with the snow turning to rain as we approached our camp and for a good night's rest before the return trip to the trailhead.

    We broke camp the following morning with Felice leading our party back to the trailhead at Whitney Portal. Daniela and Stefania met us there: Felice greeted them with a proud stride and a big warm smile of accomplishment.[9]

Not long after his return from California Felice contributed an article to *Alpi Giulie* on one of his heroes, Luigi Amedeo, Duke of the Abruzzi who was the uncle of the former viceroy in Ethiopia.[10] Luigi was an explorer and mountaineer. In 1899 he led the first Italian expedition to the Arctic; leaving his tent one night to train the dog-team he suffered frostbite to two fingers which had to be amputated on the spot to prevent gangrene. Pierre Dayné, much impressed by the duke's polar exploits, was driven to make his own mark in Antarctica; to his great surprise he met Luigi Amedeo in Madeira, not long after the French expedition of which he was a member had set out from Le Havre.[11] In 1976 Felice and Stefania aboard the Lindblad Explorer sailed below the Luigi Peak that Dayné had named a few months after that encounter in Madeira. In 1906 the duke led the first European expedition to the Mountains of the Moon in Africa and was the first to climb thirteen peaks in Ruwenzori Range. In 1909 he attempted to climb K2 but could only reach a ridge at nearly 7000 metres: that ridge, named after him, was on the route taken by the Italians who conquered the mountain in 1954. Luigi Amedeo who had been tasked in 1893 to quell unrest in Somalia, returned to that country in 1918 and set up experimental agricultural villages; he died there in 1933.

    In 1985 the National Mountain Museum in Turin published a tome on Alpine literature with a solid chapter by Felice on another of his heroes, Julius Kugy, for whom mountaineering was more than an athletic activity, it was something spiritual ('the best climber I ever knew was my pet monkey Benjamin').[12] The following year, the two hundredth anniversary of the first ascent of Mont Blanc, witnessed a debate on how best to protect the famous mountain. Roberto Osio, a noted climber from Lombardy, met with Felice and Carlo Alberto Pinelli, film director and climber: the three of them agreed on the need to draw international attention to the degradation of mountains around the world, brought on by globalisation, tourism, improved means of transport and a growing desire by more and more people to have access to them. As a result thirty or more mountaineers met in Courmayeur and produced a manifesto relating to Mont Blanc. In Biella the following year a new movement was born, Mountain Wilderness. Its scope was set out in the final document – the Biella Theses – which sought protection for 'any untouched mountain environment where anyone who so wishes may come into contact with the wide-open spaces, experience solitude, silence, rhythms, natural dimensions, laws and dangers.' Felice was one of the three moderators of the meeting, and one of the founder members, of Mountain Wilderness.[13]

***

The Antarctic treaty has two categories of membership, those who are Consultative Parties and those who are not: Felice liked to refer to these two groups as first and second division, as if they were football teams. The first group are the original twelve signatories to the treaty, plus those that demonstrate their interest in Antarctica by conducting substantial research activity there, notably by establishing a permanent base or sending expeditions. Once the Italian government became interested in Antarctica it was determined to be in this group. It was ready in principle to invest the necessary funds for the scientific expeditions, for the hire of a polar ship and for setting up a research station in Antarctica; and it discovered that New Zealand could be a worthy partner. In practice however it was not easy for Italy to move quickly, for political and economic reasons: an early problem was the selection of an existing, abandoned station as an Italian base which for various reasons then proved unusable, leading to an eventual choice of a site for a base in the Ross Sea, 350 kilometres from the New

Zealand base. Negotiations in 1983 and 1984 resulted in New Zealand's being satisfied that Italy was committed to undertaking a scientific program in that part of the continent which would fit in well with its own program, and it sought from Italy a formal agreement to this effect. Italian efforts were subject to various delays; meanwhile a number of other countries including Brazil, China, India and Uruguay were taking a real interest in Antarctica. Italy accordingly had a pressing need to begin implementing its Antarctic program both to qualify as a member of the elite group of parties as well as to convince New Zealand to look no further for a partner in its Antarctic activities: in 1984 New Zealand, under some budget strain, was keen to find another country willing to share the cost of a polar vessel.[14]

In 1985 Felice wrote another article for *Il Piccolo* in which he gave an account of an Antarctic Treaty Consultative Meeting in Brussels, attended by the full members: seated behind them were fourteen 'second division' members. The latter had signed the treaty but had not yet qualified for full-member status as they had not established either a substantial scientific research program or a permanent base on the continent. However the Italian delegate was able to inform the meeting that on 10 June the parliament had authorised the setting up of a national program of scientific and technological research in Antarctica; this program would enable an initial expedition to leave in December for New Zealand, whose government had given assurances of full cooperation; furthermore in 1986-88 a second expedition would begin the establishment of a permanent base. Felice asserted that the next Consultative Meeting in two years' time would address the issue of Italy's having fulfilled all the requirements for full membership.

In this article he was being somewhat optimistic. Italy and New Zealand were yet to reach total agreement on their relationship; there were delays in implementing the program of scientific and technological research; New Zealand was not wholly comfortable with Italy's choice of Terra Nova Bay as the site for its base in

Antarctica; and its practice of preparing for expeditions at least twelve months in advance had led to its requiring of Italy full details on itineraries, the number and specialisations of participants, the equipment being brought and the nature of the research programs. According to Polarnet, the CNR journal, in September 1985:

> a diplomatic mission led by Ambassador Felice Benuzzi was despatched to Wellington to provide details on Italy's commitment to Antarctica for the years ahead. The New Zealand authorities were satisfied with the program that was laid out, which as they had anticipated in 1984 would enable the shared use of ships so reducing their reliance on American ones as well as joint research activities with researchers being sent to the Italian base.[15]

This was a fine example of Felice's skills as a negotiator, at a decisive moment in Italy's Antarctic campaign; for him this triumph was perhaps the greatest of his diplomatic career.

Felice visited New Zealand several times in the 1980s: in return for the help New Zealand had provided in achieving its goals in Antarctica, Italy did what it could in support of New Zealand's own endeavours with the various Antarctica-related bodies and in the Ross Sea. An International Antarctic Centre had been established in Christchurch as headquarters of the research programs undertaken by New Zealand, the United States and Italy, with offices, storage facilities and workshops, and the functions of gathering, analysing and circulating scientific and environmental information on Antarctica.[16]

In three articles in *Il Piccolo* in 1986 Felice described the progress being made towards establishing a permanent Italian base: the first scientific expedition in the southern summer of 1985/86 had identified a suitable site at the Gerlache Inlet in Terra Nova Bay and the second in the summer of 1986/87 would commence construction. Felice concluded his third article on 8 October delighted that in all of this Italy had effectively met the requirements and would apply to be a Consultative Party at the next meeting, in 1987: 'In other words we will be in the first division in future arrangements for a human presence on the continent which nature seemed determined to prevent. We will be on equal footing with the other majors.'

For that crucial meeting, held in Rio de Janeiro from 5 to 16 October 1987, the Ministry of Foreign Affairs wanted its head of delegation to be a senior serving diplomatic officer and it designated the Ambassador in Brazil, Antonio Ciarrapico: Felice however was number two on the delegation. At this Fourteenth Antarctic Treaty Consultative Meeting Italy was accepted as a full member. The agenda was full of matters of interest to Italy, including the human impact on the Antarctic environment, the effects of tourism and non-governmental expeditions there, and progress being made towards a convention that would effectively prevent the exploitation of Antarctic mineral resources. Each delegation formally addressed the meeting. The Italian speech noted that since 1985 Italian scientists had worked at stations of other countries mainly in the field of geology, meteorology and marine biology. It also emphasised 'our debt of gratitude to those who have assisted them with their invaluable experience, above all the New Zealanders.'[17]

One of the scientists most involved in Italy's program of Antarctic research was Marcello Manzoni, a geologist who had been a member of the first expedition to Antarctica in 1968, organised jointly by the National Council of Research and the Italian Alpine Club.[18] Manzoni and mountaineer Ignazio Piussi had spent three weeks exploring glaciers and slopes of the Antarctic ice-cap where no one had ever been before.[19] Manzoni was on the delegation in Rio, and had been much impressed by Ambassador Benuzzi, recalling him not only as the complete diplomat but also as a man with a quirky sense of humour. With a big grin he had introduced himself saying, 'Sono Felice!' There was a double ambiguity, because it could mean 'I am happy!' and it could also mean they ought to be immediately on first name terms. The latter was not the case: the scientist was deferential to the ambassador, who always addressed Manzoni by his surname.

Felice had envied Manzoni his explorations, since his own visits had been on cruise ships, with limited opportunities to move about on land. Manzoni explained that a good deal of pressure had since come, not least from New Zealand, to exclude future uncontrolled wanderings, or anything resembling sport. Grabbing his elbow Felice replied, 'Manzoni, you can't imagine the deals that can be done. True, we are indebted to them over Antarctica. But we also buy three million lamb cutlets from them.' Manzoni did not ask for clarification of this cryptic remark. He was in any case much taken by the lordly Dr Benuzzi's common touch. Buying cooked crayfish on the beach, Felice had treated the urchin who was selling them with respect as though this was a high class restaurant. He disappeared one weekend and on the Monday told Manzoni he had been out to see the baroque churches at Ouro Preto, 400 kilometres north, on a bus crammed with ordinary folk, quite a few of whom were clutching poultry. Manzoni, struck by the casual and unconcerned account he was listening to, could not imagine other ambassadors doing what this one had done.

The following January the two of them were on another Antarctic delegation together, this time in Wellington, New Zealand. This was at the eleventh and penultimate session of informal negotiations for an international agreement regulating mineral resources. It was the first meeting in which Italy took part, and Felice was head of delegation. After six years the end was in sight of some difficult arguments over issues such as compensation payable by the party responsible for any harm done to the ecosystem. Also on the delegation was legal expert Professor Francesco Francioni. He remembered Felice as more than a diplomat: he was cultivated, a writer, naturalist, explorer and humanist. Asked about the negotiations the professor said they were delicate ones not only on account of the ecological matters under discussion but also because of claims made by some for territorial sovereignty in Antarctica. Dr Benuzzi was completely on top of the negotiations.

At one embarrassing moment the German delegation had insisted that among the convention's official languages there must be also German. Felice took the floor to heap praise on the language of Goethe which in his view was absolutely on a par with the language of Dante. All present could see at once that if German were included so too should Italian, and perhaps other languages. In the face of this victory for Benuzzi diplomacy the German delegation withdrew its proposal.[20]

Professor Francioni was at two Antarctic meetings where Felice was head of delegation. If any discussion had political elements then the ambassador took charge, consulting Francioni on technical and juridical matters; very graciously he gave his colleague the lead on discussions over the complex legal aspects related to mineral exploitation. It was not always so with other heads of delegation, according to the professor. He got on well with Felice and they spent some pleasant evenings together. Stefania also came to the meeting in Wellington and Francioni remembered how intelligent and sociable she was. On a couple of occasions they invited young people to join them, and Felice was convivial and at home in their company. From Christchurch he and Stefania took the bus to the Mount Cook area, and on the way had to stop while thousands of sheep crossed the road. At the Hermitage Felice found one of the guides from twenty years earlier and he showed them round. For Stefania that trip, the only time she visited New Zealand, was wonderful.

As in Rio, Felice left town one weekend on an adventure that surprised the other members of the delegation when they heard about it later. He made his way to Ohakune, on the south-west slopes of Ruapehu, an active volcano and the highest mountain in New Zealand's North Island. He had failed in an effort to climb it, in September 1985. On that occasion he had just missed the coach in Wellington. The stationmaster had got a staff member to drive him in his own car to the next stop, twenty kilometres away: this could only happen in New Zealand, Felice reflected. On arrival he was met by Lisle Irwin, ranger at the Tongariro National Park, who took one look at the Italian's shabby gear and paying him the ultimate compliment said, 'you're a man of the mountains.' Heavy rain, unfortunately, had prevented their making the ascent. This time all went well. Felice and Lisle took things steadily, up to the glacier. Here Lisle cut a few steps with his axe and the cracking sound it made was for Felice 'a music that I dared not hope to hear again in my lifetime.' They reached Ruapehu's crater, filled with pale green water streaked in pink and yellow, whose temperature was between 40 and 60 degrees. It was not possible for them to continue on to the summit as they would have required crampons, and more time than they had at their disposal. Felice concluded his tale of this enterprise, published in *Alpi Giulie* and dated Ohakune, 24 January, 1988:

> It is always sad going down, especially for someone knowing it is the last time for them to set foot on a mountain that they always longed for and finally got to know. But I have settled my account with Ruapehu. Tonight at Leslie and Helen's house I'll go out into their garden with its strange and fragrant smells and looking up I'll find the Southern Cross. I'll give it my last farewell.[21]

It seems odd that Felice did not think it likely he would be back in New Zealand in less than six months, to head the delegation at the final session of the negotiations that would see the adoption of the Convention on the Regulation of the Antarctic Mineral Resource Activities. Perhaps he had a premonition, the way his mother Berta frequently had. In any case the health of this 78-year old was not excellent and it was the reason why he declined to make another journey to the other side of the world.

CHAPTER 21 NOTES

[1] *Più che sassi* p. 146.
[2] Telephone conversation with Marini 17.5.2013; see also *Point Lenana*, pp. 431-433.
[3] *Alpi Giulie,* 73-1 (1979) pp. 7-17.

[4] Conversation with Stefania, Daniela and Silvia, Città della Pieve 13.10.2012; with Stefania and Daniela 9.5.2013; see also *Point Lenana*, pp. 434.

[5] *Rivista di studi politici Internazionali* Vol XLVII No 2 1980 pp. 224-236: *Il Trattato sull'Antartide*; *Il Piccolo* 22.6.1980: *Anche l'Italia entrerà nel Trattato Antartico*.

[6] Desio, A. & Benuzzi, F. (1984), 'L'Antartide notizie geografiche, economiche, naturalistiche', Memorie della Società Geografica Italiana Torino: UTET 1984 – with chapter 3 by Marcello Manzoni, *Gli elementi geografici*. Felice contributed Chapter 9 *Il Trattato sull'Antartide* and asserted (p. 228): 'Non posso chiudere questa nota senza esprimere l'auspicio che il nostro governo intraprenda al più presto i passi necessari per l'adesione dell'Italia alla convenzione per la conserva delle risorse marine viventi dell'Antartide.' (I cannot finish without expressing the hope that our government will move as soon as possible to have Italy adhere to the convention on the protection of Antarctic marine resources.)

[7] The article paying homage to Tucci, *Quelle rose di Indira*, under the by-line of Felice Benuzzi, was published two years later: *Il Piccolo* 18.4.1986.

[8] *Mattia Zurbriggen, guida alpina: le sue imprese, i suoi uomini, i suoi monti* di Felice Benuzzi: Museo Nazionale della Montagna 'Duca degli Abruzzi', Torino 1987 pp. 45-46; *Alpi Giulie*, 75-1(1981): *Mattia Zurbriggen guida di giulio Kugy*.

[9] Email of 2 February 2013.

[10] *Alpi Giulie*, vol. 79-1(1985): *il Duca degli Abruzzi alpinista*.

[11] Chabod, A. & Blanc, S. (2008), *La montagna abita a Valsavarenche, Firenze:* il Valico, p. 83.

[12] *Letteratura dell'Alpinismo* Museo Nazionale della Montagna 'Duca degli Abruzzi', Torino 1985 pp. 33-40: *Julius Kugy Scrittore*.

[13] Labande, F. (2004), *Sauver la montagne,* Editions Olizane, pp. 152-153: 'En 1986, le président du CAI est Roberto Osio. Discret, mais déterminé, Osio juge qu'il est grand temps de prendre une initiative face au déferlement d'aggressions sur le milieu montagnard. Il trouve du répondant en la personne de Felice Benuzzi et de Carlo Alberto Pinelli, et tous trois vont organiser le rassemblement de Courmayeur (In 1986 Robert Osio, the cautious but determined president of the Italian Alpine Club, decided the time was right to take steps to protect the mountain environment from the attacks now unleashed against it. In full agreement with him were Felice Benuzzi and Carlo Alberto Pinelli, and the three of them set about organizing the Courmayeur meeting).'

[14] A full account of Italy's involvement in Antarctica from the outset can be found in *L'Italia e l'Antartide: Le origini del Programma Nazionale di Ricerche in Antartide* by Emanuele Gori: Polarnet Technical Report Scientific and Technical report series PTR-3/2001.

[15] Polarnet Technical Report series PTR-3/2001 p. 67.

[16] The basis was thus laid for lasting cooperation. The New Zealand Government publication *New Zealand Antarctic and Southern Ocean Science: Direction and Priorities 2010-2020* states 'New Zealand pools logistics with the US and Italian Antarctic programmes which use Christchurch as their gateway to Antarctica and this collaboration is an important strand to New Zealand's relationships with both these

countries.'

[17] Report of the Fourteenth Antarctic Treaty Consultative Meeting (ATCM XIV), Rio de Janeiro, Brazil, 05 Oct 1987 - 16 Oct 1987.

[18] Manzoni *La natura dell'Antartide* op. cit.; Tamburelli, G. (2008), *The Antarctic Legal System: The Protection of the Environment of the Polar Regions,* Giuffrè, p. xi highlights contribution of Marcello Manzoni and Carlo Stocchino in the Ross Sea in 1984; *Point Lenana*, pp. 439-441.

[19] The full story of those three weeks in 1968 is told in Manzoni, M. (2012), *Zingari in Antartide,* Alpine Studio.

[20] Francioni, F. & Scovazzi, T. (1989), '*La convenzione di Wellington sulle risorse minerarie antartiche',* Rivista di diritto internazionale 72(1), pp. 27-41; email Francioni author 30.1.2013; interview with Professor Francioni 20.5.2013.

[21] *Alpi Giulie* 1988 N. 82/1 pp. 3-8: *Ruapehu*. Correspondence with Irwin December 2012-January 2013. On 7.1.2013 this in an email on why Felice had referred to him as Leslie: 'The confusion over my name is something that happens to me all the time. "Lisle" is short for Carlisle. It happens so often that I don't notice or don't bother correcting people.'

With the Queensland University climbers (left to right) John Comino, Felice, Geoff Goadby, Alan Frost and (in front) Peter Barnes, 1954

22

EXIT

For some years Felice had been in indifferent health. Stefania said that in a sense he had come to terms with his mortality and knew that his life might end any time: but he had no intention of changing anything, and carried on travelling and going up mountains. He had trouble with his hearing, and on a couple of occasions had told her that he missed a lot during meetings and it might be time to stop going to them.[1]

Stefania had detected another reason for his increasing reluctance to go to conferences, namely the seeming lack of appreciation by the Foreign Ministry for the efforts he put into to work on Antarctica. Those efforts were to come to their culmination at the October 1987 meeting in Rio de Janeiro when Italy would have its political victory and be accepted as a Consultative Party, a full member of the Antarctic treaty system: but Felice was not to be head of delegation. Three months later he headed the team at a technical meeting in Wellington, and in a personal sense that was certainly satisfying. But it seems he considered it would simply not be worth it to go back in June 1988 for a meeting at which member states would sign an agreement to regulate the exploitation of Antarctic mineral resources. He may well have guessed that this convention would never actually come into force.[2]

Instead, on 1 July, he flew to Madrid on a mission which he actually enjoyed a lot. Spain had joined the treaty system in 1982, one year after Italy, and had sent scientific expeditions to

Antarctica in the southern summers of 1986-87 and 1987-88 so that it, too, was now in a position to apply for full membership. It asked Italy if it was prepared to share its recent experiences, and as a consequence the Ministry of Foreign Affairs sent Felice. Stefania explained that his plane arrived late in Madrid, and when he and the party he was leading entered the meeting room:

> everybody stood up and applauded him. He was astonished, and went bright red. As always he had made every preparation and he delivered a fine speech. Despite his time in Uruguay he still had reservations about his Spanish and so got the Foreign Ministry to translate his speech for him. He delivered it in Spanish and it was a great success.

It was a Friday and as was now his habit on such occasions he left the capital next day with a colleague on an excursion to Toledo, a city that he and Stefania had visited in 1972 when they were posted to Paris.[3]

On Sunday evening Felice returned to Rome. Next morning, 4 July, he did the short walk to the Farnesina and submitted the paperwork and receipts for reimbursement of his travelling expenses. Back home he had lunch with Stefania. He got up from the table saying he would tell her about Toledo later, took a few steps and then suddenly collapsed. Stefania heard the thump in the kitchen and rushed to help him. Leaning over him she asked how he was, he tried to say something but a minute later he was dead.

For Stefania the shock was awful, but she accepted that he had not suffered at all, and had died at home. She at once rang Daniela who had come back from the United States with Alan and Annalivia only a short while before. That very morning Felice had wished them a safe journey as they set out from Rome for the small property they had bought in Puglia, and they had hardly arrived when they heard he had died. Stefania also called Silvia who was then in Calabria. All of them rushed back to Rome.

Felice was buried in the family tomb at Dro alongside his parents and two of his brothers. His friend Dario Marini returned to Trieste to find waiting for him a postcard from Felice, sent from Madrid, saying he was at an Antarctic meeting and looked forward to seeing him in September. *Alpi Giulie*, which had run Felice's article on Ruapehu in its first issue for 1988 now in its second issue had an obituary by Marini which began: 'On 4 July 1988, in his home in Rome, the sudden death occurred of Felice Benuzzi, a figure at the highest level of mountain literature and a mountaineer with a long and illustrious career.' After describing his accomplishments it ended: 'For Stefania Benuzzi nothing will fill the emptiness left by such a companion but she will have had the privilege of having spent a long and happy life alongside a man who was in every sense extraordinary.'[4]

Over the following months Stefania dedicated herself to looking after some of the inevitable loose ends. One task she set herself was to type the manuscript of *Più che sassi*. Since Felice had told her it needed a little more work initially she circulated a few copies only among friends. One copy of the unpublished work was placed in the safekeeping of the National Mountain Museum in Turin.[5]

Marini had rightly mentioned in his obituary that Felice and Stefania had been married a long time: in fact it would have been their fiftieth anniversary just two months later. Stefania had been with her husband on practically all of the adventurous excursions he had undertaken during and subsequent to his diplomatic career. She had helped him make presentable all the handwritten drafts of articles to be submitted to newspapers and journals. She had stuck by him in difficult times. In Berlin, especially, she had developed contacts that were professionally useful to him. It had not always been easy. She had health problems which aggravated the trials of life in hot countries, and she suffered from a congenital problem with one leg which deteriorated in later life, impairing her mobility. She had had to cope with Felice's perfectionist professional standards, his obsession with mountains and his wish to control most situations, as well as his responses to approaches by women who found him attractive.

All those who knew them both had the greatest admiration for her. Like him she was bright and cultured and perfectly fluent in three languages. And, as also displayed when on her own and with a baby in Africa, she was his equal in bravery. With a strong character and a restlessness of spirit she was now able to cope with life on her own. The opportunity came with Mountain Wilderness.[6] Stefania, too, had caught mountain fever. The first meeting after the foundation of the organisation was to take place at Evian in France that October, and she was keen to attend. When she arrived she was warmly welcomed by all present who had such fond memories of Felice. At the official lunch she was placed alongside President Roberto Osio. Next to her, symbolically, was an empty chair, in honour of Felice. Halfway through the meal founder member Carlo Alberto Pinelli came and sat beside her. Knowing her linguistic capabilities he offered her a paid job as secretary for Mountain Wilderness: this she accepted with alacrity, although she refused to take any salary.

For many years Stefania worked for Mountain Wilderness. Pinelli had the highest regard for her skill in judging people, knowing straight away if a person was or was not reliable. To begin with her tasks were mainly in translating but quite soon she made herself indispensable in the office as coordinator of global activities. She had a direct and energetic style, and got on best with the men she had to deal with, some of whom had international reputations and sizeable egos. A member who was also a tour organiser and guide said though she was in fairly poor physical shape she devoted great energy to the organisation and was clearly devoted to the husband she had lost. She was 'a lady who was always attentive and accessible especially to young members, modest and humble as only those rich in heart can be.'[7]

***

In Kenya in 1995 various ceremonies were arranged to mark the fiftieth anniversary of the end of the Second World War. The Italian ambassador in Nairobi had the idea of commemorating Felice's achievement, and invited the members of his family to attend. Stefania, Daniela and Silvia flew to Nairobi in November. There was a big reception at the embassy and an exhibition at the Italian cultural institute. They then travelled to Nyeri, where almost seven hundred Italian prisoners were buried, together with the Duke of Aosta.[8] They carried on to Nanyuki to visit the site of the POW camp, only to discover that virtually no trace of it remained. To their surprise and gratification, when they entered the nearby Naro Moru Lodge and said who they were, this caused quite a stir. In Kenya apparently Benuzzi was a name favourably known to a good many people.[9]

At some point they met Bongo Woodley, who like his father before him was now the senior warden in charge of Mt Kenya National Park. In 1974 Bill Woodley had flown Felice around the mountain. Now his son was to fly the three Benuzzi ladies one by one in a small plane over the same general area. They met at the aerodrome at dawn, and the weather was bad, with low clouds. It was only on their last day in Kenya that the clouds finally and fortunately lifted. The weather threatened to deteriorate and so in haste Bongo took off with Stefania. After circling high up and around Mt Kenya he brought her down and took off next with Daniela and then Silvia. For the first time these three were able to appreciate fully the distance from the camp to the forests, and the ruggedness of the terrain. The foolhardiness of Felice's entire project hit them. It was clear that none of the POW climbers could have had any proper notion of what they were up against. That they had successfully managed it now seemed a miracle.

Reflecting on all this many years later Silvia remembered her father, when talking about what he had done, saying he felt then like Adam at the beginning of everything. She thought that innocence, ignorance and paradise were all somehow wrapped up in this for him; but in any case what had happened to him up there had been in part spiritual and transcendental and had changed his life. Some of this comes through at the end of the chapter entitled 'The Unknown' in *No Picnic on Mount Kenya*, and they are the very last words in the Italian version:

> Every step led to new discoveries, and we were continually in a state of amazed admiration and gratitude. It was as though we were living at the beginning of time, before men had begun to give names to things.[10]

The 1943 escapade clearly lent itself to film treatment. The matter had been brought up by director Pinelli when he and Stefania had their conversation in 1988. With her full permission he in due course made a highly professional documentary called *Double Dream on the Equator*. This film narrated the achievement of Felice and his companions and illustrated it with footage of an expedition organised by Mountain Wilderness in 2002 in which Pinelli and mountaineer Fausto de Stefani followed more or less their route to the top of Mount Kenya.[11]

Already half a century earlier there had been talk of a film. In a letter from Karachi dated 13 December 1955, Felice had written to Peter Barnes, one of the students he had climbed with in Queensland: 'You will perhaps be interested in knowing that some Italian film-people are planning to make a film out of my Kenya book. God knows what a frightful love story they will be mixing into it.' Stefania recalled that six years later Felice was in New York for discussions on Alto Adige: an Italian entrepreneur had approached him then and persuaded him to sign over the film rights, which were then onsold to 20th Century Fox.

In September 1994 the movie *The Ascent* was released, directed by Donald Shebib. Drawing its inspiration from the 1943 escapade, the screenplay moved away from it radically: the story was now of a race to the summit, and in the background was a beautiful widow. The Benuzzi family despaired. Stefania insisted that Felice's name be removed entirely from the credits; she could not however prevent the blurb referring to a 'real-life adventure.' She commented that Felice at the time of course had plenty of other things on his mind, but still he never had any head for business.

In 1953 an episode of 'Robert Montgomery Presents' in the United States was based on an adaptation of *No Picnic on Mount Kenya*, starring George Chandler. While Felice was at the OECD in Paris in the 1960s he responded positively to another approach for a film which while not telling his story might depict a quirky Italian mountain-climbing feat, one challenging fate and harsh British POW camp conditions. Nothing came of this, nor of a proposal by mountaineer and film-maker Rick Ridgeway, who wrote the introduction to a 1989 edition of Felice's book and directed the summit scenes of *The Ascent*. In 2008 film director Gabriele Iacovone made a factually correct version of *Fuga Sul Kenya*, under that title. In the end the Benuzzi family were able to reacquire the film rights.

Felice's book is his principal and lasting legacy. His extraordinary enterprise has inspired many mountaineers from Italy to New Zealand to travel to Kenya and climb the mountain which will be permanently linked to his name. Other people have gone out of their way to follow in his footsteps, including the authors of the 2013 book *Point Lenana*.

On 7 March 2013 in the magnificent setting of the Palazzo Senatorio at the Campidoglio in Rome an event was held to mark seventy years since Felice's achievement: according to the invitation this was 'an unforgettable escape which will always remain a landmark in human daring.' The event, entitled 'Seventeen Days of Freedom,' was organised by Mountain Wilderness.[12] More than a hundred people were present, including noted mountain-climbers Fausto De Stefani and Kurt Diemberger. It began with a screening of Pinelli's documentary of climbing Mt Kenya and was followed by a round table meeting with speeches in honour of Felice. Stefania had been granted rare permission to be driven up to the front door on the hill above the ancient Forum, and was wheeled in to the centre of the front row. Many tributes were also paid to her.

Stefania, at the age of 97, had become increasingly immobile, and her health – although not her mind, which remained wonderfully keen until the end – went into decline. She had been looking forward to this occasion. She played her part and derived satisfaction from it. Two months later she passed away at her home in Città della Pieve in Umbria.

CHAPTER 22 NOTES

[1] *Point Lenana*, pp. 443-446 gives a good account of the events of July 1988.

[2] Felice headed the Italian delegation to the eleventh and penultimate meeting preparing for the Convention on the Regulation of Antarctic Mineral Resources in Wellington from 18-29 January 1988; Rothwell op. cit. p. 135.

[3] *Il Piccolo* 25.1.1973: *Fa risplendere l'arte più pura del Greco*.

[4] Telephone conversation with Marini 17.5.2013; *Alpi Giulie*, vol. 82-2(1988); *Point Lenana*, p. 443.

[5] Conversation with Stefania, Daniela and Silvia, Città della Pieve 13.10.2012. See Introduction, note 4.

[6] See Introduction, note 9.

[7] See http://lucagianotti.wordpress.com/leggere-coi-piedi/.

[8] In the war cemetery at Kiganjo near Nyeri are 368 Commonwealth graves. At Mathari, 5 kilometres away, the Italian War Memorial Church has a sanctuary that houses the remains of 676 mostly Italian soldiers. In front of the altar is the marble tomb of the Duke of Aosta.

[9] Conversation with Stefania, Daniela and Silvia, Città della Pieve 13.10.2012; *Point Lenana*, pp. 587-588.

[10] *No Picnic on Mt Kenya* p. 151; *Fuga sul Kenya* p. 330.

[11] *Doppio Sogno all'Equatore* by Carlo Alberto Pinelli, 2002; Silvia Benuzzi, 13.10.2012: 'Pinelli takes the same route father took, and that's why the doppio sogno, because it is the story of my father but it is also the story of making the same route.'

[12] See www.mountainblog.it/diciassette-giorni-di-liberta-roma-7-*marzo-2013*/.

23

LEGACY

In his tribute to Felice upon his death in July 1988 Dario Marini was right to highlight his significance as a mountain-writer and a mountain-climber, in that order. Certainly the scaling of Mt Kenya by a malnourished prisoner of war with no map and only makeshift equipment was an almost unbelievable feat: but we remember Felice for his book. Though he had a mania for mountains, climbed on several continents, began as a boy and carried on until just before he died, he was not an outstanding mountaineer. In 2007 Marini reflected once more on Felice's real contribution. The book he wrote was utterly memorable 'above all for the understated way in which it told of a difficult and dangerous enterprise, without any self-promotion or hyperbole that is all too common in tales of mountaineering.' Marini however in that later article wanted to bring to the attention of his readers the unpublished *Più che sassi* memoirs in which Felice was able to write in an original way about 'mountaineering as something spiritually uplifting that can fortify a trouble soul, an aspect beyond the experience of those who go collecting the world's highest peaks or climb with their eyes on their watch.'[1]

The quintessential element of the *More than rocks* memoirs was the 'more', the something extra. The central chapter of *No Picnic on Mount Kenya* is an interlude which begins 'Mountains, like people, have their history. They too are born, grow, decay and die.' Felice says one cannot claim that they love, 'but it is true —

and how true – that they are loved.' In this chapter he analyses the fascination that this mountain had initially for Africans with their myths and legends and then for European explorers and those desiring to climb it. As a boy he had gone with his father Nino up Triglav 'and we placed our feet on the top of the king of the Julian Alps, the mountain sacred to the Slovenes.' In that aftermath of the First World War Felice and his companions were aware of the battles recently fought in those mountains which they were taught to view as 'now silent witnesses to tragedies, heroisms and unspeakable sufferings' – but they gave no critical thought at all to the fact that a large Slav presence was now here in Trieste's hinterland, within Italy's new borders. Afterwards he perhaps felt guilty about that. In any case in his adult life he made every effort to comprehend the ancient and the contemporary history behind every mountain he climbed. In his final months as a POW he visited a volcanic crater in Kenya and was highly intrigued by tales of the Wanderobo, without managing to discover whether they were real people or part of local superstitions. In Australia he wanted to know about Aboriginal lore relating to the weird rocky peaks in Queensland and wrote that 'one needs to understand nature in the antipodes which of course is so utterly different from our own, and to appreciate it.' He learned of the volcanoes in New Zealand's North Island that 'once were warriors and rivals, and the fire they nursed in their hearts was none other than their love for the beautiful Pehanga.' Writing of his ascent of Mount Olympus he was well aware without having to spell it out that this was the dwelling-place of the gods.

In the prologue to his memoirs Felice said it was hard for him as a writer to 'capture or lock in a moment which is still throbbing with life, and light.' It was practically an obsession for him to first find these moments and then to put them on display. As a boy he yearned to break out of hemmed-in Trieste and travel to exotic places. As an adult he wanted to share with everyone the moments he had discovered in for example Antarctica which he visited twice, and wrote about with titles to his articles like 'The continent of solitude' and 'On the frontiers of white silence.' He was perpetually on the lookout for the extraordinary. It was not enough to visit Easter Island with its bizarre stone monoliths: the key point of interest for him there was the islander who decided to eat his brother, and the encounters he had with these two who both luckily survived. Felice was fascinated by exceptional people like the explorers and mountaineers who had risked everything, and he longed to do something similar. He was not impressed by the experienced mountaineer in the POW camp who reckoned it was impossible, insane even, to climb Mount Kenya: 'He was a realist and when all is said and done it was he who was right; I am an incurable idealist, or possibly a madman, as he had it.'[2]

Felice did know how to capture the moments of throbbing life. In his memoirs he wrote of the 1920s, when there were many more people living in the valleys than today, and far fewer people on their way to the summits. He wrote of 3 a.m. arrivals at tiny stations, of trudging hour after hour on the hard snow of country roads to get to the foothills, of steep paths up in the moonlight and then the final climb. He was able to capture the ecstasy of reaching the summit, not easy to imagine for anyone who has never done it – perhaps the best comparison would be a cocaine or heroin high. In a 1980 article for *Alpi Giulie* he described the moment he reached the top of Zuc del Boor with Emilio Comici:

> In the Canale del Ferro valley below us a bluish smoke spread over the village roofs and the flowers on the fruit trees were a gossamer veil over the fresh green fields. This was spring sweetly exulting: and then gusts of breeze brought all the way up to us the tolling of bells for the first Easter Mass: Rejoice, rejoice, Alleluia![3]

Whenever he planned to tackle a mountain Felice would always try and find out about the early efforts to scale it and and the first successful reaching of the summit, and as a writer was keen to pass this information on. As a POW he was tormented by what he did *not* know about Mt Kenya, and he wrote 'Krapf and Teleky,

Shipton, Wyn Harris and Tilman, Gregory and Mackinder and his European alpine guides had all made huge efforts to understand the mountain: but for us it was if they had never even existed! ...Our ignorance proved an insuperable handicap from the point of view of material achievement.'⁴ Before attempting Illimani in Bolivia he talked about the mountain over dinner with some who knew it very well: from one of them he heard the legend of the Indian who vanished after getting too close to the throne of the god Viracocha. Felice had read how Sir Martin Conway, conqueror of Illimani, climbing with Italian guides had come across an ancient woollen rope, making him think there might be some truth in the legend; what Conway did not know was that Carlos Wiener had preceded him twenty years earlier. Someone else at the dinner told Felice of the Italian mountaineer Carlo Nembrini who fell to his death up there in 1973.

None of the climbers who had gone before him were more important to Felice than Julius Kugy; he wrote often about him and agreed completely with Willy Merkl (a German mountaineer who later died on Nanga Parbat) that 'Kugy's book is our bible and for us he is the prophet Elias.'⁵ He first heard about him on his early excursions with Nino and after that would watch 'with respectful curiosity when the imposing figure wrapped in a green loden coat made his way along the Corso in Trieste.' Felice was awed by Kugy's achievements at a time when, in Kugy's own words, 'many peaks did not even have a local name and apart from one or two of the main ones all those Alps were virgin.' He was awed, too, by Kugy's whole approach: he had started out as a botanist, and for him the best information was to be had from shepherds and hunters, as well as from the mountain guides whom he held in great esteem. Kugy's equipment was rudimentary, an axe to make steps in the ice, a rope. Once after scrutinising a difficult rockface he wrote: 'I thought about using pitons and I had some in my rucksack. But it would have given me no pleasure to get to the top using artificial means, and those pitons are right now still rusting in my cupboard.'⁶

Kugy's book, *Aus dem leben eines Bergsteigers*, came out in 1925 and the teenaged Felice read it soon afterwards, underlining page after page. He loved its very title which translates literally as 'from the life of a mountain climber' because it perfectly summed up Kugy the man, who abhorred anything pompous and who took as his first principle that a mountaineer must be 'truthful, noble and modest.' Felice wholly accepted Kugy's belief that truthfulness in mountain-climbing is that spiritual element which can make us rise above ourselves, and he believed that for Kugy mountains were a sanctuary. He admired his hero's fresh, spontaneous prose. In 1985 Felice contributed a chapter entitled 'Julius Kugy, writer' for *Alpine Literature*, published in Turin. He quoted no excerpts from Kugy's book but had he wanted to he could have chosen none better than this paragraph describing an incident on Jof Fuart, a mountain that Felice knew well:

> In the ravine there were, indeed, the expected overhangs, which explained why the chamois avoid this gully. At two points they were so high that we had to form a triple *Steigbaum*, or human tree. I took the lowest place, Josz stood on my shoulders, while the agile Oitzinger as the lightest climbed up over us. At the second step, however, he had to stand on Josz's head, in order to reach the decisive handhold, and in so doing he slipped, and was within an ace of falling. He recovered his balance with extraordinary skill, and finally swung himself up. But the swaying crown, which he represented in this critical moment, set the tree-stem below into violent oscillation. At first the gravity of the situation struck us all, and especially the burdened base of the tree; but an instant later we realised its extraordinarily comic side. It must have looked like three clumsy bears executing a crazed danse macabre against the vertical cliffs.[7]

According to Kugy there is more to be learned from failures in the mountains than from victories, and he found the notion of 'conquest' distasteful. His advice was to weigh the chances as carefully as possible, and go ahead only if these justified it. This good sense was to become Felice's own philosophy, although he was not yet ready for it when he and Nino failed to reach the summit of Monte Nero:

> And so my first alpine outing ended up, perhaps instructively,
> in an unachieved goal: it was the first and would not be the last
> time that happened. How many matters like that have I had in
> my life! How many proofs of my limitations![8]

Felice never got to the top of Illimani or Ruapehu, and Mt Cook
was a total failure. But the mother of all unachieved goals was
Batian. On 8 February 1943, as the three POWs made their way
down, he brooded on the huge disappointment. It is a key passage
in *Fuga sul Kenya* as it throws light on his restless character. At the
same time it offers readers, and not just those with an interest in
climbing, thoughts on dealing with some comparable frustration
or regret. Felice twice asks himself: Really and truly what did we
achieve? As mountaineers, nothing significant, at the very best
an honourable failure. Because at Point Lenana, the high point
we reached, we could see that any tourist could get up there, no
technical skill at all required. Our plan had been for a single mighty
effort that would somehow solve the whole awful prison situation
we were in: but were completely mistaken and deluded. There
is no point whatever in trying to wring out of some action more
than it's capable of providing, and to make a holy grail of it is quite
insane. He went on:

> So now just pick up your rucksack and get back down to the
> camp. Accept that there is something gnawing away inside you
> that can never be satisfied, a yearning for the impossible and
> the eternal, accept that it's part of your faith, that it's central to
> the human condition. It will go on tormenting you to the end of
> your days, this idea that you have somehow let yourself down.
> No Mt Kenya can give you the thing you will only ever achieve
> at the supreme instant: your own self.[9]

These thoughts take up two pages in the Italian version, but
only two paragraphs in *No Picnic on Mount Kenya*.[10] Five years
separated the two books, which tell the identical story but in
two quite different ways. The Italian is more spontaneous, and
emotional. This is shown earlier, when in the English book Felice
does not dwell at great length on the terrible and crushing boredom

in the camp which descends on him between his first glimpse of Mt Kenya and his brilliant idea to climb it: he merely says that the past was finished; there was nothing more to think about, only the present existed, unavoidable, overwhelming, it was easy to understand how people go mad. In Italian he has twice as much to say on this, concluding: 'What is to be done about it? Who are you anyway? Where's your name? You're a number. Nothing. A huge lump in your throat but you can't even cry.'[11]

Felice Benuzzi was an important writer in the field of mountaineering and adventure. He contributed six major articles for *L'Universo*, the quality review of the Military Geographic Institute in Florence, eleven for *Alpi Giulie* of the Trieste branch of the Italian Alpine Club and fifty or so for the Trieste daily newspaper. He wrote on Antarctica for the *International Political Studies Review* in Rome, and in 1985 on the first aerial exploration in southern Patagonia for a volume published by the National Mountain Museum in Turin. That institution in 1987 also published his book *Mattia Zurbriggen, alpine guide: his achievements, his men and his mountains*, which begins with a quote from Sainte Beuve: 'When you put the life of a key figure under scrutiny you have to dare everything, see everything, look at everything and at the very least point out everything.' Felice ends his book greatly disappointed that no newspaper or journal, not even a mountaineering one, had 'written a single word to remember the sad physical and moral decline and the tragic loss of a man who had been one of the greatest alpine guides of his era, an honour to his profession in four continents.'

In 1971 one of Felice's first articles published by *Il Piccolo* was inspired by the 'typically British cool and cautious' report in the *Daily Telegraph* of the death of the explorer Frederick Spencer Chapman: for almost four years in the Second World War Chapman had risked his life on a daily basis as a guerrilla in the jungles behind Japanese lines. At the end of his article Felice tells of a speech made by Chapman to the Alpine Club in London 'entitled, with just about the most beautiful understatement that I know: 'Travels in Japanese-occupied Malaya'.'[12] That was Felice's ideal: to describe the fantastic in neutral terms. It was *No Picnic on Mount Kenya* with its wonderfully modest title that made him famous. It was written deliberately for the English reader, and it was crammed with understatement. He used simple language, although it is that of a person of learning, and he tells his story as if anyone could have done it. But his is a totally Italian story, deriving from Italian genius and Italian know-how. Felice Benuzzi's book is a book of war and a book of sport, but it is much much more. It is a model of alpine literature, and it does honour to Italy.

CHAPTER 23 NOTES

[1] Marini's article is entitled *Benuzzi, la montagna come medicina dell'anima*, on page 6 of the April-June edition of *Alpinismo goriziano 2/2007*, the quarterly review of the Gorizia branch of CAI, the Italian Alpine Club. Alongside are substantial extracts from *Più che sassi*, under the title *Non solo sassi*, by Felice Benuzzi. Further extracts are published in the July-September edition: *Alpinismo goriziano 3/2007*.
[2] *No Picnic on Mt Kenya* p. 28; *Fuga sul Kenya* p. 34.
[3] *Alpi Giulie* Vol 74 – 1980: *Cinquant'anni fa con Emilio Comici sul Zucc dal Boor d'inverno* p. 16.
[4] The exclamation is in *Fuga sul Kenya* pp. 329-330. *No Picnic on Mt Kenya* p. 150 has the more restrained "Of all this we were at the time profoundly ignorant.'
[5] *Più che sassi* p. 18; Luciano Santin quotes Felice in an article *Julius Kugy Scrittore* in *Lo Scarpone* N 4/2008: marzo-aprile 2008 – supplemento bimestrale a la Rivista del Club Alpino Italiano, p. 19.
[6] Kugy op. cit. p. 95.
[7] Kugy op. cit. p. 122.
[8] Più che sassi p. 16.
[9] The final words (in *Fuga sul Kenya* pp. 260-262) echo Nietzsche, who in *Thus Spake Zarathustra* describes an eternal, timeless instant of supreme blessedness, one preceded by despair: despair and redemption are both overcome in an abyss of light, when time stands still. Felice never refers anywhere to Nietzsche, but he would have known that his uncle Valerio had published a translation of some of Nietzsche's letters (*Nietzsche, Friedrich: Lettere scelte e frammenti epistolari* – Prefazione e traduzione di Valerio Benuzzi: Carabba, 1914). Some of Felice's articles in *Il Frontespizio* (notably *Teutones* and *Disfacitori*, see Chapter 4, note 9) reflect Nietzschean elements. His aspiration for purity does not seem so different from Zarathustra's 'O heaven above me, thou pure, thou deep heaven! Thou abyss of light! Gazing on thee, I tremble with

divine desires. Up to thy height to toss myself – that is MY depth! In thy purity to hide myself – that is MINE innocence!' (*Thus Spake Zarathustra* chapter XLVIII).

[10] *No Picnic on Mt Kenya* p. 203.

[11] *No Picnic on Mt Kenya* p. 24; *Fuga sul Kenya* pp. 29-31.

[12] Il Piccolo 17.9.1971: Morte d'un uomo d'avventura.

Felice and the Dalai Lama 1980

24

CONCLUSION

The prisoner of war who climbed Mt Kenya in 1943 with two friends was an ordinary man. Felice Benuzzi was a father, and a government official whose outside interest was mountaineering: in the camp there was nothing remarkable about any of that. Most POWs dreamed of escaping and a few did manage to slip out for a few days of freedom before their recapture. But only three who considered themselves a bit crazy set off through a jungle full of animals to an ice-capped mountaintop, with the aim of returning to prison. This is the story of the man whose idea it was, and who achieved the near-incredible.

Felice grew up in a city that was successively ruled by an emperor, a king, a dictator, a foreign army and by occupation forces before becoming what Trieste is today. When he left the city in 1930 two contrasting urges drove him, one into the wider world and the other back up into the Alps. From his parents he learned caution, and to set aside politics: but his grandfather and uncle, fiercely Italian and ready to take risks, also influenced him. In the early years of fascism Felice went with the flow but at a certain moment he rebelled in his own way and married a Jewess. It was a risk not unlike one a mountaineer might make, gripping the rockface with the depths below, determined to go on.

In Ethiopia he was at first a diligent colonial civil servant and then, when war came, he was valiant as a soldier. In prison he faced something hellish, and may have been reminded of the first verse of Dante's *Inferno*, for he was familiar with and often quoted the great poet: in any case in this grim mid-point in his life Felice did something radical. His escape was part defiance, part pilgrimage.

Afterwards he was a changed man, self-assured, one of the few in any community who would now be a leader, rather than one of the led. He came to terms with his imprisonment, which had three more years to run; he resolved to write about his adventure, and was helped in this by British residents in Kenya. When Italy surrendered later that year he embraced the king's decision, rejected fascism, and collaborated with the former enemy. He hoped for a democratic future for his country, and now took interest in national and international affairs. As a diplomat from 1948 until his retirement in 1976 he was loyal to the government of the day and was consistently rated outstanding by the Foreign Ministry. While other colleagues received earlier promotions Felice refused to compromise for some career advantage and his guiding principle was to be able to sleep well at night.

Elements of inflexibility show through in his character, and for a number of people he seemed austere, even introverted. His family, too, had to put up with some long silences and with his reluctance to share with them the goings-on at the office. But there was another side of his character that was warm and lively. He got on well with poor and ordinary people, he enjoyed himself in company, he had a wicked sense of humour. It was not always easy for others to understand these two sides of him and often his jokey remarks caused some bafflement.

According to Stefania there was a dualism in her husband: a Teutonic aspiring for purity perhaps acquired from his Austrian forebears, set against a dominant, Latin element.[1] Between these two aspects, there was harmony. Felice was never unpredictable or impulsive or capricious, and on the contrary any action he took was always after due deliberation. Nevertheless fundamental to his character was a great restlessness, both physical and intellectual, which he himself acknowledged and often spoke about. He felt compelled to see the world, and understand it. As a tourist the spectacle did not satisfy him, he was drawn also to local history, even the myths of the place; if it was a wilderness, he sought to enter into its very magic.

He looked, too, into the human condition. At the beginning of his book he writes of a special aptness in the term 'concentration camp' which was the normal Italian phrase for such a place of internment: here humanity was squeezed together and preserved in a concentrated state, young and old, healthy and sick, smart and stupid, good and bad. It was not a discovery that gave him much comfort: in that laboratory he witnessed an excess of mediocrity and fanaticism. His preference had always been to examine instead the motivations and actions of great people, and especially the experiences of mountaineers, their challenges, their successes and also their failures. Here he found inspiration and humility, too: reading of their accomplishments made him realise, as he wrote near the end of his memoirs, that he was no more than a chronic mountain rambler. The inexplicable suicide of the explorer Frederick Spencer Chapman whom he greatly admired he had to put down to 'that impulse which is the absolute hallmark of humanity: contradiction.'[2] Reflecting on the often difficult life of the famous mountaineer Eric Shipton, Felice concluded: 'There is nothing that we don't pay for – including the realisation of what we are really worth.'[3]

Felice explained life to himself in terms of the individual, not in terms of religion or society or politics; one had to choose a good path and follow it to the best of one's ability. He opted for the mountains, and his choice had general application: it was a rugged path but following it the individual could rise above the ordinary, take risks and tough decisions, and by staying the course get the chance for a spectacular reward. He wanted everyone to appreciate mountains as he did, and was glad climbing had become so popular.[4] Sometimes – once after his highest climb of all, in Bolivia, and again after one of his easiest on Mt Olympus – he offered advice, especially for young climbers. Near the end of

Più che sassi memoirs he asked rhetorically:

> Is there any more worthy purpose in our life than that of gifting to others what we have received and what has become part of us? To offer to others the fruits of our experience, however poor, battered and sodden they may be?

A moment earlier in those memoirs Felice had pondered on the strangest of contradictions, one that he had recently come across and that he found disturbing: in heraldry the very centre of the shield is known as the 'heart' or the 'abyss,' both terms being equally valid.[5] How could this be, he wondered. What equivalence was there? What power could drag the heart from its own abyss, to comfort it and fire it and exalt it – unless this very contradiction represented the core of the id, and explained everything.

Felice recognised only too well the fiery urge to climb up to the summit, and the icy and immediate reality of the void, into which his hero Emilio Comici had plummeted – on the one hand the heart which throbbed with life and humanity, on the other the abyss of physical and spiritual destruction. He had no answer for their terrible identity, but knew that in his most melancholy and desperate times, it had been in mountains that he had found comfort, healing and perhaps salvation.

Such a powerful force of attraction, or sublimation, Felice believed, might well lie where earth ends and heaven begins.

What he has bequeathed us is the memorable story of how a man in his own darkness made it up into starlight.

CHAPTER 24 NOTES

[1] On 12.10.2012 Stefania told the author (see Introduction, note 3) 'there's a sort of dualism in him. Otherwise probably I wouldn't have fallen in love with him.' On 9.5.2013, with their daughter Daniela, the matter was further discussed.
[2] *Il Piccolo* 17.9.1971: Morte d'un uomo d'avventura.
[3] *Il Piccolo* 20.12.1977: L'ultimo degli esploratori.
[4] In his 1986 article *Su e giu' per l'America* (Alpi Giulie p. 16) he tells how an American climber on Mt Whitney had quizzed him on alpine facilities in Europe, wanting to know: 'everything from the via ferrata to chalets, guides and porters, cablecars and

ski lifts'; Felice comments how different the attitude in New Zealand where such things are disdained. For them 'we are a spoiled lot, lacking in sporting vigour. The pragmatic Americans, however, give us full approval.' Felice had a certain nostalgia for that New Zealand attitude, but he could see how the world had moved on.
[5] *Più che sassi* p. 147.

Acknowledgements

When in June 2012 I conceived the idea of this biography I sought help from Ambassador Stefano Stefanini in the Italian Foreign Ministry. He spoke with his colleague Stefano Baldi, responsible for a compendium of Italian diplomats including Felice Benuzzi whose works had been published. By coincidence Dr Baldi had just for the first time met Daniela Benuzzi in a bookshop in Città della Pieve where they both lived. As a consequence by August I was in regular contact with Daniela and her mother, and in October met with Stefania, Daniela and Silvia Benuzzi. Since then the family has offered me every possible support, including access to their records of their husband and father. I had long conversations on different occasions with them all, notably with Stefania until she sadly passed away in May 2013.

The Italian Ministry of Foreign Affairs subsequently provided me with further valuable assistance, and I am particularly grateful to Dr Stefania Ruggeri, coordinator of the Ministry's historical archives, who gave me access to Felice Benuzzi's personal files.

I am indebted to those who knew Felice Benuzzi and shared with me their memories of him, most notably Professor Marcello Manzoni, a colleague on Antarctic issues; Dr Manzoni read closely and commented in detail on the final text of this book. Professor Francesco Francioni in Florence, an Antarctic expert, was similarly of much assistance. I am especially grateful to Moray Graham for his insights into the time he spent as a boy with Felice in Kenya and his recollections of meeting the Benuzzi family more than once in later years. Giampaolo Colella contributed substantially to the chapter on Felice's final posting as Ambassador to Uruguay. Sergio Romano, a senior colleague in the Ministry of Foreign Affairs, drew in particular on their time together in Paris. Dario Marini, who wrote the definitive obituary for Felice in 1988, provided useful recollections, advice and editorial comment.

Research in Italy was advanced substantially as a result of help received from Roberto Bui in Bologna who has written extensively about Felice Benuzzi and his times, and from Daniela Gangale in Florence who furnished me with information on *Il Frontespizio*. At the Istituto Geografico Militare I received assistance from Colonel Ugo Amendola and Alessandra Cristofari. In Turin the staff at the National Mountain Museum could not have been more cooperative; Lina Maria Vitale and Luisa Szauber at the Biblioteca Nazionale Universitaria met all my requests and Pietro Crivellaro provided worthwhile commentary. In Trieste the Archivio di Stato furnished me with copies of newspaper articles by Felice, and Pietro Spirito at *Il Piccolo* was obliging and informative. I pay special tribute to Sergio Duda and Luciano Santin in the mountaineering fraternity of Trieste, and to Fabio Malusà who assisted me in countless ways. Others to whom the name Felice Benuzzi was immensely familiar and who gave me the benefit of their wisdom were Maurizio Serra, Ludovico Sella, Carlo Alberto Pinelli and Mirella Tenderini.

A number of friends eminently qualified to do so encouraged me along the way, read some or all of what I wrote and offered commentary and sometimes hospitality. They included Lynne and Brian Chatterton in Umbria, Ubaldo Alifuoco in Vicenza and Gianfranco Cresciani in Sydney.

It would have been hard to cover adequately Felice's time in Africa without the help of those who had direct family knowledge and relevant expertise. Accordingly I thank Bongo Woodley, Ettore and Adrian Balletto, John Temple and Glyn Roberts for responding so fully to my correspondence. An interesting contribution was also made by George Brose.

In Australia Peter Barnes provided direct memories of having climbed with Felice in Queensland, as well as photographs and copies of correspondence. Enrico Taglietti in Canberra described to me his friendship and collaboration with Felice half a century earlier. Michael Meadows gave me a number of useful leads and copies of extracts from Bert Salmon's diaries. Professor Richard Bosworth recalled interviewing Felice in the late 1980s on Italian migration to Australia.

In New Zealand Felice's final climb, up Mt Ruapehu, was fondly remembered by his companion Lisle Irwin. Others who told what they knew were Alan Hemmings, Harry Keys, Chris Harris, Graeme Ayres, Stuart Prior and Graham Langton.

Finally I wish to thank Gary and Jean Smith in Seattle for a detailed description and photographs from the time they went up Mt Whitney with Felice in 1984.

Bibliography

Alcock, A.E. (1970), *The history of the South Tyrol question*, London: Michael Joseph.

Antonsich, M. (2006), 'Addis Abeba caput viarium. La rete stradale del Duce', *Rivista Italiana di Geopolitica*, 3, 133-144.

Ara, A. (1974), *Ricerche sugli austro-italiani e l'ultima Austria*, Roma: ELIA.

Arreguín-Toft, I. (2005), *How the Weak Win Wars: A Theory of Asymmetric Conflict*, Cambridge University Press.

Barbarani, E. (2012), *Chi ha ucciso Lumi Videla?*, Milano: Mursia.

Ben-Ghiat, R. (2004), *Fascist Modernities: Italy, 1922-45*, Berkeley: University of California Press.

Ben-Ghiat, R. (2005), 'Italian universities Under Fascism', *Universities Under Dictatorships*, Michael Grüttner & John Connelly (eds), Philadelphia: University of Pennsylvania Press.

Ben-Ghiat, R. (1995), 'Fascism, Writing, and Memory: The Realist Aesthetic in Italy, 1930-50', *The Journal of Modern History*, Vol. 67, No. 3, The University of Chicago Press.

Bertone, E. (2004), *Quegli anni del Novecento: storie di partigiani, soldati, contrabbandieri e frati*, BLU Edizioni.

Bevilacqua, P., De Clementi, A. & Franzina E. (eds) (2001), *Storia dell'emigrazione italiana: Arrivi*, Roma: Donzelli.

Blinkhorn, M. (2006), *Mussolini and Fascist Italy*, Routledge.

Bocca, G. (1997), *Storia d'Italia nella guerra fascista 1940-1943*, Mondadori.

Bonatti, W. (2001), *The Mountains of My Life*, New York: Modern Library.

Borgomaneri, L. (1997), *Hitler a Milano. I crimini di Theodor Saeveche capo della Gestapo*, Rome: Datanews.

Borruso, P. (2003), *L'Africa al confino: la deportazione etiopica in Italia, 1937-39*, Manduria: Lacaita.

Bosworth, R.J.B. (1998), *The Italian Dictatorship: Problems and Perspectives in the Interpretation of Mussolini and Fascism*, Arnold.

Bosworth, R.J.B. (2013), *Italy and the Wider World: 1860-1960*, Routledge.

Botta, F. (2009), *Seduzione e coercizione in Adriatico. Reti, attori e strategie*, Milano: FrancoAngeli.

Buzzati, D. (2010), *I fuorilegge della montagna. Cime, uomini, imprese*, Mondadori

Canali, M. (2004), *Le spie del Regime*, Bologna: Il Mulino.

Canavero, A. (2003), *Alcide De Gasperi: cristiano, democratico, europeo*, Rubbettino.

Cecini, S. (2007), 'La realizzazione della rete stradale in Africa orientale italiana

(1936-41), *Dimensioni e problemi della ricerca storica* 1/2007.

Cervani, G. (1983), *Stato e società a Trieste nel secolo XIX : problemi e documenti*, Udine: Del Bianco.

Chabod, A. & Blanc, S. (2008), *La montagna abita a Valsavarenche*, Firenze: il Valico.

Charlton, K., Jones, B. & Favaro, P. (2007), *The Contribution of Enrico Taglietti to Canberra's Architecture*, Royal Australian Institute of Architects, ACT Chapter.

Comberiati, D. (2009), *Una diaspora infinita: l'ebraismo nella narrativa di Erminia Dell'Oro*, Utrecht: Italianistica Ultraiectina.

Corazzi, P. (1984), *Etiopia. 1938-1946: guerriglia e filo spinato*, Milano: Mursia

Corvaja, S. (2001), *Hitler and Mussolini: The Secret Meetings*, New York: Enigma Books.

Costa Bona, E. (1995), *Dalla guerra alla pace: Italia-Francia: 1940-1947*, FrancoAngeli Storia.

Cox, G. (1977), *The race for Trieste*, William Kimber.

Cresciani, G. (2011), *Trieste goes to Australia*, Padana Press.

Cuomo, P. (2012), *Il miraggio danubiano: Austria e Italia, politica ed economia, 1918-1936*, FrancoAngeli.

Curti G. (2009) (ed), *Carlo Riccardo Monaco un giurista poliedrico al servizio della pace attraverso il diritto*, Milano: Giuffrè.

De Masi, P. (2013), *Santiago. 1 febbraio 1973-27 gennaio 1974*, Roma: Bonanno.

Del Boca, A. (1982), *Gli italiani in Africa orientale: La caduta dell'impero*, Laterza.

Dennis, A. & Potton, C. (1984), *The alpine world of Mount Cook*, National Park 1984 Dept. of Lands and Survey.

Desio, A. & Benuzzi, F. (1984), 'L'Antartide notizie geografiche, economiche, naturalistiche', *Memorie della Società Geografica Italiana*, Torino: UTET.

Di Gregorio, A. (2012), *Epurazioni e protezione della democrazia. Esperienze e modelli di «giustizia post-autoritaria*, FrancoAngeli.

Du Bois, W.E.B. (2007), *Africa, Its Geography, People and Products and Africa-Its Place in Modern History*, Oxford University Press.

Duranti, S. (2008), *Lo spirito gregario: i gruppi universitari fascisti tra politica e propaganda, 1930-1940*, Donzelli.

Elkner, C. (2005), *Enemy Aliens: The Internment of Italian Migrants in Australia During the Second World War*, Connor Court.

Favaro, P. (2009), *Drawn to Canberra: The Architectural Language of Enrico Taglietti*, University of New South Wales.

Ferrari, M. (1996), 'Cooperatori e non cooperatori', *Italia 1939-1945: storia e memoria*, Carlotti, Anna Lisa (ed), Milano: Vita e Pensiero.

Ferraro, G. (2010), *Enciclopedia dello spionaggio nella seconda guerra mondiale*, Roma: Sandro Teti.

Fischer, G. (1989), *Enemy Aliens: Internment and the Homefront Experience in Australia 1914-1920*, St. Lucia.

Francioni, F. & Scovazzi, T. (1996), *International Law for Antarctica*, The Hague: Kluwer Law International.

Francioni, F. & Scovazzi, T. (1989), 'La convenzione di Wellington sulle risorse minerarie antartiche', *Rivista di diritto internazionale* 72(1).

Fullerton, S. (2009), *Brief Encounters: Literary Travellers in Australia 1836-1939*, Picador Australia.

Gaiga, L. (2000), *L'Africa di Angelo: Angelo Tarantino vescovo d'Africa e missionario colombiano*, Editrice Missionaria Italiana.

Genova, L. (2012), *Cieli d'Africa*, pubblicato dall'Autore.

Gentile, S. (2010), *Le Leggi Razziali: scienza giuridica, norme, circolari*, Milano: EDUCatt.

Gilbert, M. & Nilsson, R.K. (2007), *Historical Dictionary of Modern Italy*, Scarecrow Press.

Gillette, A. (2003), *Racial theories in fascist Italy*, Routledge.

Goodchild, J.M. (2014), 'Exploitation of Displaced European Refugees', *War and Displacement in the Twentieth Century: Global Conflicts*, Sandra Barkhof & Angela K. Smith (eds), Routledge.

Haile, G.M. (2002), *Ya-Ingliz Gize or British Paramountcy in Dire Dawa (Ethiopia), 1941-1946: Notes Towards History 2002*, Vol 9, No 2, 47-82, Michigan State University: Northeast African Studies.

Hametz, M.E. (2005), *Making Trieste Italian, 1918-1954*, Boydell & Brewer.

Henze, P.B. (2000), *Layers of Time: A History of Ethiopia*, C. Hurst & Co.

Holman, D. (1978), *Elephants at sundown: the story of Bill Woodley*, W.H.Allen.

Houston, C.S., Bates R.H. & Wickwire J. (2008), *K2, The Savage Mountain: The Classic True Story of Disaster and Survival on the World's Second-Highest Mountain*, Globe Pequot Press.

Ion, A.H. & Errington, E.J. (1993), *Great Powers and Little Wars: The Limits of Power*, Greenwood Publishing Group.

Jupp, J. (2001), *The Australian People: An Encyclopedia of the Nation, Its People and Their Origins*, Cambridge University Press.

Kaufman, E. (1979), *Uruguay in Transition: From civilian to military rule*, Transaction Publishers.

Kugy, J. (1934), *Alpine pilgrimage,* transl. H.E.G.Tyndale, London: J. Murray.

La Rovere, L. (1999), 'Fascist Groups in Italian Universities: An Organization at the Service of the Totalitarian State', *Journal of Contemporary History*, Vol. 34, No. 3, 457-475.

La Rovere, L. & Bongiovanni, B. (2003), *Storia dei Guf: organizzazione, politica e miti della gioventù universitaria fascista 1919-1943*, Bollati Boringhieri.

Labande, F. (2004), *Sauver la montagne*, Editions Olizane.

Lacedelli, L. & Cenacchi, G. (2006), *K2: The Price of Conquest*, Mountaineers Books.

Laurie, R., Stevens, B. & Weller, P. (2001), *The Engine Room of Government: The Queensland Premier's Department 1859-2001*, University of Queensland Press.

Lonza, B. (1973), *La dedizione di Trieste all'Austria*, Trieste: Edizioni Italo Svevo.

Lowry, B. (1999), *Armistice 1918*, Kent State University Press.

Mahoney, M. (1992), *Harry Ayres: Mountain Guide*, Whitcoulls.

Manzoni, M. (2012), *Zingari in Antartide*, Alpine Studio.

Manzoni, M. (2001), *La natura dell'Antartide*, Springer Science & Business Media.

Martucci, M. (2005), *Hitler turista: viaggio in Italia*, Greco & Greco.

Menczer , B. (1994), *Tensions of Order & Freedom: Catholic Political Thought, 1789-1848*, Transaction Publishers.

Michaelis, M. (1978), *Mussolini and the Jews : German-Italian relations and the Jewish question in Italy, 1922-1945*, Oxford: Clarendon Press.

Monteleone, R. (1971), *Il movimento socialista nel Trentino. 1894-1914*, Roma: Editori Riuniti.

Moore, B. & Fedeorowich, K. (2002), *The British Empire and Italian Prisoners of War*, Palgrave Macmillan.

Motta, G. (2012), *The Italian Military Governorship in South Tyrol and the Rise of Fascism*, Edizioni Nuova Cultura.

Novello, M.G. & Zamoni, D. (2010), *Sotto un'unica bandiera: la Croce rossa italiana nella Seconda Guerra mondiale*, Marvia.

O'Brien, I.M. (2006), 'Internments in Australia during World War Two', *The Great Mistakes of Australian History*, UNSW Press.

O'Kelly, S. (2002), *Amedeo: The True Story of an Italian's War in Abyssinia*, Harper Collins.

Olivieri, L.M. (2009), *Swat: Storia d'una frontiera*, Roma: IsIao.

Podestà, G.L. (2004), *L'emigrazione Italiana in Africa Orientale - il Corno d'Africa* http://www.ilcornodafrica.it/rds-01emigrazione.pdf.

Podestà, G.L. (2009) 'Le città dell'impero. La fondazione di una nuova civiltà italiana in Africa orientale', *Lo sguardo della storia economica sull'edilizia urbana*, Michela Barbot, Andrea Caracausi & Paola Lanaro (eds), Università Roma TRE.

Powers, R. S. (2012), *Protest, Power, and Change: An Encyclopedia of Nonviolent Action from ACT-UP to Women's Suffrage*, Routledge.

Preti, L. (2004), *Impero fascista: africani ed ebrei*, Mursia.

Quarantotti Gambini, P.A. (1967), *Endgame 1945: Victory, Retribution, Liberation*, Mondadori.

Rodogno, D. (2006), *Fascism's European Empire: Italian Occupation During the Second World War*, Cambridge University Press.

Roggero, R. (2006), *Oneri e onori: le verità militari e politiche della guerra di liberazione in Italia*, Greco & Greco.

Roncalli, M. (1999) (ed), 'Giuseppe De Luca - Fausto Minelli', *Carteggio*, vol. 1 Roma: Edizioni di Storia e Letteratura.

Ros, A. (2012), *The Post-Dictatorship Generation in Argentina, Chile, and Uruguay: Collective Memory and Cultural Production*, Palgrave Macmillan.

Rossi, M. (2011), *Tutela dei diritti umani e realpolitik. L'Italia delle Nazioni Unite (1955-1976)*, CEDAM.

Rothwell, D. (1996), *The Polar Regions and the Development of International Law*, Cambridge University Press.

Rusinow, D.L. (1969), *Italy's Austrian heritage, 1919-1946*, Oxford: Clarendon Press.

Salvante, M. (2010), 'Violated Domesticity in Italian East Africa, 1937-40',

Domestic Violence and the Law in Colonial and Postcolonial Africa, Ohio University Press.

Sbacchi, A. (1985), *Ethiopia under Mussolini : fascism and the colonial experience*, London: Zed Books.

Sbacchi, A. (1980), *Il colonialismo italiano in Etiopia 1936-1940*, Milano: Mursia.

Sbacchi, A. (1997), *Legacy of Bitterness: Ethiopia and Fascist Italy, 1935-1941*, Red Sea Press.

Sbacchi, A. (1977), 'Italy and the treatment of the Ethiopian Aristocracy 1937-1940', *The International Journal of African Historical Studies*, Vol. 10, No. 2, 209-241.

Scarano, F. (2012), *Tra Mussolini e Hitler: le opzioni dei sudtirolesi nella politica estera*, FrancoAngeli.

Schäfer, B. (2010), *The East German State and the Catholic Church, 1945-1989*, Berghahn Books.

Shawcross, W. (2012), *Counting One's Blessings*, Macmillan.

Shinn, D.H. & Ofcansky, T. P. (2013), *Historical Dictionary of Ethiopia*, Scarecrow Press.

Simone, G. (2012), *Il guardasigilli del regime: l'itinerario politico e culturale di Alfredo Rocco*, FrancoAngeli.

Sluga, G.(2001), *The Problem of Trieste and the Italo-Yugoslav Border: Difference, Identity, and Sovereignty in Twentieth-Century Europe*, SUNY Press.

Spadoni, P.S. (1996), *I prigionieri italiani in Africa* in *Italia 1939-1945: storia e memoria*, Carlotti, Anna Lisa (ed), Vita e Pensiero.

Stafford, D. (2010), *Endgame 1945: Victory, Retribution, Liberation*, Hachette UK.

Tamburelli, G. (2008), *The Antarctic Legal System: The Protection of the Environment of the Polar Regions*, Giuffrè Editore.

Toscano, M. (1975), *Alto Adige, South Tyrol: Italy's frontier with the German world*, Baltimore: Johns Hopkins University Press.

Toscano, M. (1967), *Storia diplomatica della questione dell'Alto Adige*, Bari: Laterza.

Vianello-Chiodo, M. (2012), *Under-Soldier*, AuthorHouse.

Vinci, A. (1992) (ed), *Trieste in guerra: gli anni 1938-1943*, Istituto regionale per la storia del movimento di liberazione nel Friuli-Venezia Giulia.

Wu Ming 1 & Santachiara, R. (2013), *Point Lenana* , Einaudi.

Zagnoni, S. (1993), 'L' attività dell'Incis. Le case degli "uomini bianchi", *Architettura italiana d'oltremare 1870-1940*, G. Gresleri, P.G. Massaretti and S. Zagoni (eds), Venezia: Marsilio.

Zanin, U. (2007), *Giacomo Emilio Benuzzi ingegnere nell'impero austro-ungarico*, Il Sommolago Comune di Dro.

INDEX

Milton Keynes UK
Ingram Content Group UK Ltd.
UKHW020803150823
426904UK00016B/683